HOW TO FIND LOVE, SEX & INTIMACY AFTER 50
A Woman's Guide

HOW TO FIND LOVE, SEX & INTIMACY AFTER 50

A Woman's Guide

Dr. Matti Gershenfeld
and Judith Newman

Produced by the Philip Lief Group, Inc.
FAWCETT COLUMBINE
New York

A Fawcett Columbine Book
Published by Ballantine Books
Copyright © 1991 by Dr. Matti Gershenfeld and
Judith Newman

Grateful acknowledgment is made to the following for permission to reprint previously published material: Little, Brown and Company: Excerpt from *Love, Sex, and Aging: A Consumer's Union Report* by the Consumers Reports Editors and Edward Brecher, 1984.
Viking Penguin and Gerald Duckworth & Co. Ltd: Four lines from "Pictures in the Smoke" from *The Portable Dorothy Parker* by Dorothy Parker, introduction by Brenda Gill. Copyright 1926, renewed © 1954 by Dorothy Parker. "Pictures in the Smoke" was published in Great Britain by Gerald Duckworth & Co. Ltd. in *The Collected Dorothy Parker*. Reprinted by permission of Viking Penguin, a division of Penguin Books USA Inc. and Gerald Duckworth & Co. Ltd.
Warner/Chappell Music, Inc.: Four lines from the lyrics of "Anything Goes" by Cole Porter. Copyright 1934 by Warner Bros. Inc. (Renewed) All rights reserved. Used by permission.

Produced by the Philip Lief Group, Inc.

Library of Congress Catalog Card Number: 90-85060

ISBN: 0-449-90518-7

Cover design by Sheryl Kagan
Manufactured in the United States of America
First Edition: August 1991

10 9 8 7 6 5 4 3 2 1

To the first group of "Golden Girls" from whom
I learned much about women between
the ages of fifty and sixty-five.
—*Matti Gershenfeld*

To my parents
—*Judith Newman*

Acknowledgments

This book could never have happened without some unusually caring, supportive people. First, I want to express my appreciation to Robin Feller, of the Philip Lief Group, for conceiving of this project and convincing me to write the book. Judith Newman is an intelligent, wonderful writer who made writing this book one of the most gratifying and easy projects in which I've been involved; I spoke and she wrote—a great combination. I am especially grateful to our editor, Ginny Faber, who really wanted to understand this subject way beyond working on the project; she was continuously affirming and supportive. Other special people who helped make the book possible are Mary Gaynor, a longtime friend and associate who got the foundation grant that started us on working with women fifty to sixty-five. Also, to Milly Behrend, the administrator at the Couples Learning Center who handled administration of the project and even proofed and read copy. In all, they were a great group of women and a joy to work with.

And special thanks to my family who are supportive of every project I undertake, and to Paula Leder, my ever conscientious and always dependable administrative assistant.

—*Matti Gershenfeld*

Thanks to Nancy Kalish, the world's best editor and worst driver; to Robyn Feller at Philip Lief and Ginny Faber at Ballantine, who made our words flow a lot more smoothly than we could have on our own; to David Galef, who got me into this mess; and to Don, who provided invaluable research assistance.

—*Judith Newman*

Contents

Contents

Preface

"Why aren't women's magazines writing about the issues I'm dealing with?"

As a practicing psychotherapist and educator, I've heard this question asked repeatedly by women over fifty—women like you who are just as interested in love, relationships, and sex as twenty- and thirty-year-olds. Your concerns, however, are different. Your *feelings* are different.

Women are divorcing later than ever before; they are being widowed at a time when they still have twenty or thirty healthy years ahead of them; they are facing changes in their lives they never thought they would have to face alone. *How to Find Love, Sex, and Intimacy After 50: A Woman's Guide* is the first book to address the very specific needs of mature women who are looking for a romantic relationship or are already in a new one. The need for this book became glaringly apparent to me several years ago when I began teaching a course at the Couples Learning Center in Philadelphia called "On Being a Golden Girl."

When I introduced the class, I expected *some* enthusiasm from Learning Center students. What I didn't expect was an article about the course in the *Philadelphia Inquirer*, which created so much interest that the number of course selections I taught first doubled, then quadrupled, and finally sextupled! Instead of the enrollment of ten or fifteen students that I had expected, hundreds of women signed up. Clearly women of this age, going through major conflicts in their lives, were tired of being told by the media that they were too old to be worrying about frivolous things like sex and relationships—why didn't they just curl up with a cat and a good book?

Well, I hope this is one of the "good books" you curl up with—it may help you change your life.

MATTI GERSHENFELD

HOW TO FIND LOVE, SEX & INTIMACY AFTER 50
A Woman's Guide

ॐ

1

"Golden Girls": You're Not a Girl, and the Years Aren't Always Golden

Many foxes grow gray, but few grow old.
                                    —BENJAMIN FRANKLIN

Fifty. Fifty-five. Sixty. These are what many people call "the golden years." Your children are grown, your career is at its peak. Your major worries are behind you, and now, maybe you're planning for retirement. You've spent a lifetime caring for others; now others are going to care for you. Time to put your feet up, relax, and enjoy the fruits of all that hard work. And if you ever feel a little lonely, well, all you have to do is reach out and touch someone—just like those jolly folks on the television commercials.

This is what our culture says you can expect at this stage of your life. It's all so easy.

What? You mean that's not the way *your* life is? Really?

Welcome to the club.

Meet Lily. Now fifty-five, Lily went through a horrendous divorce fourteen years ago that left her in emotional ruin. Although she has reluctantly dated a few men since, she has not been to bed with anyone since her ex-husand. Now, Lily has recently met a divorced man who is crazy about her. He has been wining and dining her for weeks, and Lily knows he wants and expects to make love soon.

She is terrified. Since she last had sex, she has gained fifteen pounds, her breasts and buttocks have succumbed to the laws of gravity, and she has developed varicose veins on her legs that look like the New Jersey interstate system. She thinks she loves Bert, and part of her wants to go to bed with him, but the idea of baring her body fills her with dread. She is also worried she will fail to perform well—that she won't have an orgasm, or *he* won't, and it will be her fault. She is thinking of breaking off the relationship.

Then there's Liz. After five miserable years of widowhood she believed she had finally found happiness in the form of Jay, a widower, whom she met through a personals ad in a local newspaper. They liked each other instantly and began dating more and more, even though they lived two hours away from each other. Soon Jay began spending nights at Liz's house. Liz loved the arrangement, but both her thirty-four-year-old son and his wife did not. They considered her too old for what they termed her "wild sexual behavior," and told her so. This made Liz feel terrible, but it really hurt when they refused to invite Jay to Thanksgiving dinner at their house. Liz felt frustrated, forced to choose between her son and her friend. She chose Jay, but her estrangement from the family has definitely put a pall on the relationship. She wonders,

Why can't my family be happy for me? Why do I have to choose?

Janet, at sixty, would like to be in a relationship with a man, but it all feels difficult and overwhelming to her. She's just not sure if she's ready.

If, like Lily, Liz, and Janet, your life after fifty doesn't resemble a Hallmark greeting card, you're reading the right book. This is one of the first works to examine the lives of many women over fifty not as psychologists have told us they should be, but as they actually *are*. Not peaceful, but tumultuous. Not restful, but terribly active. Not always embraced by a close family unit, but sometimes splintered and disjointed. Millions of American women who thought they had put the stress—and excitement!—of dating, romance, and new love behind them are now confronting situations they thought they would never have to face again. Sometimes you're going to find that you feel like a kid again. And being a kid, as you'll remember, wasn't always fun.

Here are some statistics you may not know, compiled in 1987 by Resources for Midlife and Older Women Inc. in Washington, D.C.:

• More than 48 million Americans, or 21 percent of the population, are over fifty-five years old. By the year 2000 this will be the nation's fastest-growing age segment.
• Women aged forty-five to fifty-four are about twice as likely to be widowed or divorced as men. Women over fifty-five are more than three times as likely.
• Eighty-five percent of wives outlive their husbands. The average age of widowhood is fifty-six.

- Twenty-five percent of women outlive their eldest son.
- Eleven percent of divorced women over fifty remarry.
- Court awards of marital property upon divorce average 30 percent to the wife and 70 percent to the husband.
- Upon divorce the average man's standard of living goes up 42 percent, while the women's and children's drop 73 percent.
- Only 18 percent of divorced women over forty are awarded alimony. Only 62 percent of mothers over forty are awarded child support.
- The median income of married women is still less than $11,000 a year, regardless of what their husbands make.

If you are a woman between the ages of fifty and sixty-five, you are a member of a unique generation, utterly different from women born before and after you. First there's the physical difference. At the turn of this century the average life expectancy for a woman was fifty; for a man it was forty-eight. Today the average woman lives to be seventy-eight, and the average man, seventy.[1] Couples at that time had six to eight children; the average couple today has two to three. This means that women in the early 1900s would usually not live to raise all their children to adulthood—whereas most women today have finished their major childrearing responsibilities by the age of forty-five.

So at fifty not only is today's woman *not* dead—she is

[1]Riley, M. W. "Women, Men, and the Lengthening Life Course." In A. S. Rossi, ed. *Gender and the Life Course* (New York: Aldine, 1984, pp. 97–113).

usually free of her childrearing role, in very good health, and, whether working or not, has twenty-five to thirty active years ahead of her.

This reminds us of the story of a man who asked a young boy how old he was. The boy responded, "That's hard to say, sir. According to my latest school tests, I have a psychological age of eleven. Anatomically I'm seven; mentally I'm nine. But I suppose you refer to my chronological age. That's eight—but nobody pays any attention to that nowadays."

That's pretty much the way things are with you today.

Next there's an enormous difference in the expectations men and women have of each other. If you were born in the twenties or thirties, you grew up with models of womenhood vastly different from those today. Today's girls have Jane Fonda; you had Betty Grable. Today's girls have Cher; you had Ann Sheridan. Women in movies who were assertive and independent were rare—and were usually punished for their behavior. (After all, all Joan Crawford, Bette Davis, or Katharine Hepburn ever really needed was a *man* to tame them!) And where were the models for women in business, science, politics? Virtually nonexistent.

How about the men you looked up to? These were men with convictions, who were fighting a war that our entire nation fervently believed in. In the movies they were Gary Cooper, Cary Grant, Jimmy Stewart. (Just try to imagine Phil Donahue being a hero when you were a teenager!) If the real-life models weren't such paragons, most, at least, seemed to have a stronger sense of responsibility and integrity—and a better-defined sense of their roles—than men do today. And even if a woman didn't have as many choices and rights, she at least knew what behavior was expected of her. For example there were girls who did and girls who didn't—and we all knew what happened to the girls who did! Compare that to today, when the girls who wouldn't have now do.

There's also the extraordinary change in life-style. Before 1960 divorce was rare. And when it did occur, it was almost always within the first five years of marriage. Only 4 percent of women married more than fifteen years got a divorce. By 1970 that number had ballooned to 25 percent. *By 1980, it had leaped again to 40 percent.*

Can you imagine any woman taking pride in being called "Ms." back in the 1950s? The title would have seemed almost an insult, perhaps because society placed even more emphasis than it does today on being a "Mrs."

So, vast societal changes have taken place—and as these changes have occurred, psychologists have begun to take a closer look at life for women between fifty and sixty-five. They're discovering that, like infancy, adolescence, or young adulthood, the years from fifty to sixty-five are a period of development all their own.

When scientists were first studying adult development, they decided that the years from twenty-one to sixty-five were all part of one stage, the plateau of adulthood. The idea was that you stayed the same—an almost comical notion, considering what we now know about adult development. After researchers finally ditched that theory, they reassessed those years and broke them into various stages:[2] sixteen to twenty-one,

[2]Roger L. Gould, *Transformations: Growth and Change in Adulthood* (New York: Simon and Schuster, 1978).

twenty-two to twenty-eight, twenty-nine to thirty-four, thirty-five to forty-five, and then. . . . At this point, like hounds that lost the scent of the fox, they stopped in their tracks and snuffled around, looking puzzled. Most of these sociologists and psychologists were in their mid-forties. Looking ahead for themselves, they concluded that they had made it through all the rough stages and that, basically, there was not too much more developing to be done. As a result they wrote about the years between forty-five and sixty-five as periods of resolution.

They also came up with a number of generalizations about adult development in order to support their theories. Here are a few of them, culled from *Adult Development* by Judy Arin-Krupp, Ph.D.:

- Adults enter their fifties feeling comfortable with themselves. There is the feeling, "I am in my prime."
- Marital satisfaction is high. There is autonomy and mutuality in the relationship.
- Parents are no longer perceived as the cause of personal problems.
- Men are more concerned with their health and their bodies than women are.
- Divorce is rare, especially after the mid-fifties.

How many people fifty to sixty-five do *you* know for whom these statements are true? The way we live today flies in the face of these assumptions.

Here's a more likely scenario:

The major relationships in your life are undergoing radical change. You've spent the last twenty-five years working, keeping a house, raising children—and now you are widowed or divorced. As a result your finances are in flux. Your children are grown, but your nurturing responsibilities are not over: with life expectancies growing ever-longer, you have one or two elderly parents whom you care for. Yet, while you're still attending to their needs, your children may not be attending to yours—they are more self-involved and less family-oriented than you'd hoped.

You are part of what we call the "sandwich generation," caught between looking after your elderly parents and trying to relate to your adult children.

You look in the mirror and you may not be thrilled with what you see. Your mind and heart feel like thirty, but those are definitely sixty-year-old bulges around the hips! If you are married, the issues you are facing are not necessarily the same ones confronting your spouse. He may be worried about his virility, career status, how much money he's put away, and what he's achieved. But in this culture he's considered more attractive than you, more valued, and more sought after. Your value seems directly related to the portrait in the mirror.

If you're widowed, you may believe you can never start over.

If you're divorced, you may feel you'll never marry again—while your husband will find a new love and be remarried in six months.

You leaf through women's magazines looking for articles that apply to you. But every article about love and sex is geared toward women young enough to be your daughter. The fashions are for women who can fit neatly into a straw. Even the makeup, the triple-rich under-eye cell renewal cream geared for "more mature" skin, defines "more mature" as "twenty-five or older." (*Really* mature skin, we are led to believe, is beyond hope. Better hightail it to the plastic surgeon.) The occasional article clearly targeted to the middle-aged or older woman is usually about something depressing—Alzheimer's disease, menopause, osteoporosis.

So, if popular entertainment (magazines, television, films) is any guide, women your age barely exist as loving, sexual beings. And when they *do* exist, they're gossamer fantasies who, like Dorian Gray, have mysteriously bypassed the changes of time, such as Joan Collins, Tina Turner, Linda Evans—miraculous exceptions to society's rule that sexuality is only properly expressed by women in their twenties and thirties.

Yet *you* are just as interested in love, intimacy, and sex as women half your age, but with a slightly different twist. Your needs and concerns are simply not the same as those of women twenty to thirty years younger. You may be looking for a relationship with an older (or younger!) man, and you want to know how the new, liberated rules of relationships apply to you.

The appearance of *Lear's*, the magazine created several years ago "For the Woman Who Wasn't Born Yesterday," is a testament to the redefinition (and celebration) of the over-fifty woman. A magazine like *Lear's* is possible in large part because of several interesting discoveries among advertisers. In the past the popular theory was that young, newly married women handle the household money and will buy what they see on ad pages of magazines; older women, by contrast, have bought what they need and don't handle the household expenses anyway. Suddenly advertisers have caught on to the fact that people over fifty-five have a total annual income of $416 billion, and almost *twice* the discretionary spending power of those under thirty-five.

The renewal of interest in the over-fifty woman also explains the popularity of the television sitcom "Golden Girls." Here are three fifty-plus women, two divorced and one widowed, who have banded together to form a family and who are anything but stay-at-home biddies: they are busy, smart (well, except for Rose!), wisecracking, warm, and—most shocking—sexy! It may not be the most realistic show on television, but what a departure from the average sitcom, where any woman over fifty is usually the butt of "desperate woman on the prowl" jokes.

Nevertheless we still live in a youth culture—just look at the new magazine *Longevity*, which is entirely devoted to articles about staying young as long as possible. The problem with this attitude is that it grossly undervalues the past. Sometimes we treat the past as an impediment to be overcome, instead of recognizing the strengths we can draw from it. But we have to be able to use our experience to help us do what we want to do now.

What have you overcome that you're proud of and that can help you in the future?

This book is designed to help you examine the major issues in your life—self-definition, friendship, loneliness, attractiveness, and relationships—and help you live that life more successfully. It's primarily for women who have been widowed or divorced and are now having to ask themselves these questions:

- Who am I today?
- Am I the person I want to be?
- If I'm not, how do I want to change?
- What can I do to change?
- How do I feel about my friends?

- How can I make new friends?
- Do I want another man in my life? (or, for a few, Do I want a woman?)
- How do I find another person to share my life with?
- How can I make myself as attractive as possible?
- Am I capable of a new sexual relationship at this stage?
- Is sex going to be different now?
- What's important to me in a new relationship?
- How can I overcome loneliness?
- How can I have new relationships without alienating my children, or my friends?
- Is change even *possible* at this stage of my life?

During the course of this book, you will be meeting many women—women who, like Liz, Lily, and Janet, you'll recognize. They are the stories of my private clients, and of students from the Couples Learning Center in suburban Philadelphia, Pennsylvania.

They are asking themselves an important question: Since when did age prevent great human endeavor and accomplishments? After all, between the ages of seventy and eighty-three:

- Commodore Vanderbilt amassed an additional $10 million to his fortune.
- Verdi, at eighty-three, produced his magnificent "Te Deum," "Stabat Mater," and "Ave Maria."
- Oliver Wendell Holmes, at seventy-nine, wrote "Over the Teacups."
- Tennyson, at eighty-three, wrote "Crossing the Bar."
- Jessica Tandy, at eighty, won her first Best Actress Oscar for *Driving Miss Daisy.*
- Rex Harrison played the lead in George Bernard Shaw's *Heartbreak House* at seventy-five.

- Barbara McClintock won the Nobel Prize for medicine at eighty-one.
- Beryl Bainbridge started bike racing professionally in her thirties. Now, in her sixties, she's still competing—very successfully.

Remember, the average woman lives to be seventy-eight. What are you going to be doing twenty or twenty-five years from now? It's time to begin building skills for the future.

For millions of women today, turning fifty is not the happily-ever-after end of a chapter but rather the beginning of a whole new book. Answering these questions, and shaping a new life for yourself, is what this book is all about.

Before you begin reading, it may be useful for you to take stock of some of the problems confronting you right now. Please fill out the two following exercises before you read any further.

Life-style-Problem Checklist

Check (X) which of these apply to you:

NONE   SOME   A LOT

1. I have medical, dental, or
   health problems *(circle which)*.
2. I worry about my health.
3. I have a problem with alcohol,
   drugs, or other addictive
   substances.
4. I have trouble with physical
   appearance: face, hair, body,
   clothes *(circle which)*.

NONE   SOME   A LOT

5. I often feel "down," bad, or sad.
6. I often feel tense, nervous, anxious.
7. I have trouble getting over past hurts or resentments.
8. I often feel exhausted, that I don't have enough energy.
9. I have bad eating habits.
10. I have trouble with relationships: children, spouse/partner, parents, relatives, or friends *(circle which)*.
11. I have trouble with sexual relationships.
12. I am often too hard on myself or others.
13. I have trouble with being assertive enough.
14. I am often unable to relax.
15. I often feel guilty.
16. I often feel lonely.
17. I often feel dissatisfied with my job or career.
18. I have trouble finding meaning in life.
19. I am often too easily discouraged.
20. I have trouble imagining what I want in life.
21. I have trouble making decisions.
22. I don't have enough fun or time for fun.

NONE   SOME   A LOT

23. I don't sleep well at night.
24. I don't get regular physical exercise.
25. I have trouble finding time for myself.
26. I have trouble handling criticism or being too dependent.
27. I find it difficult to control my behavior.
28. I have trouble deciding what my religious beliefs are.
29. I have trouble loving or feeling loved *(circle which)*.
30. I have problems with my conscience.

Circle which number is the biggest problem. Add any comments about that problem here.

Life Inventory

This exercise, adapted from *Values Clarification*, by Simon, Howe, and Kirschenbaum, asks you to look at some of the major themes and events of your life. Answer each question briefly, in writing if possible.

1. What was the happiest year or period in your life?

2. What things do you do well?

3. Describe a turning point in your life.

4. What has been the lowest point in your life?

5. What are some things you would like to stop doing?

6. What are some things you would really like to get better at?

7. Describe some peak experience you have had.

8. Describe some peak experience you would like to have.

9. What are some things you would like to start doing now, right at this time in your life?

Learning About You

Fill in the blanks with a few words:

1. One of my pleasures is to . . .

2. I feel best when people . . .

3. If I had a million dollars, I would . . .

4. Secretly, I wish . . .

5. On vacations I like to . . .

6. Many people don't agree with me, but . . .

7. My bluest days are . . .

8. I am best at . . .

9. People can hurt my feelings most by . . .

10. When people depend on me, I . . .

11. I get angry when . . .

12. I have accomplished . . .

13. I feel warmest toward a person when . . .

14. My appearance . . .

15. What I want most in life is . . .

16. When someone hurts me . . .

17. In a difficult situation, I . . .

18. I often find myself . . .

19. I have difficulty trying to deal with . . .

20. I used to be . . .

21. My greatest strength is . . .

22. I am most concerned about . . .

Six months from now, and then one year from now, look back at your responses and answer these questions one more time.

If you're unhappy with some of your answers, and you think you just *can't* change, read on.

The first step is to examine the obstacles you put in your own path. That's where we'll begin.

2

Of Course I Want a Relationship! (Don't I?)

Our doubts are traitors
And make us lose the good we oft might win
By fearing to attempt.
                    —SHAKESPEARE,
                    Measure for Measure, I.iv.77

Kate is a tall, Irish beauty with wavy black hair, green eyes, and a pert nose. At fifty-three, she retains a special aura of youth and vigor, and she often wears shades of green that set off her dramatic coloring.

The older of two daughters, Kate grew up with a mother who was very dependent on her father. He died of a heart attack when her mother was fifty-four. Finding living alone unbearable, Kate's mother came to live with Kate and her family. After about six months, however, Kate's husband insisted his mother-in-law couldn't make her home with them any longer. She then moved into the other daughter's home. Kate's mother never dated, saying she was through with "all that."

Kate's husband, an insurance salesman, was a practiced flirt who never let marriage slow him down. When Kate was forty-seven, he got into a serious relationship with another woman and finally asked for a divorce. There were six years of bitter negotiations before the divorce was final. She has spent the time not wanting to grant a divorce. Like her mother, she's terrified of being alone.

Today Kate makes halfhearted attempts at going out to meet men, but, despite her attractiveness, never gets involved enough for a man to ask her out. She recently entered therapy because she is fearful that she will end up like her mother. In the six years since her husband left, she has never had a single date.

Ask Kate why she hasn't dated, and she will offer myriad reasons, most of which sound perfectly rational. The problem is, they are all smoke screens for one real reason: fear.

She says she wants to meet someone—and then she says, "BUT . . ." *But* she's too old. *But* she's not the kind of woman to. *But* she's doomed to disappointment.

To Kate, thinking about dates has become a constant source of tension. She has never really asked herself the primary question: Do I *want* to date? And if I do, why?

In order for a relationship to go from being an idle dream to a reality, you have to identify the obstacles that are standing in your path and systematically figure out ways of overcoming them.

Have you ever gone to a horse show and watched the experienced riders "walk the course—" that is, walk step by step, *on foot*, around the series of obstacles they and their horses will be jumping over later? You'll notice that the less experienced riders often don't do this—they'll just look at the course from a distance and map it out in their minds. But the real pros want to learn every inch of that course, every hurdle; they want to know what the dirt will feel like under their mounts' hooves. These folks jumping six-foot fences are risk takers, but they're *calculated*-risk takers. They will examine the obstacles from every conceivable angle, and then they'll jump.

And it's pretty much the same with you.

We all tend to be able to deal more easily with relatively unemotional problems—say, deciding to go back to school. If this were your goal, you would probably roll up your sleeves and make a list. You would decide what you want to study, what school you want to go to, whether it has a program for older adults, how you can pay for the classes (take an extra job? cash in a stock?), whether the classes meet at convenient times, and so forth.

Why should looking for a mate be any different? Because you know there will always be some college that will accept you—but you're not quite sure if there will be someone who will accept you romantically and, yes, sexually. It's a scary decision, and everything in you has been trained to say no.

This behavior reminds us of an old navy story: When Rear Admiral Samuel Francis Du Pont explained to his superior officer, Admiral David Farragut, the reason why he had failed to take his ships into Charleston Harbor in 1863, Farragut heard him through to the end and then said, "Admiral, there is one explanation that you have not given." "What is that?" asked Du Pont. "It's this. You did not believe that you could do it."

Here are some of the most common rationalizations that stand in the way of starting a relationship:

1. *"There will never be anyone like Harry."*
You sent him through school; together you endured years of colds and broken bones with the kids. He paid the bills on time and brought you flowers when you had a bad day. He may have been the only man you slept with. He may have died in your arms.

Yvonne is a handsome, black-haired fifty-five-year-old widow of Persian descent. She looks formidable, even a little fierce, but dissolves into girlish laughter at the slightest provocation—like when friends tell her she's a dead ringer for Imelda Marcos. Since her husband's death nine years ago, she's suffered from the "Harry syndrome"—the fear that no one can ever live up to the memory of her late husband.

But in her calmest moments Yvonne admits that she has conveniently forgotten many of the difficulties of her marriage—including her husband's gambling problems which ended in bankruptcy proceedings just before his death from chronic heart disease nine years ago. Still, she has deified Sam, preferring to remember him as she *wished* he had been rather than as he was in real life. Before she can move on with her life, Yvonne must reach a point where she can look at her marriage as it really was. By denying her very real anger at being abandoned—first financially during Sam's life and then by his death—Yvonne feels a certain apathy. Which, she reasons, is better than feeling pain.

Like Yvonne, many women tend to cling to the memory of their late or ex-husbands, seeing only the good. It's a subtle way of convincing yourself that change is not necessary. After all, if *that* relationship was as good as any relationship gets, what's the point of trying for another one?

What Yvonne and other women in her situation don't realize is that maintaining the idealization is simply a way of avoiding a new relationship. Any imperfection in a new partner means you are settling for less than the "real thing." It means you don't have to communicate with, adapt to, or understand another person; and it means you can live in the past, with a lonely present and an even lonelier future.

2. *"All the men look so old."*

They wear baggy pants and have hair coming out of their ears. They moan and wheeze and complain about bursitis. They've got wrinkles on their wrinkles.

Well, some do and some don't. A lot of women have grown up with the idea that the physical attractiveness of the man they're with mirrors their own attractiveness. Therefore if they're out with a man who looks considerably older, they reason, it means *they* look old!

As Liz told us about Jay, the widower whom she's now happily dating: "We met through the personals, so I didn't know what to expect. And he was so . . . old! I mean, he wasn't old in spirit or outlook, but he had all these wrinkles. And he was bald. He greeted me at the restaurant on our first date wearing a badly faded, wrinkled sport shirt and bell-bottom trousers. That was almost our *last* date."

Part of meeting men at this stage of your life is reevaluating your own biases about age. What, after all, *is* "old"?

3. *"I don't want to hear about his wife and children."*

If you were dating in high school, you'd ask him what team he was on. If you were in college, you'd ask,

"What's your major?" As with so many aspects of your life, the small talk is different now—for one thing it's less small. The issues in your lives that are important have changed drastically. He has an entire life history for you to learn, and he may be eager to share it with you.

"I remember the first time Jay told me about some of his wife's funny habits. They were just little things— like every time she saw a red Chevy from the fifties, she would squeal, jump in the air, and give Jay a kiss. Even Jay didn't know why she did it—she would never tell him. His theory was that she lost her virginity in a car like that. Anyway I felt that I had no right to know these things. And when he told me more personal things, I felt as if I had sneaked into her house and was rummaging around her underwear drawer. Jay didn't understand why these revelations made me angry."

Part of maturing and forming a family unit is erecting barriers to outsiders. Many women have not discussed details of another person's life (or their own), outside of their family circle, for years. This kind of intimacy can be frightening. But if you want to get to know him, it simply doesn't make sense to limit your discussion to his golf game.

4. *"I'm only interested in men who are very successful. Who wants to struggle now?"*

Later in these pages you'll meet couples who have struggled over disparities in salary and/or ambition. It's a particularly dicey subject, because financial security *does* play a much more important role in your life now than it did when you were twenty-five.

5. *"Would Cary Grant not pay for Grace Kelly's dinner? When we go out together,* he *pays."*

Some of the most sweeping changes in the dynamics between men and women over the last twenty-five years involve money. You are in a generation of women who have been firmly brought up to believe that, on some level, money equals love, and not being paid for is the same as not being cared about.

We're not saying that you should entirely abandon that belief. But we will be reconsidering some of these notions in the course of this book.

6. *"I simply will not go to anything with the word* singles *in it—bar, dance, lecture, talk, bingo game, nature hike,* anything. *The only men who show up for these events are freeloaders and nerds. And to make it worse, there are ten lady barricudas for every one so-called man. No, I'll only give my number to friends, and they can give it to any friends they have."*

Guess what? *Nobody* likes to go to a singles event, for three very good reasons: (1) More women than men *do* attend these events; (2) Prince Charming isn't likely to be hanging around; the guy who believes powder-blue leisure suits are making a comeback *is*; and (3) most singles evenings are guaranteed to make you feel like you're fifty-three going on fourteen.

"At my first synagogue-sponsored singles dance I spent half the evening cowering in a corner, and the other half in the bathroom, checking to see if my panty line showed," laughed sixty-year-old Ruth, a short, buxom brunette with sleek, straight hair and huge, sparkling eyes.

Finally someone came over and asked Ruth to dance: "Because he was several inches shorter than me, I spent the whole time worrying about where he was placing his hands and wondering how much time it took him every morning to artfully conceal his bald spot."

Many of the women who disdain singles activities are the very same ones who complain about being uncomfortable at evenings where everyone is in a couple. Being at a singles event is an admission of *wanting* someone—and that admission in itself is extremely uncomfortable.

We'll talk at length in chapter 4 about singles activities, and the many alternative places to meet men.

7. *"I can tell in a minute whether I'll be interested."*

Could Cleopatra tell about Marc Antony in a minute? Could Héloise tell about Abelard? Was Juliet sure about Romeo?

Well, yes—and look what happened to them! The point is that feeling that flush of excitement at the first meeting is no guarantee of anything except that your hormones are still in working order. As we all know, the girl who married the high school football hero was not necessarily the one with the best marriage (maybe *you* were the one who married the football hero!).

"The first time I laid eyes on Jack, I thought, 'Now there's a guy I'd trust with my dogs and children,' " says Lorraine, a stylish, chain-smoking sixty-three-year-old. "Not exactly the kind of feeling that made my heart pound. But looking back on it, I'm so glad I gave him a chance."

Of course there is such a thing as "chemistry," and it would be silly to deny that it is not important. There are times when the chemistry between you and a man is simply not there, no matter what you do. But one of the most enduring myths about women in this culture involves their so-called intuition. We're told from an early age that we have some magical ability to "know" a person from the very beginning, and that we should trust these initial feelings. Perhaps for this reason women, more than men, stick with their first impressions and are reluctant to alter their feelings about an individual—even when all evidence points to a very different conclusion.

So we're the ones who stick around long after a man starts treating us badly—and we're also the ones who decide, with very little information (other than our much vaunted "intuition") whether he's "right" for us or not.

In truth these snap decisions are just another way we limit our options in life. Options, after all, can be as frustrating and disturbing as they are desirable. (You know what we mean if you, like us, have ever spent half an hour in the cereal section of the supermarket trying to figure out what brand you'll buy *this* time!)

8. *"I want someone with my interests."*
Of course you do. But the question is, Just how many interests must you have in common? Lots of women say to themselves, "If he doesn't love bridge, if we don't both love the same opera, if he didn't cry when he saw *Awakenings*, then *forget it*; he'll never understand me."

Some interests should be shared. If, for example, breeding Abyssinian long-haired guinea pigs is your lifelong hobby and you have dozens of them at home, the guy better like guinea pigs, or at least not have allergies. Most interests, however, do not have to be mutual. Jack's idea of a good time on weekends is restoring a Sherman tank he had bought twenty years ago; Lorraine likes to spend her Saturday afternoons at the movies. After several months of bickering at the beginning of their relationship, they agreed to disagree.

We'll be exploring how you can make your differences with a new man a positive factor in your life.

9. *"He has to live in my town. I'm not uprooting my life for anybody."*

This is an argument some women use against traveling or taking vacations in the hopes of meeting someone. Sure, long-distance relationships are difficult and unlikely. But again, by saying no, you're closing off your possibilities.

Ruth was so adamant about meeting a man who lived near her, in Westchester, that when a friend invited her to a party in New Jersey, to meet a friend who was "perfect" for her, she was reluctant to go. "What's the point?" she thought. Then she reconsidered and decided she'd cross that bridge when she came to it.

Ruth began dating, and although the relationship ended, for a while she crossed that bridge—the George Washington Bridge!—many times.

10. *"I want a man who can support me. Why should I spend the money I intend to leave to my children?"*

Your man may be asking himself the *very same* question, and his reasons are as legitimate as yours. At this stage in their lives, many men are reluctant to take on the full support of another person. And there may be many reasons for this feeling, reasons that may or may not be a genuine obstacle to a relationship.

This is yet another way the women's movement has changed men's values and attitudes. You must ask yourself, Is it just a matter of pride, obsolete and outdated, that's making me object to splitting costs? Do I have as much money as he? (Of course there is always the possibility that he does have scads of money and that he *is* cheap! But again, that's a separate issue.)

11. *"I'm not giving up my job for any man; I have a life of my own."*

This can be tricky. When Phyllis, a plump fifty-five-year-old widow, met Bob, she had been working for twenty years as the head of research at an advertising agency; he had just sold his graphics design firm. He was ready to leave the Northeast and move to Florida; Phyllis still loved her work and knew that finding a similar position in Miami would be very difficult: "I would just go crazy down there with nothing to do."

Bob is still living in New Jersey. He is anxious to leave, but desperately wants Phyllis to come with him. Phyllis cares for him deeply, but can't yet make the break from work. The problem is still unresolved, although they are trying to work out an agreement that she will join him in a year, when she has full retirement benefits. He's not sure he wants to wait.

There is no immediate answer to this kind of situation. But over the course of this book we hope we'll give you the tools necessary to decide for yourself whether your work is absolutely necessary to your well-being or if you're using a job as an excuse for veering away from commitment.

12. *"He had a heart attack last year. I don't want to be with anyone who has health problems."*

Understandably widows often fear going through the horror of watching another cherished person become ill and perhaps die. Before she met Jay, Liz was terrified of being with a man who had any health problem. She wanted to know what she was in for on the first date, but of course she knew it was too soon to ask. So at the earliest opportunity she would snoop through his mail (looking for Blue Cross forms, not love letters!) and the medicine chest. "If I found any 'serious' medication or insurance claims, that was *it*," she exclaims. She never felt obliged to mention that she herself took medication for high blood pressure.

So not only does the man have to be rich and famous, he has to be in perfect health too! Whether medical problems are genuinely an obstacle to the relationship or merely an excuse to stay away is a question you should ask yourself. (On this subject I'm biased: my father had his first heart attack at forty-two; he died at eighty-one!)

13. *"I want* commitment—*someone who's interested in marriage."*

You may always harbor the feeling you grew up with: that marriage equals commitment. But ask yourself, What does *commitment* mean to you at this point in your life? It's no longer about having children together, for example. Nor is it necessarily about sharing financial bonds. Instead commitment is a matter of love, trust, and companionship, which are not always contracted by the state.

Ruth grew up in a very orthodox Jewish household, where getting married and having children as early as possible were high priorities for the good Jewish woman. But during many unhappy years of marriage, difficulties with her husband made her lose faith—both in herself and, just as traumatically, in God.

After her husband left her, and as she slowly began to recover, Ruth began to rediscover the depth of her feeling for her religion. She began attending services Friday night, Saturday morning, and several days during the week, time permitting. It was at a weekday-morning synagogue service that she first met Ben, who was saying prayers for his just-deceased wife. Some weeks later, after the service, they talked together over coffee. Soon having coffee together became a regular part of their morning ritual.

In the last year their relationship has blossomed; meeting Ben has helped Ruth shed her depression *and* about sixty pounds. But Ruth is also confronting—and may ultimately reject—a deeply held belief: that marriage is an essential element of a romantic relationship between a man and a woman. Yet although she believes it's somehow her duty, Ruth really doesn't want to remarry. Ben is certainly financially secure, but she makes more than $150,000 a year and doesn't really want to be obliged to share her wealth and all of her free time. Both keep their own homes, dine together three nights a week, and spend weekends together, usually at Ruth's. For now Ruth is thrilled with the relationship, but the issue of marriage preys on her mind. She is sixty years old, and both her parents are dead. Yet every day she wonders, "What would my mother think?"

Ruth might be asking herself that question for a very long time, but so far she has not let it become an impediment to her relationship. More often these days it's the men who are avoiding marriage. Many are afraid of marriage because they worry about the division of property—like you, they're concerned about their children's inheritance. Thus an increasing number of older couples choose to live together rather than marry. What would have been a source of gossip, even scandal, twenty years ago is now commonplace.

In this book we'll be reevaluating many of the dearly

held beliefs you may have about marriage and commitment. Many may still feel right for you; others may not.

14. *"Why bother? After a few dates with me he'll just want to go out with a twenty-five-year-old."*

That old joke about a man looking at his fifty-year-old wife and saying, "I'm going to turn you in for two twenty-five-year-olds" is just that—an old joke. Here are the facts: in the first marriage most men marry women who are an average of two years younger than they are. In the second marriage most men marry women who are an average of three years younger *than their first wives.* That's only five years younger than they are.

The vast majority of men *do not* marry women half their age, even though they may "test the waters" by going out with them. If he, like you, is just getting back into the dating scene, he may feel the need to test his prowess by seeing if he can attract young women. Ultimately, however, he probably wants a mature companion as much as you do.

But the possibility of rejection on the grounds of age is one of the most deep-seated fears a woman carries into a new relationship. It's a confirmation of all our worst nightmares that because we can no longer bear children, we have become unviable—not *vital*, not *sexual*—in every other way. It's a small wonder that many women over fifty think their age precludes them from finding happiness with another man.

Age really *is* relative. In certain areas of your life you may feel considerably older or younger than you really are. Here is a questionnaire that may help you gauge your own feelings toward your age. There are no "right" or "wrong" answers. We just ask you to look at your own responses, and see how you actually feel, relative to your real age.

1. When I get up in the morning, I feel
   0++10++20++30++40++50++60++70++80++

2. When I look at myself in the mirror, I feel
   0++10++20++30++40++50++60++70++80++

3. Before I look at myself in the mirror, I feel
   0++10++20++30++40++50++60++70++80++

4. With a man I'm romantically interested in, I act
   0++10++20++30++40++50++60++70++80++

5. Doing exercise, I feel
   0++10++20++30++40++50++60++70++80++

6. At work I feel
   0++10++20++30++40++50++60++70++80++

7. Playing with children makes me feel
   0++10++20++30++40++50++60++70++80++

8. In bed with a man I can be
   0++10++20++30++40++50++60++70++80++

9. Going to see a doctor makes me feel
   0++10++20++30++40++50++60++70++80++

10. Reading about women in this book makes me feel

    0++10++20++30++40++50++60++70++80++

Fill in the blanks:

11. The activity that makes me feel oldest is _____

12. The activity that makes me feel youngest is _____

13. The biggest age difference between how I feel and how I actually perform is _____

14. The activity that makes for this difference is _____

15. What I resent most about younger women is _____

True/False [check one]:

16. You're only as old as you feel.
    True_____
    False _____

17. Many women like older men.
    True _____
    False _____

18. Many men like older women.
    True _____
    False _____

19. Age is reversible.
    True _____
    False_____

20. The older you are, the better you get.
    True _____
    False _____

Give this quiz to friends who are approximately your age, but whom you consider "youthful" or "crotchety"— and see how their answers stack up against yours.

15. *"It's disgusting the way women go after men—I could never be that aggressive."*

Yes, there *are* some women who regularly read obituary notices and immediately contact the bereaved to offer "comfort." Lorraine recalls a friend who made going to funerals kind of a hobby. She would hear that someone's wife had died, and she would find out as much about the woman as she possibly could. Then she would show up in some slinky black number that would have been more suitable for the Copacabana than a funeral. Hovering around the husband of the deceased, she would insist that she was an old friend of the wife's from high school. "You mean Shirley never mentioned me?" she would ask, incredulous. Usually the husband, not wanting the woman to feel bad, would quickly assure her that, yes indeed, Shirley did mention her frequently. Then the two would be off and running. The woman got many dates this way. "But after about a year of this," adds Lorraine, "some men caught on. People started calling her 'that professional FOB— Friend of the Bereaved.' It was kind of a joke around town—if she didn't show up at someone's funeral, the guy had to be a real loser."

Of course *your* behavior doesn't have to be a black-and-white choice between vulture and dove, but, as you will see, you can be more assertive in finding a mate than you were allowed to be years ago.

16. *"I want friends—people to do things with—and I'm not sure a man is the answer. He'll expect so much more from me. If he's from my generation, he'll expect to be*

*waited on. Who needs all that trouble? I love my free-
dom."*

Some women welcome the chance to fuss over a man
again, but if you're not one of them, you have nothing
to apologize for. "Jack had a very traditional wife who
loved to cook and clean, and he always felt it was somehow 'wrong' to enter into this domestic sphere," says
Lorraine. "And I had very similar feelings about traditionally 'male' activities. But when his wife died, he
finally acknowledged how much he loved to cook. When
we first started seeing each other, I had to convince
him that I wasn't insulted if he wanted to take over in
the kitchen. Now when we're together, he does all the
cooking. And I've fixed all the leaky sinks in his house!"

Maybe your new man is looking for Donna Reed; then
again, maybe he's looking for Margaret Thatcher. You
don't know, and you're not going to know unless you
spend time with him. Just because he grew up as part
of the same generation as you, it's as wrong for you
immediately to assume you know what he wants as he
would be in assuming he knows what *you* want.

17. *"God, I haven't had sex in such a long time." "I've
only done it with one person." "I don't know if I'm any
good." "If sex is part of it, it's not for me." "I'll just
wait until I meet a really rich man on heavy blood pressure medication who won't want to do it." "Even the
thought of how I'll look naked—aaaargh."*

Sound familiar? Embarking on a new sexual relationship *is* one of the scariest things you'll have to face.
It's uncharted territory.

"The first time Ben and I went to bed together, it
was like being a virgin all over again—only this time
the equipment wasn't all bright and shiny and new,"

says Ruth with a laugh. "It was terrifying for so many reasons. First, I hadn't been to bed with a man in years; and second, even though I wanted him and thought I was in love, everything in my religious upbringing told me it was *wrong* to go to bed with a man outside of marriage. All sorts of weird thoughts occurred to me. At one point I almost asked Ben if a man's penis shrinks with age, along with the rest of him. Luckily I thought better of it. Ben told me later that he just assumed a woman couldn't have an orgasm if she was postmenopausal. We laugh about it now, but it's amazing how misinformed two adults can be. As ignorant as teenagers—only now there's a whole new bunch of things to be ignorant about!"

Just because you've driven one car for the last ten years doesn't mean you can't drive another (even if it's a stick shift instead of an automatic!). You can learn, if you want to—and you will. (More about this later.)

18. *"Even if he holds my hand, it's scary. I think of myself as still married to my husband."*

You grew up believing marriage is forever, that you and your husband would go through life arm in arm, in sickness and in health, for richer and poorer, and all the rest. And when you said, " 'Til death do us part," you somehow envisioned the two of you going *together*. And now *this*—widowhood, divorce.

So, at this stage, separation seems overwhelming and impossible to overcome—yet it must be.

Charlotte and Edward met at camp as teenagers and went together for years before they married. They had four children and always had a lot in common. Their kids always jokingly called them Ozzie and Harriet, and secretly Charlotte thought of them that way too. And if their sex life was never exactly fireworks, well, Charlotte thought to herself, it probably wasn't dazzling for Ozzie and Harriet either.

At sixty-four Edward developed Alzheimer's. Charlotte spent two years caring for his every need, until finally he had to be hospitalized. During the years of his illness she was forced to take over all the household tasks he had managed during their marriage: She took care of their financial affairs, sold their house, learned to relate to their "couple friends" alone. She missed her husband terribly, but she had to admit she didn't miss the sexual demands he had placed on her.

When he died three years ago, at first Charlotte couldn't even think about another man—particularly when she thought about . . . *that.* She dated a few times, with little interest or success. Always, when it came to the point of that first kiss, she could feel herself cringing involuntarily. She was only sixty, and very vital and attractive; but when it came to dating, she felt old and awkward. Yet, she had to admit, part of her wanted to see if sex was . . . different with another person. Better maybe? Now she is determined to find out. Although she still hasn't gone to bed with another man, she has gone on a few dates with a widower, who is, as she describes it, "touchy-feely: he always has his arms around me, or is holding my hand, or brushing against my cheek. And for the first time I like it!" Cheating on your husband is disloyal. It is *not* disloyal to go out with someone after he's gone. If you're a widow, he's dead, you're alive. If you're divorced, you must break the bond, and part of that bond is physical. Overcoming this barrier will take time, but for many women it's crucial to getting on with their lives.

19. *"My husband left after twenty-five years. How dare he! I thought I knew him through and through. I don't know if I'll ever be able to trust a man again. I'll be used, and I'll end up hurt."*

Life, as you know by now, does not come with guarantees. Women, more than men, tend to stay in dead marriages—for the kids, for financial reasons, for fear of loneliness. You think that if you hang in there, he will too. But your marriage ended for a multitude of reasons that only time and healing will allow you to understand. You may be hurt. You may be furious. But as we'll show you, you can let yourself be overcome by your emotions to the point of paralysis, or you can use those feelings to motivate yourself in new and positive directions.

This book is about learning to harness those emotions. Moving beyond your obstacles. Taking anger and turning it into drive. Taking sadness and turning it into compassion.

Taking risks and turning your life around.

But even before you can take those risks, you should understand how what you're looking for today is not necessarily the same as what you needed the first time you were considering relationships with men. That's the focus of our next chapter.

3

Dating and Relationships: What You Wanted Then, What You Need Now

No wise man [person] ever wished to be younger.
—JONATHAN SWIFT

Sitting in the cozy little fern-and-teakwood café, waiting for Ralph to show up, Alberta checked her lipstick for the tenth time. She smoothed down her carefully arranged blond hair. She noticed, with alarm, a chip on her newly lacquered nails. At about the same time she realized her panty hose were clutching her like a vise. She made a mental note: Next time, buy Large instead of Medium. Alberta sighed. At fifty-seven dating wasn't what it used to be.

Alberta's mind meandered back to that very first date. She had been fourteen. First her parents had thoroughly checked the boy out. His qualifications: He was a sophisticated older man of sixteen, whose family owned a nearby farm and who once impressed her by lifting up the front end of a horse. After he was deemed acceptable, at least for an evening, they were allowed to go to a restaurant unchaperoned. Junior—that was his name, and his father's name, and his grandfather's name. A family of Juniors. Alberta wondered if there had ever been a senior.

Anyway Junior wanted to go to a local bar, which was filled with couples in dark corners, kissing and holding hands. Occasionally, Alberta had been told, hands could stray. She opted for the Schraft's about a mile from her house—far enough to feel separated from her family, but not too far that she couldn't run home if necessary.

Junior talked and talked. From a distance of over forty years she couldn't recall too much of what he'd said. But, come to think of it, she probably couldn't remember the day after either. She had taken her glasses off the moment they got in the restaurant and spent the whole time hoping she was looking deeply into his eyes, although she might have been staring at his forehead. Junior lectured her about a new brand of hog feed. She wondered if he thought she was pretty.

After dinner (he paid of course, and Alberta realized as she thought of her own wallet stuffed with bills that a girl wouldn't have even *thought* about bringing money with her on a date), they went for a long walk around the local reservoir. This, she knew, was strictly forbidden by her parents, making their time together all the more delicious. She seems to remember hearing music wafting through the air from the radio of a car parked nearby—the words were, "I'll be with you in apple blossom time." Junior promised her a ride on the new tractor his family was buying as soon as they'd saved up the money. Then he grabbed her hand—which was drenched with sweat—and kissed her.

Alberta was suddenly jolted back to the present. Ralph's bright, too-even smile (dentures?) was radiating in her direction. She had met him at the zoo—the only thing she knew they had in common was a fondness for reptiles. He told her about his trip to the Galápagos Islands to see the monitor lizards; she noticed that he had bright eyes and, despite having just come from the gorilla exhibit next door, smelled good.

So here she was. Nobody ever told her she would be dating at fifty-seven. Nobody ever told her her parents wouldn't be around to make sure this was the kind of boy she should be seeing. Maybe she should have asked her children to accompany her? Now, forty-three years later, Alberta desperately wanted a chaperone. And why, why, did she have to pick a restaurant that was so *bright*, when a dark place would have been so much kinder to her skin?

As Ralph sat down, Alberta realized that the only thing this date had in common with that evening with Junior was her sweaty hands.

Dating can be exciting. More often it is nerve-racking. One thing it is *not* is comfortable.

Welcome (back!) to dating. And you thought you'd never again hear yourself utter the words "Last night, my date and I . . ."

If you're already actively looking for a relationship, we'll tell you some things you've probably already experienced for yourself. If you're about to begin the search, or even just considering the possibility, we'll confirm a few suspicions you've probably had all along. Dating was never a picnic, of course—but at least when you were twenty, you believed you had brought along all the right goodies!

What you want from a relationship now is different

from what you wanted when you were twenty. And recognizing the way your needs have changed could make the difference between dating fun and fiascos.

Am I the Only One Looking?

"When I was a young girl, I had a regular routine on first dates," said Lise, a fifty-four-year-old divorcée who's a Carol Channing look-alike. "I would pick one of my single girlfriends to come with me to the restaurant where I was meeting the guy. She would sit at a different table and sort of watch us. We had a prearranged set of signals. If, after a certain period of time, I still liked him, I would cough once into my hand, and she could leave. If I coughed twice, it meant, "Get me out of here," at which point she would come over and remind me that, gee, didn't I have a dentist appointment now and what was I doing here? Now, if *she* answered my double cough with a loud cough of her own, it meant, "Hey, you might not like him, but I think he's cute. I'm going to come over and introduce myself, and you can find a reason to take off.""

If only she had this system now, Lise says ruefully, she would feel better about dating. "But just about everyone I know is either married or not ready to date. They're very interested in what I'm doing, but they don't want to get involved."

The fact is, while your friends may be excited by your dating—while they may even love to live vicariously through your experiences—it may be very hard for them to understand what you're going through. You're at a point when you're getting to know new people and feeling most vulnerable, but who do you turn to for advice?

"When you were twenty, all of your friends were going through the same little ordeals," says Lise. "But now ... who do I share my experiences with? My children? It's awkward. And my friends, who may have had their last date twenty-five years ago, aren't giving me the kind of advice that pertains to today."

Lise remembers telling a friend who has been happily married for twenty-five years about one rather pleasant date. She began the story with, "I picked him up at his house, and. ..." Dismayed, her friend interrupted her. "How could you pick *him* up? That's *his* job. He probably immediately thought you were one of those woman who would, oh, I don't know, choose your own dinner off the menu without first asking him what he thought was best." Lise chuckled, and, wanting to irritate her friend a little more, told her that she had ordered for him—and that she had bought dinner that night. "That finished her," Lise recalls with a grin. "She was apoplectic." Lise finally mentioned that this man was a funeral director and that the reason she picked him up in her car was that she didn't feel like spending the night driving around in a hearse. "Hearing that, my friend calmed down a little," says Lise. "It was the only excuse that made sense to her."

What Happened to the Old Crowd?

In addition to not having the support network of single friends you once had, you also probably don't have "the old gang" that would make dating easier and more comfortable by initiating group activities.

"In college I was part of this cliquish, intellectual crowd. We all wore black, smoked cigarettes, and thought Dostoyevski was a cockeyed optimist," says Erica, fifty, whose dramatic, dark features still look right with sari pants and a caftan. "Basically, though, we were a bunch of scared virgins. Only boys who respected womanhood were allowed into our circle, and these were never boys we dated. Secretly I think we all yearned to go out with the captain of the football team."

Erica recalls the advantages of hanging out with this crowd. "When I was getting to know someone, I could bring them around for inspection. I might not listen to my friends' opinions, but at least I knew they cared. And we had this little club, where we would sit in a dark room, light candles and read poetry, listening to Miles Davis. Whenever one of us had a boy we were interested in, we invited him to the club to see how he got along with the others. We thought we were being terribly cool, but in fact we were doing what everyone else was doing: getting to know men without the pressures of one-on-one dating. There was definitely safety in numbers. No matter how badly some man treated me, no matter what kind of an ass I made of myself, I could always go back to the group for assurance."

Today Erica wishes she had a group of people to date with. "Carrying on an interesting yet nonthreatening conversation with a virtual stranger for hours—sometimes it's tough," she laughs. "Lots of times I wish I could make like Mr. Spock on *Star Trek* and do a Vulcan mind meld—just *know* what that person is thinking, without all the chatter."

When you are given the opportunity to go out in a group situation, Erica notes, the other members of the group are usually couples. "There have been times when I've been really excited about a new man and I want to sort of bill and coo," says Erica. "I could do that if I were with people in a similar stage in their relationships. But if I'm with friends who've been married twenty years, it's a little unseemly. They make me feel like an oversexed old lady."

One time Erica's enthusiasm got her into *real* trouble. She and her date, David, were out for the evening with a married couple, acquaintances of her ex-husband's with whom she had remained friends. "We were all chatting away, and I was sort of playing footsie with David under the table. I thought I was being very ladylike and subtle, but after a few glasses of wine I wondered why Arnold, the old friend of my husband, was staring at me. But David looked at me lovingly every now and then and I assumed everything was okay."

The following day, at the newspaper where Erica worked, she received an impassioned note from Arnold. It began, "Erica, my sweet, I always knew you were fond of me, and I must say the feelings are mutual. Please, I know how strong your feelings must be, but I don't want either of us to be hurt. I am married, and although I always expected more from a marriage . . ."

"It went on like this for some time, and finally ended with the suggestion we meet in his office, on a night when his wife was out of town, to 'discuss things,'" Erica says. "Apparently I had spent an entire evening playing footsie with *Arnold*."

It was an unfortunate yet funny little incident, and reminded Erica of how much this kind of overt physical affection is missing in the lives of most married couples. Although she was always brought up to believe that public displays of affection are in bad taste, now Erica actually makes a point of being physically affectionate in public. "I mean, I don't paw the other person. But I believe that most men my age really *love* having a woman holding their hand and making a fuss, particularly if they've just been divorced. It's been something missing in their lives for many years."

No Fix-Ups

When you were in your teens and twenties, you could sometimes swear there was a secret organization out there whose sole purpose on this planet was to fix you up on dates—usually with weirdos. Mom, Dad, brothers, sisters, neighbors, well-meaning aunts and uncles . . . and then there were your girlfriends, who always had "this great guy. I love him like a brother, really, but I know he's just the man for you." They may have all worn their pants belted somewhere around their chest, but, hey, as all those matchmakers would say . . . you just never know.

You still "just never know." But now, there aren't as many suitable people to fix you up with. "In the good old days, you could look around your classroom and know that, theoretically at least, everyone was ripe for the picking," notes Erica. Even boys with girlfriends, if you were a tiny bit naughty, were fair game. Now, though, available men are rationed like nylons during wartime. "And while there may be some women who will go after men in unhappy marriages, it's not like giving cow eyes to the guy who's been going steady with the class cheerleader. That kind of behavior is shunned by society—and rightly so."

Moreover, many people, even when they know available men, are unwilling to stick out their necks to fix you up. "Sometimes friends who would like to play matchmaker hesitate because they're afraid that their choice of a mate for you might reflect badly on them in some way," says Lise. "For example, if you don't like the person in question, they're worried that you (or the man) will think they don't understand what you're all about."

Lise is remarkably good with languages and speaks seven fluently. Recently a well-meaning friend fixed her up with a man she knew, recently divorced, who had spent many years working at the U.N. "She thought we'd be a perfect match, because we were both so interested in languages. I was delighted and really looked forward to our time together." Unfortunately the man in question was not only not delighted—he was insulted. He thought the friend had put them together as a sort of "test" of his skills. "He approached me like we were in some sort of competition," recalls Lise. " 'How many languages do you speak? Oh, seven? Oh, I see, the *easy* ones. And how fluently? *Oh?*' "

By the middle of the date the man got up to go to the men's room, and Lise looked around the restaurant, half-expecting a bell to signal the end of Round One. To make matters worse, Lise's well-intentioned matchmaker later accused her of being "aggressive" and "threatening" with their friend. "They never fixed me up with anyone else again," she said with a sigh.

What Will Mom and Dad Think? Here's the Good News—They Won't!

There's at least one way dating has changed for the better: You probably won't have to worry about your parents' opinion anymore.

"When I was seventeen, my parents were so strict, I

was afraid to bring home anyone but 'the good neighborhood boy,' " says Lorraine, who has just struggled
through her second divorce. "So generally I dated future accountants, lawyers, doctors . . . the kind of boy
who thought he was getting a big reward if your parents were charming to him. But guess what? I married
two 'good boys' in a row, and I found out that as they
got older, they weren't always so good! All those years
of having to be perfect made them want to live a little
in middle age. Both of them decided to break loose with
twenty-year-old girls—the kind of 'fast girl' they would
have been too scared to date when they were young."

Now, Lorraine thinks, she has learned her lesson. "I
look for the kind of men who've already done their
share of living. Lots of the boys who fancied themselves
as Errol Flynn when they were eighteen are now looking for a little peace in their lives. They've *had* the
chicks and cuties—now they want a responsible, interesting partner."

Some women internalize their parents' opinions so
deeply that they reject perfectly good prospects because
they know they're not the types their parents would've
liked. "I haven't been to church in years, but when a
friend convinced me I should start dating a few years
after my husband left me, I refused three offers because
the men weren't Catholic," says Kate, whose deep-blue
eyes well with tears at the memory. "It was ridiculous.
It's not as if I anticipated fights over how we would
raise our future children. There wouldn't *be* any future
children, so what was I hesitant about?"

Others new to the dating scene need validation of
their own feelings so badly that they substitute their
children's approval for that of their parents. "Vinnie
was sweet, warm, sensitive . . . just a little rough

around the edges," says Lise, who has since dated other men, none of whom she's liked as much as Vinnie. "Okay, so maybe he didn't know the right fork to use with his salad. He really cared for *me*. But when my kids said Vinnie was uncouth, that he wasn't smart enough for me, I was devastated. It was like they had pressed some button." Lise's mother used to complain that she liked men who would rather use their muscles than their minds. "Well, that may be true, but aren't I entitled to like that sort of man? If I want to sit around and discuss the tense political situation between Albanians and Serbians in Yugoslavia, I can call my friends. If I wanted my car fixed or a great back rub, I could call Vinnie."

We're not suggesting, of course, that you start looking for prospective mates in the county jail. It's just that the so-called standards your parents and friends held up for you when you first dated may no longer apply, for several reasons.

First, you may be thinking of the future with a prospective date, but it's a different kind of future than the one you needed at eighteen. "Edmund sells shoes. He's extremely interested in politics, he invests his money well, he's wonderful to me and I adore him—but he sells shoes," says Frances, a sixty-three-year-old radiologist whose previous husband, also a physician, died. "Now, if we were in our twenties, I would never have looked at Edmund twice. I wouldn't have been *able* to look at Edmund, because my parents—my father was a judge, my mother an accountant—would have put the Kabosh on the thing right away. But ambition, or lack of ambition, doesn't really count for all that much when you're in your mid-sixties."

One of the loveliest things about dating during your

middle years is that you don't have to worry about what that boy is going to be when he grows up. He doesn't necessarily have to be a good provider. He doesn't necessarily have to be good with children. You're not planning fifty years ahead—instead it's five, or ten, or fifteen. The emphasis is on what he brings to your life *now*, which you can judge with far more accuracy.

Moreover, as Marybeth, a friend of Kate's who also believed she could never accept a man who wasn't Catholic, recently discovered, religion and ethnic background may be far less important. "I never thought that as a strictly raised Catholic I'd ever find myself with a Jewish man," she marvels. "But then I met Irving, and, at least for now, everything seems to click into place. When he first told me I was the *shiksa* he'd always dreamed of, I admit I had to look up the word, and the first time I invited him to my son's house for Christmas, he had a certain amount of trouble with it. But now things have progressed. He dipped Easter eggs with my grandchildren, and I enjoy being with his family as he conducts a Passover Seder, even though neither of us would ever think of actually converting to the other's religion. There would have been lots of conflicts about this sort of thing when we were younger, but his kids from his previous marriage are Jewish, mine are Catholic, and it's fine."

The Body—Beautiful??

When Lise first began dating, the first priority to her and most of her friends was very clear: The closer a guy's resemblance to Tyrone Power, the better.

"God, we were picky in those days," Lise remembers.

"He had to be tall and dark, with a wide chest and big hands." Later, when things got more serious, it wasn't only his hands that had to be big. "When I think about it now, I squirm. I guess I was what people today call a size queen," Lise murmurs sheepishly. "We never talked about it directly, we just ... well, a couple of my friends and I in college would do a sort of 'postmortem' after that first time. We would sit around a table and hold up various objects—a banana, a lipstick, that sort of thing, and, with every object held up, the one who had just been with the guy had to indicate if her friends were getting 'warmer' or 'colder.' "

Not only are there undeniably fewer men available today, there are even *fewer* men with a full head of hair and muscular body. Fortunately for most women, these attributes simply aren't as important as they once were. "I used to think baldness was kind of icky," says Alberta. "Now I sort of subscribe to the saying a bald friend of mine has on his T-shirt: 'God made a few perfect heads—on the rest he put hair.' "

Coming to accept the imperfections in the bodies of others can be much, much easier than accepting the imperfections in yourself—and for this reason making love holds newfound worries.

You wonder, Will your body excite him? "I made the mistake of going shopping recently in a place where they have three-way mirrors—and, darling, my thighs look like they're made of cottage cheese," says Lorraine. Lorraine is seriously considering plastic surgery as a means of correcting the so-called problem (we'll talk more about plastic surgery in chapter 11), but most women have neither the resources nor the desire to take such measures.

"There are these ads in magazines for some sort of

face cream that feature a beautiful woman, maybe in her mid-thirties, saying 'I won't grow old without a fight,' " Erica comments. "Everything in our society tells us that no matter how wonderful we are as human beings, we can't expect to be as desirable as a twenty-year-old. Well, desirability encompasses a lot of things, doesn't it? This," says Erica firmly, "is a body that has *lived*."

In fact for those women really worried about their own bodies, the thought of an older man who's in really great shape is a worrisome prospect. "You took a nice body for granted when you were young," Erica continues. "Now if a man my age has rippling muscles, I know he really had to work at it. I may be happy that he's interested in his health, but it also makes me ask myself, 'Is he preoccupied with his body? Does he spend most of his life at the gym? And what will he think of *my* body? Is he going to expect me to look like *that*?' Exercise is not my top interest or priority. Being in great shape says more about a man's life and values than it used to—and sometimes it says things a woman doesn't want to hear."

In addition to worrying about their bodies, many women—especially those who haven't made love for a long time—worry that they have "forgotten how," or that they will never be able to please anyone who's not "used to" them.

"When we were young, we were both pretty sure that everything would work," says Alberta. "I mean, it might not be ecstasy, and we might worry whether we would know all the right things to do. But we didn't think much about sexual response on a *physical* level. As one man I've been seeing told me, 'Hell, when I was eighteen, I could get an erection any time—and lots of times it was embarrassing, to say the least.' "

While all this may sound pretty disconcerting, the good news is that tenderness, touching, hugging, and kissing may be genuinely more important—to both women *and* men—than orgasm. "Sex is no longer a goal that isn't reached if one or both of us doesn't climax," notes Erica. "And that's great. It makes sex like going on holiday: Half the fun is getting there." (For some reason men have regarded the fact that it may take them longer to reach orgasm as a drawback; but have they asked themselves why so many younger women prefer older lovers?)

What Matters More Now

While many issues that were important in your youth seem less important now, there are of course several that are much, much more important.

Health, for example. It's no longer something that can be taken for granted. Even if there was sickness in youth, it was taken a lot more lightly. "If you found out that a boy you were crazy about had diabetes when he was fifteen, you thought, 'So what?' " says Erica.

In fact many of us grew up with the idea that there was something romantic about a person with a health problem—and that our involvement with that person would somehow ennoble us. Susan Sontag wrote brilliantly about the romance of certain diseases in *Illness as Metaphor*—the notion that tuberculosis purified the soul, for example, for poets like Keats and in novels like Thomas Mann's *The Magic Mountain*. But Sontag never wrote about the glamour of, say, chronic arthritis.

"When I was young, I always imagined myself faithfully attending some man whose ailing body was merely an appendage to his brilliant mind," says Erica. That is, until recently, when she started dating someone who was formerly a heavy smoker and had been battling emphysema for years. "Believe me, there's nothing romantic about being with a man who always has to be within shouting distance of an oxygen tank."

If you know, when you're beginning to see someone, that he has a health problem, you immediately ask yourself, "How serious is the problem? Is it something that might strike him down any minute? Am I going to find myself nursing someone I don't even know that well, out of guilt? Will there be stays in the hospital? Will there be huge hospital bills? My health isn't perfect . . . what if *I* get sick?"—and so on.

Those who have already suffered through a loved one's illness or death are especially prone to take the health issue seriously. As Yvonne, a fifty-five-year-old widow who watched her first husband die in a slow and painful struggle with heart disease, said, "The next death I endure will be my own."

Equally frightening and guilt-inducing is the possibility of burdening someone else with *your* health problems. Years of unchecked high blood pressure caused irreversible damage to the blood vessels in Liz's eyes. She's on medication now, but she fears that her eyesight could become much worse. "And then what would happen to Jay?" she worries. "After losing his first wife, he'd have a blind lady on his hands."

In addition to health, money plays a much bigger

role in the scheme of things now. A poor man at twenty-five is very different than a poor man at sixty-five. Chances are that at this point he's not going to get that big promotion. "Well, after all, it does say something about a man's character when he hasn't saved for a rainy day," explains Frances, whose beau, Edmund, has invested his money very carefully. Other women think not having saved a lot actually says something nice about a man's character. "After my first husband, Herb—the kind of man who'd cut his own hair rather than spend twenty bucks on a decent haircut—being with someone who couldn't save money would be kind of a relief," says Lise, who added quickly, "Provided of course he'd spend it on *me!*"

If you are well-off, you may have more freedom of choice than you did when you were younger. "I come from a fairly wealthy family, and I married two increasingly affluent men," says Naomi, an immaculately groomed brunette who now divides her time between her Fifth Avenue town house and her beach house in the Hamptons. "I admit that when John divorced me, there was a huge settlement, and I knew I'd never have to worry about money again. But it was strange. Even the thought of trying to find a man in my financial bracket was exhausting. Why should I put myself through it? I guess, at first, I thought any man without money who liked me would be interested only because of my money. My parents had always told me that anyone who didn't have at least as much money as we did was a gold digger. So I had two miserable marriages to rich men I didn't really love, and who didn't love me."

Eventually Naomi met Bob, a seventy-year-old widower, now retired, who had owned a small business in

London. "Of course he had no money to speak of, and I had lots of doubts," she says. But her crush won out, and he and Naomi are now together. She does pay for those weekends on Costa del Sol or their intimate lunches at Lutèce; but his generosity, says Naomi, shines through in many nonfinancial but nevertheless crucial ways. "He tells me he loves being a kept man, and actually I love keeping him," she laughs.

The Most Important Thing That's Changed Since You Were Young: YOU

Clearly there is good reason that what you need from a relationship has changed since you were in your teens and twenties: You are a different person. While this may seem obvious, many women refuse to take this factor into account and discount the changes they see in themselves as just a result of "crankiness" or "old age."

Don't be surprised, for example, if you are not as adaptable as you once were. "I get angry at myself sometimes because I seem to be a stick-in-the-mud," opines Phyllis. "When I went out with a basketball player in high school, I went to every game and cheered, even though I didn't see the point of a bunch of very tall men throwing a ball into a hoop. Now if some man I'm seeing wanted to take me to a basketball game, I'd just say I'd be bored to death, and I know it. But I'm afraid a lot of men would lose interest in me and think I'm a boring crank."

Being less adaptable doesn't necessarily mean being disagreeable or "old"—it means you know yourself better than you did in earlier years. You're much clearer about what you like and what you dislike. There's no reason to apologize for that. By all means, whenever you have the slightest inkling that you'll enjoy some new activity, bravo! Go ahead and try it. But feeling compelled to "go along" with something that is offensive or bores you to tears is something you can do without—one of the many benefits of growing older that you can be proud of. (As Noel Coward once said, "The pleasures that once were heaven/Look silly at sixty-seven!")

It's not only what you're looking for in a relationship that has changed. It's the overall concept of the dating game that has changed as well. And the first rule is knowing how to make the distinction between being an active participant in getting a man's attention and being a *huntress*. Keep in mind that the saying about the sexes still, to some extent, holds true: "He chased her and chased her until she caught him!"

So, where are you going to find these magnificent dates? That's the subject of the next chapter.

4

1,001 Places (Well, at Least 22) to Meet the Right Man

The typical eye overlooks the ninety percent good in any idea because of the ten percent bad that the conventional eye never fails to see.
—CHARLES KETTERING

It's Friday night. Everything is ready: the bowl of Doritos is within easy reach, the butter-pecan Häagen Dazs is waiting for you in the freezer. *White Heat* has just ended on the tube; James Cagney is screaming "On top of the world, Ma" as you switch the channel to a cable station where telepsychic Madame Lenora will explain what the future has in store for you, if you just dial 964-4678 (that's YO-GHOST). You glance at the calendar next to your bed and mark this day with a big X. There are many X's on your Friday nights—forty-two, to be exact.

Next week, you promise yourself, you *will* go out. Next week you'll really make an effort to do something different with your life—because, as your friends and family so frequently tell you, Mr. Right doesn't make house calls.

When it comes to meeting men, sometimes even the most imaginative women are stymied. Well, there are bars, you figure, but that scene is awful; and then there are friends who promise to fix you up. You'll just have to wait for them to get to work.

You could be waiting a very long time.

There are many places to meet men who won't make you feel like you're wearing a huge billboard that reads, Undignified, Unattractive, Embarrassed, Desperate. We're not saying there's a sort of male-rich Shangri La just around the corner; but there are plenty of avenues open for the enterprising woman who, most importantly, has admitted to herself that meeting a man is her (very legitimate) goal and that she wants to do it in the most sophisticated way possible.

A Where-to-Meet-Men Brainstorming Session

At one point in my class at the Couples Learning Center, I will ask women to brainstorm ideas about where they can meet men. By "brainstorming" I don't mean going ahead with the single weirdest idea you've ever had—as in, "Hey, I know! Enlist for a secret commando unit in the Israeli army! Bet there are plenty of available men there!" But I do mean *letting yourself* come up with those ideas. Let yourself think of a quantity of ideas before quality. And let yourself focus all your mental energies on the possibilities before you, without putting lots of no's in your path. You tune out that nasty little critic sitting on your left shoulder (you know him—he looks a lot like Dick Cavett, or perhaps your former husband) and tune in to that cockeyed optimist whispering in your other ear.

Every creative person, from the advertising man to the scientist, knows that the best ideas often come from entertaining *all* possibilities first, testing them out, and then, when there is more solid information or experience by which one can form judgments, narrowing them down to the ideas that work. So, brainstorming is the first step in finding the ideas that work for you.

Usually, when my students brainstorm at the beginning of the course, their list of man-finding locales looks something like this:

- Bars
- Introduction through a friend
- Luck

Not very inspiring! By the end of the class, however, the list has expanded five- or even ten-fold, as your list will be by the end of this chapter. Here's the list from Sylvia. Sylvia is an endlessly cheerful, bespectacled fifty-nine-year-old office manager who has always been the "good daughter" in her family, remaining single throughout her life and taking care of her ailing, demanding parents until they both died last year. She came into the class thinking that meeting a man was as likely as winning the lottery; she left the class with this list of alternatives:

_____ going to singles bars
_____ joining singles groups
_____ taking dancing lessons
_____ taking adult education courses
_____ placing personals ads

_____ answering personals ads
_____ signing up with a dating service
_____ asking friends for introductions
_____ asking relatives for introductions
_____ meeting men at work
_____ learning to hang glide
_____ striking up conversations at the supermarket
_____ traveling
_____ joining a health club
_____ joining Weight Watchers
_____ joining one of those religions that sells things at airports
_____ wearing a button saying "I'm not free, but I'm reasonable"

We'll start with the most familiar answer to the where-do-you-meet-them question, and then move on to happier hunting grounds. But before you read this chapter, make a list of the places you think you can meet men. Then, when you're finished, have a little brainstorming session with yourself, or with some of your friends—see what ideas you can come up with that would be just right for *you*.

The Bars

The first place many women think about meeting men is the singles bar. And because singles bars are the first place in a woman's man-searching experience, they may be her last.

The singles bar is an almost universally unhappy experience. We say "almost," because there are certain to be some drop-dead beautiful Linda Evans look-alikes out there who have sat down at bars and found the men of their dreams. Or, perhaps there is a woman whose dream man is a guy in skintight polyester pants and gold chains, who smells like Old Spice and whose idea of classical music is "Louie, Louie."

For the rest of us, however, an evening at the average singles bar is a recipe for disaster. You are competing for male attention with women half your age in an environment where looks count for virtually everything, because there is really no other information for men to base their judgments on. Worse still, you are meeting them in a place where, likely as not, they don't have all their wits about them.

If you are a knock-out . . . if you can respond to men who are cruising like twenty-five-year-olds . . . if you enjoy making flirtatious eye contact with strangers . . . and if you can go with a friend who's equally attractive—by all means, go to a bar.

Or, maybe you just want the meat market experience. As long as you're there, you might as well play the game correctly. Here's how to get the most out of your evening:

1. Find the most popular "over-thirty-five" places. Don't assume that *anytime* is a good time to go—check and see when the older crowd gathers. There are usually specific nights.

2. If someone looks at you, look directly back at him. "When I went to a singles bar and I got a glance, I would look demurely down, hoping I resembled Mary Pickford," says Erica. "I had to keep reminding myself that I was not a blushing sixteen-year-old anymore, and these days the direct approach is best." Most women, like Erica, tend to turn away. Remember that a man's ego in a bar is as

breakable as the wineglasses. He's risking rejection even more than you. This does not mean that you have to immediately sidle over to him, purring, "Hey, sailor." It just means that if you like the looks of him, you have to look friendly and *accessible*.

3. Don't just randomly plop yourself down at the bar. Look the place over first. (Erica reports that she used to pretend she was looking for a friend while really "casing the joint" for any attractive men. If there were none, she would leave.) If there is an appealing man, sit next to him. Smile. Be inviting. Even strike up a conversation— about anything. See how it goes. Tell yourself you're building skills, talking to men you don't know yet.

4. If you talk to someone, he may very well ask for your phone number. That does not mean he will call!

Some women learn this lesson the hard way. Dawn is a very attractive fifty-five-year-old with long dark hair and sparkling brown eyes who was known as the long-legged beauty of her small Texas hometown. Her dad owned the local watering hole, where she was the belle of the bar for most of her teen years; so one would think she would be well versed in bar behavior.

Perhaps precisely because she *should* know better, Dawn has been burned more than most women. After her second marriage, of nineteen years, ended in divorce, she insisted, despite the pleas of friends and family, that bars would be the place she would meet her next man—after all, hadn't she met her first two husbands there?

But the first few encounters she had were disappointing, if not downright depressing. The men who liked her seemed like dolts, and the men she liked took her number but never, never called. In fact by not allowing herself to "compete" in a fairer arena (and because she had only her old successes with which to compare this experience), Dawn felt she had lost everything—her looks, her charm, her witty repartee.

In fact, usually the man won't call. The idea is to get you to think he'll call, just so that the evening doesn't end on a bad note. It's just too difficult and dehumanizing to say, "Listen, there's no chemistry here, so why not just leave things as they are and not pretend there's something more?" Most men feel it's better to go through the little let-me-have-your-number ritual. It's their way of saying, "Thanks for talking to me tonight."

5. Don't play the equally nasty woman's game: giving an incorrect phone number to a man, just because you find him unattractive and want to discourage him. Some women go even farther. One woman we know would annoy her ex-husband by giving out his phone number. In fact she gave it to so many people that he ended up leaving a message on his answering machine saying, "This is the home of Herman. If you're looking for Lily, her number is _____."

It's far better, though admittedly more difficult, to simply say, "I really enjoyed talking to you, but I'm not giving out my number right now. Thanks so much for the compliment anyway."

Above all, do not feel bad if you try the bar scene and it's terrible—feeling as you do, you're certainly in good company. If nothing else, by going to a bar you will build valuable social skills and get to practice talking to strangers.

A Twist on the Concept: Piano Bars

If you still feel compelled to try your luck at bars, you might seek out piano bars in your area. Often there is a more congenial, less "cruise-y" atmosphere at a piano bar, where people's minds are occupied—not by how cute the blonde looks in a leather miniskirt but by remembering the ninth verse in Cole Porter's "You're the Top."

Kate, the divorced Irish woman who is still too frightened to go on one-on-one dates with men, enjoys spending at least one night a week at a piano bar. She is, by her own admission, "tone deaf"—but she knows the lyrics to *everything*. This talent makes her a popular figure in the local piano bar near her home, a sort of one-woman trivia computer. "I've also made a tidy sum of money knowing lyrics," she adds. "People will bet me. I haven't lost yet." Piano bars are fun as you sing together and laugh together; it's a great place to build a group of "regulars."

Singles Events

We've said it before and we'll say it again: Most desirable men have a squadron of people fixing them up—they are not likely to show up at the average event targeted for singles. The few men who do come tend to be attention-hungry and love being fawned upon by the women. But *do* at least try a singles evening in your area; like going to a bar, it will be good for building social skills and may enable you to meet interesting women . . . who have interesting brothers or friends!

Dances are, of course, a particularly popular event

for singles. If you enjoy dancing but are intimidated by the potential intimacy of the situation, avoid couples dancing and look for folk or square dancing. It can be Israeli, Irish, Greek—anything that involves dancing as a *group*.

Sylvia reports that her twice-weekly folk dancing classes help her get rid of some of her fears of physical contact with men. "I've been so scared of the . . . intimacy . . . side of a relationship for so long, because I've had so little experience," she says. "Just having to hold hands with strange men for an hour twice a week and occasionally having someone put their arm around me is great. It's helping me get over some of those fears."

And who knows how good a dancer you'll become? There's a group of over-fifty (sometimes way over fifty) women in Long Island, New York, who call themselves the Golden Songsters. They formed a sort of tap dancing club fourteen years ago; and now, wearing tight-fitting bodices that show every curve, baby-blue satin skirts, and feather boas, they've actually taken their show on the road!

Meeting Men Through Relatives

Remember how annoyed you used to be when your Aunt Agatha tried to fix you up with her best friend's boy, the one with the oily scalp and the nervous tic? Now of course you yearn for an Aunt Agatha. She may not have always been on the mark as a matchmaker, but at least she had your best interests at heart.

For those of us lucky enough to have relatives who want to fix us up, it's an ideal way to meet men. There are even times when the relative becomes the date. When Jacqueline's husband died, a second cousin on her husband's side came to pay his condolences. Her husband had left some of his financial affairs in a terrible state, and this cousin, a lawyer, not only helped her—they started to date!

While you may once have been ambivalent about family functions—weddings, anniversaries, bar mitzvahs, confirmations, and, yes, even funerals—they're not to be overlooked as likely places to make new acquaintances. Whereas you were once seated at tables with other couples, you may now find yourself sitting at a singles table. Many newly single women complain that this makes social interaction awkward with still-married friends and relatives—but sitting with other singles might, in fact, help you make additional single women friends, and sometimes even male friends.

The Personals

Years ago answering or placing a personals ad (it was likely to be called a "Lonely Hearts" ad back then) meant one thing: *You were desperate.* You would sit there and try to decode each ad: "DWM, looks like Sean Connery, loves good food, great wine, long walks on the beach, seeking sleek, chic, adventurous companion who feels equally at home in jeans or evening gown." Translated, this meant a bald, fat guy who drank too much and would rather go for a cheap day at the beach than spend his money on theater and restaurants. He probably wanted you to cook. He was looking for Katharine Hepburn as she appeared in *The Philadelphia Story.* But Katharine also had to be "adventurous," meaning she had to be willing to do things in bed that require an advanced degree from the Flying Wallenda Academy of Circus Arts.

Fortunately personals have gone legit. Sure, you still have to read between the lines (we all know what "Rubenesque" means), but there are so many people just like you taking out personals ads these days. And the publications that have these columns no longer only have titles like *MANdate* and *Girls Will Be Girls*. For instance, have you seen the number of personals ads in the *New York Review of Books* lately? There are more people for you to discuss Schopenhauer with than you ever thought possible.

The personals worked for Liz, sixty, and Jay, seventy-two. Liz and eight of her friends decided to put an ad in the local paper. It began: "Nine merry widows seek . . ." and ended with a request for photos and phone numbers. The response exceeded their wildest expectations. Over one hundred letters poured in, and the women had a ball dividing them up, deciding who was best suited for whom—and occasionally arguing over the rights to a particularly hot prospect. Liz took a look at Jay's picture, thought, "Well, maybe . . ." and put it in her "check out this one" pile. After a brief phone conversation she had a feeling that something was there, and after the first date. . . .

"God, was I nervous," she laughed. "I had seen and called him, so he already knew I thought he was attractive. But what if he took one look at me and went running in the other direction?" Fortunately he didn't, and this couple is still together.

We think there's something terribly exciting about placing and answering personals ads. If you can afford it, placing an ad might actually be preferable. It puts you in the driver's seat. While you have to make a financial investment, and while it forces you to be up-front and vulnerable about what you want, it also enables you to get a list of available men quickly. Sure, you're risking rejection, but so are they.

A few words of caution: Unfortunately this is a world where some people will prey on the vulnerable. Until you feel very comfortable with him, and perhaps have had him meet a couple of your friends, always meet the personals prospect in a public place. Also be aware that there are sweetheart swindlers out there. You might want to keep your dates inexpensive and Dutch treat until you get a sense of how he lives and what his financial situation is. Strangely enough, letting him spend wads of money on you at the beginning is also not a good idea because it makes you let your guard down too quickly. Many women see a man spending his money freely and think, "Aha, he must really care for me." This can be dangerous because those funds can dry up fast and you would be amazed at how quickly he can make you feel that it wouldn't hurt for you to foot the bills for a little while. That's also fine, but how long will that little while last?

At the Office

Endless articles have been written about the pros and cons of office romance. It is undeniably fraught with danger, as any woman who, day after day, has to face a man whom she has dated and broken up with will tell you.

The only rule here is: Know thyself pretty darn well. On the one hand, a romance with a man you work with almost guarantees similar interests and convenience (not to mention entertaining and unusual places to rendezvous!); on the other, will you be bothered seeing this person if things don't work out?

Bea, in her mid-sixties, is a petite, striking black woman, who wears her steel-gray hair in a short Afro. Her life, it seems, began after her divorce, when she decided to take her career seriously and went back to school to earn her MBA. It took four years, but she got it, and eventually landed a key managerial position at a California clothing manufacturer supervising a staff of thirty. It has been a meteoric rise for a woman who didn't complete her education until she was fifty-six!

Bea is now the utter professional from nine to five. But she has always been turned on by younger men, and she hasn't always been so successful at keeping her distance from those "sweet young things" on the job. In fact, on her last job, at age fifty-five, she had a torrid love affair with a thirty-three-year-old management trainee.

"At first I thought Bud had just seen *Harold and Maude* too many times—that I was just some sort of kinky distraction for him. But when I realized he was genuinely attracted to me, I couldn't believe my luck. I had had a very sexually repressed marriage, and here was this cute little guy not much older than one of my sons who saw *me* as a sex object. He wasn't working in my department, so I knew he wasn't playing around with me to get ahead."

Bea and Bud began taking longer and longer lunch hours and would plan business trips together. "Our best trip was a visit to a tulip farm in the Netherlands. One early morning, in a field, we showed those plants the meaning of the words, "Gather ye rosebuds while ye may . . . !"

For about a year the affair made coming to work a pleasure, but when things began to sour, Bea realized she had to choose between finding another job and losing her sanity. "Bud wanted the things other boys his age want—a wife, kids—and I couldn't give them to him. And in truth the only thing we *really* had in common was that we *loved* each other's bodies." When the affair fizzled, Bea, who considers herself the most level-headed of women, had to move on. "The point is, I wouldn't have traded that year for anything, but I hadn't given enough thought to the fact that I would probably have to leave my job. Luckily I got an even better job and things worked out for the best."

Even after her last experience Bea still flirts with the idea of another office romance, although she's trying to keep herself in check. Bea still invites young men she likes out to events she knows will interest them. "I'm probably one of the few sixty-five-year old women with season tickets to the L.A. Lakers!"

The office can be the best place to met a man—or the worst. Tread carefully.

Conventions or Professional Affiliations

Another way to use business connections for romance—and a way that's a little less risky—is to attend conventions and seminars related to your profession. In addition to the possibility of advancing yourself professionally, you will meet your colleagues and peers in a social situation where you nevertheless have the all-important reason-to-be-there. There is also the benefit of meeting people with similar interests and goals, while you avoid the hazard of running into them every day of your life.

Even at the convention or seminar, however, proceed with some caution—if you've attended these events before, you know they can be like summer camp. There are always a few people who, overnight, can become a subject of gossip and speculation throughout their industry! Bea recalls the time a friend of hers, a designer in her mid-forties, had a one-night stand with a well-known fashion journalist. "She was a little too eager to impress him, and she told him a few things she shouldn't have about her fall collection. The news about her manufacturing troubles came out in the papers the following week and gave my friend more than her share of troubles for the next few months."

Religious Organizations

Remember Ruth? As a young woman she had married a strikingly handsome man and considered it a feather in her cap that he had been interested in marrying her. They had three children. About the time the youngest child was ten, it became evident there were serious marital problems. Ruth's husband was promiscuous, staying away a week at a time, going on trips, running up huge bills. She confronted him; but sullen and indifferent, he refused to stop. Marital counseling didn't help. Finally he left her and moved out of state. After much torment they divorced, but he never paid a penny of child support, nor did he visit his children.

Severely depressed, Ruth started eating for solace. She gained sixty pounds in a matter of months. To support her children, she took a part-time job as a real estate agent. She discovered that even with her depression, she was a born saleswoman, and she began to make quite a bit of money. But neither work nor therapy eased the burden of her loneliness. Although her family had an Orthodox background, she knew little about Judaism. She began attending Friday night and Saturday morning services at a large congregation with her children. She took courses on how to read Hebrew. Meanwhile her income flourished, and she found herself making more than $150,000 a year.

For three years her life continued in this way. Then one day she met a widower whose wife had just died and who also came to the morning service to say prayers in her memory. They talked to each other over coffee afterward. Crushed by his wife's death, Ben nevertheless found it an enormous relief to talk to Ruth.

In the last year their relationship has blossomed. They have dinner together three nights each week and spend weekends together at each other's home. She has transformed her appearance, as she says, "from frump to femme fatale." And Ruth believes that "a little determination, plus a little help from God" have helped her do it.

If you have a religious bent—or even if you don't!—a church or synagogue is a wonderful alternative to the bar scene, a traditional and highly desirable place to meet people beyond your immediate social circle who are likely to share similar interests, tastes, and values.

In the past many churches and synagogues catered to the needs of younger singles. Today, however, recognizing the needs of older singles, many religious institutions have events set up precisely for the purpose of getting singles together.

There is likely to be a church or synagogue in your area that's known for its singles population. Many hold services once a week specifically for under-forty and over-forty groups, usually inviting a speaker to talk on a subject of interest and following up with an extended getting-to-know-you after-service coffee hour.

If you're not sure whether there's a church or synagogue near you that serves singles, ask around.

Libraries

Spend a Saturday morning researching the information you need to enhance your own life. Pore over those reference directories with lists of continuing-education programs, or periodicals with information about some investment you want to make. You may find yourself wrestling a like-minded individual for the same reference book.

Once Phyllis met a man she dated for several months while looking up information about rottweilers, a breed of dog she was thinking about getting. "Dan *bred* rottweilers, and he was looking up some information about a particular bloodline." Phyllis ended up with one of Dan's pups, which she still has (although Dan is a distant memory)!

Libraries also hold "Great Books" discussions, another place to meet people who enjoy reading and animated discussion.

Auctions

Every day, merchandise ranging from farming machinery to rare books goes to auction. People who come to these affairs tend to get sociable and talkative. Hint: If you're looking to meet men, don't hang out at the antique auctions. Wander through and note where there are "interesting" people—art auctions, car auctions, country auctions, you name it.

Lise did meet a man, once, at an auction of cartoon art. A noncollector herself, she was trying to buy an original cell of Porky Pig for a friend who collects vintage Warner Bros. cartoons. "There was this florid-faced man bidding furiously for the same work I wanted. He went at it tooth and nail." Eventually by their furious bidding they drove the price up to something neither of them wanted to pay, but they went out for coffee afterward to discuss the auction. "We had a great time for a few dates, and I really was impressed by him. And I knew he liked my 'fighting spirit,' as he called it. But somehow the competition between us never stopped. He would fight about *everything*. One day, when he was arguing with me about the precise latitude of the Strait of Magellan, I told him I'd had enough. It was like going out with a living, breathing Trivial Pursuit game. But it was fun for a while."

Jogging or Dog Walking

The good thing about morning hours is that they aren't customarily prime-time for "pickups." So, you can make friendly overtures with a minimum of worry about being taken for a flirt.

Phyllis had only acquired her rottweiler because she had met a man who bred them at the library; after that man was gone, she met *another* dog lover while walking her pooch. "Walking a cute dog always gets people's attention, and when Darcy was a puppy, I couldn't make it down the street without ten people stopping me. So I was used to that. And of course people who have dogs always stop each other and exchange doggy tips. What attracted me to Sam was the names he had given his two Airedales. He called them Shall and Will, because nobody could tell them apart!"

Playgrounds and Parks

Grandchildren, like dogs, are excellent decoys or conversation openers, whether you're with your own or approach someone who is with his. Weekends are probably best for meeting this way, since on those days working people as well as retirees will be out and about.

Alberta was particularly lucky: Her daughter, Amy, had identical twins. "Being a grandmother was so much more fun than being a mother. I could hand them back to their mom when they got to be too much for me," Alberta says with a laugh. "Nothing started a conversation faster than strolling out with little Lisa and Laurie in their identical playsuits. And I could tell a lot about a man by the way he reacted to them."

Behind the Wheel

Recently an enterprising older woman, Ruth Guillou, turned the horror of Los Angeles traffic jams into a plus by establishing a "Freeway Singles" club, in which members, aged eighteen to eighty, display a sign with an identification number and the club's address. Those who spot someone they'd like to meet can send a letter to the driver, in care of the club, by jotting down the identification number.

Perhaps this method of meeting people is a bit unusual. But who knows? If you're sick of traffic jams in your area, maybe it's time for *you* to start a club.

Organizations Catering to Your Interests

Thomas Edison, the inventor, seemed to know the secret of youth; he was still inventing in his eighth decade. In the 1920s Henry Ford and Edison visited the California home of their mutual friend, Luther Burbank. Burbank kept a guest book, in which his visitors would sign in. Beside the name and address spaces was a space marked "Interests." Ford watched Edison write in that place, "Everything."

Whether *your* interest is tennis, Tennyson, or tae kwon do, there is likely to be an organization of people in your area with similar leanings. (Of course if there isn't, you can always start one—but more about that later.) Joining a club or organization like this is surely a no-lose situation—the very worst that will happen is that you won't meet a man, but you'll discover a whole new group of people who care passionately about a subject that concerns you.

The key here is to choose the activity wisely and not pick it just because you think it's the best place to meet a particular kind of man. Right after her divorce Bea decided that a good way to meet men was through political involvement—a great notion that she approached in a somewhat addle-headed way. "I thought I would enjoy being around fresh, young men whose consciousnesses were raised vis-à-vis women, so I joined a group that was trying to mount a campaign for a feminist running for mayor on the Socialist ticket. Even if I didn't agree with everything the candidate said, I thought, so what? It should be an interesting group."

Bea learned an old lesson: You can't blame an idea for its followers. "These idealistic, 'politically attuned' young men and women were the biggest bunch of cranks you've ever seen. They made such a show of accepting and loving me because I was black, and the oldest woman volunteer in the organization, but when it came right down to it, all they cared about was establishing their own sphere of power. We spent more time squabbling about who should run our meetings, or who should run out and buy supplies for the office, than raising money for our candidate!"

Bea went on to join other groups that interested her, and eventually hit the jackpot with something all her friends considered not only unusual but downright crazy—an organization called Outward Bound. "Who says you can't learn to survive in the wilderness when you're over fifty? Not only did participating in an Outward Bound program introduce me to lots of single men—who were fascinated that an 'old lady' wanted to live like Thoreau!—but the achievement of completing three days by myself in the mountains gave me a kind of inner strength and peace that I never thought I possessed."

Charities and Fund-raisers

If you have the money and time, joining a charity or volunteering to help organize a fund-raiser is one of the most socially beneficial activities to participate in. You will be expected to donate not only a certain amount of your own money, but to tap the funds of friends as well—that, after all, is what the charity game is all about! But joining the board of a local dance group or museum is a surefire way to meet some of the most powerful, wealthy people in your community.

The advantage of running a fund-raiser? Many women are more comfortable in the role of host than guest, and participating in a fund-raiser gives you just this opportunity.

In areas like New York City, Washington, D.C., or Houston, boards and charities are so clearly a key to social advancement and political power that you will usually be allowed to participate on charity boards only if you have the money and connections to begin with. In smaller regions, however, entrée is somewhat easier. Ruth, for example, started out volunteering to address invitations for a fund-raiser for the local chapter of B'nai B'rith women. Her influence seemed to grow along with her workload: She eventually ended up on the regional board of directors, wining and dining with the most influential members of Philadelphia's Jewish community.

College General-Studies Programs

Many colleges and universities have general-studies programs, where nonmatriculated students can take courses in areas of their interest without necessarily working toward a degree. The courses are usually less expensive than those taken for college credit, and the hours the classes meet are geared for people holding full-time jobs.

Frequently general-studies courses are led by some of the best professors the university has to offer, because they enjoy teaching a diverse, highly motivated student population with a wide age range.

ElderHostel

ElderHostel is an umbrella organization for programs at colleges and universities in the United States and abroad especially designed for people over sixty. Four times a year the Boston-based organization puts out a catalog listing hundreds of colleges and places across the country offering educational programs for senior adults. In addition to attending the classes of their choice, participants can stay in dorms on college campuses for a cost of only about $250.00 a week.

As Naomi, the sixty-five-year-old twice-divorcée, said, "It's the closest thing to being nineteen again! I've always been interested in ancient cultures, and I've traveled around the world several times. I decided to take an intensive introductory course in archeology being offered at a university near my home. Even though I could have gone home every day, I decided to live on campus. There were about twenty people in the class from across the country who had had all kinds of previous careers. We lived together and every day we ate meals together. We got to know each other in a way that's normally impossible for people our age."

There Naomi met Bob, a retired businessman from England, who had heard about ElderHostel and decided to try the program "for a lark." Bob grimaces when Naomi mentions that, as budding archeologists, they really "dug" each other—but in fact they moved in together, shortly after their two-week program ended.

For more information about ElderHostel (and a free catalog), write to:

> ElderHostel
> 75 Federal Street
> Boston, Massachusetts 02110

High School and College Reunions

If you *really* want to feel like a kid again—for better or worse!—why not attend a high school or college reunion? Whether you go or not may depend on what you thought of yourself during those times in your life *versus* what you think now. "I was so unpopular in high school, that even at fifty-seven I had to let everyone know that I had grown up to have lots of friends," says Alberta with a laugh. "I wanted to go, but I knew people would ask me about my former husband. I wasn't sure I was ready to talk about my divorce."

But Alberta gave in to her gut feeling and went anyway. "I admit it was silly, but I dragged along half the people I knew. And—this is even stupider—I was going out with a handsome but utterly narcissistic man at the time. I knew the relationship wouldn't last, but I figured I might as well get some use out of his looks. So I pestered him to wear his gorgeous Ralph Lauren suit, and I got him a natty shirt and paisley tie so that he would look *just so*. I really did get satisfaction out of impressing all those snotty ex-cheerleaders who wouldn't let me join back then. A lot of them," adds Alberta in a happy, conspiratorial whisper, "have gotten quite *chubby*." (Someone once defined *reunion* as "a place where you meet people your own age who all look a lot older than you.")

Many women are simply scared to death by reunions: "Oh, I've grown so old, no one will recognize me" is a commonly voiced fear. Yet we know more than one couple who have met at these events. Remember, that boy who had a hopeless crush on you when he was seventeen still, in all likelihood, remembers you as you were when you were seventeen!

"So, there I was, hanging around the punch bowl, so nervous," begins Maria, a tall, intense woman known for her fiery Cuban beauty when she was a girl. She came from a working-class family that had never encouraged her to go to college, and she had only recently decided to go back to school after her husband died. "As I stood there, Alex, the scrawny class nerd, sidled over to me—only now the orthopedic shoes were gone, he had filled out nicely, and unlike the captain of the basketball team, he still had all his hair!" He'd been the butt of everyone's jokes, Maria remembered, and here he was, a molecular biologist at a major laboratory.

"He made small talk, nervously, and then all of a sudden blurted out, 'I really hoped you'd be here today. I've thought for years how much I'd like to tell you what I thought about you in high school. I was so crazy about you. But . . . you were Cuban; I was Jewish. . . . I knew my parents wouldn't approve. And . . . and you hung out with a pretty tough bunch of kids. I just couldn't tell you back then. Isn't that funny?' "

Maria didn't think it was funny at all—just touching and very, very sweet. He had recently lost his wife; she had lost her husband. They talked. And talked. They discovered that after all this time the "girl from the wrong side of the tracks" and the class brain could actually have a lot to say to each other. They're talking still—and spending long evenings together.

Widow/Widower's Support Groups and Divorce Support Groups

More and more of these groups are cropping up around the country. Sure, they sound like the ultimate downer: lots of people who've just gone through one of the most devastating periods of their lives getting together to talk, talk, talk. In fact both widow/widower and divorce groups *are* emotionally charged, but it's a place to get information, to be comfortable talking, and most important, to know you're not the only one going through this. True, you're meeting people at a difficult time, but it's also a time when they may be opening themselves up to new people and new experiences. And, especially at the widow/widower groups, you're likely to meet men who have had good, solid, loving relationships with their wives.

These groups are not just for yakking. Many of them are organized around lectures. For example someone will come in and give a lecture about easy cooking for men who have never spent much time in the kitchen, or financial planning for widows whose husbands had always taken care of money matters in their household. Biology being what it is, you're more likely to meet more interesting women than men at the widow/ widower's support groups cropping up around the country, but go anyway. And if you're comfortable there, keep going, even if you've heard that financial-planning lecture one too many times. There is a high turnover at widow/widower support groups—every time you go, you increase your chances of meeting someone new and exciting.

Social Clubs in Apartment Complexes

These days many large apartment complexes, especially those designed for the over-fifty crowd, have social clubs. Go! Even if you meet only your neighbors, it's a chance to widen your social circle. (And then again, Mr. Right could be living next door.)

Start Your Own Group!

If no group seems quite right for you, you can always do what many enterprising women around the country have done—start a group that *does* answer your needs. One woman we know, Rose, was dissatisfied with her forays into the singles scene and decided to establish a bimonthly coffee klatch at her local synagogue with the following rules: (a) you had to be over fifty; (b) you had to be single; (c) you had to bring a single man whom you were not dating. Rose reasoned that each woman had at least one man in her life who was not right for her but might be fine for someone else. "The first few meetings were hard," Rose admits. "We knew what we were all there for, but we sort of couldn't talk about it. It was awkward." But eventually the joking would begin, and things would become more relaxed. At each session they would all exchange a mimeographed sheet with their names and numbers on it.

What started one year ago as a tongue-tied group of four men and four women has ballooned into a bimonthly party with about forty participants and a long waiting list (of both women and men) to get in. Needless to say, the group has many relationship successes to boast about—and so far several marriages.

Another woman who loves to entertain holds a monthly gathering at her house called "Dinner at Eight for Twelve," to which she invites six men and six women for an intimate little soiree. The evenings actually turn a little profit: She charges a fifty-dollar-per-dinner "membership" fee.

Yet another woman we know who loves tennis reserved time on her local court one day a month and dubbed it "Singles for Doubles" day. Over-fifty tennis aficionados, she tells us, have, (ahem) a ball. . . .

The possibilities are limited only by your imagination. So, if you still think there are no places to meet men, you haven't looked in the best place of all—your mind!

Even if you're a veritable scholar on where to meet men, you still need to know how to make yourself into the very best "you" you can be—and that's the next subject we will tackle.

5

Upping the Odds of Finding Your Mate

It is not by the gray of the hair that one knows
the age of the heart.
— Sir Henry Bulwer

We hope the last chapter was an eye-opener, helping you see that there are many more places to meet a mate than you once thought possible. But now that you've opened up your mind to the range of opportunities, how do you really improve your chances of meeting this person?

The challenge that awaits you reminds us of the story of Christopher Columbus and the Spanish royal coat of arms. Before Columbus crossed the Atlantic, Europeans believed the world ended out there somewhere past Gibraltar. And Spain took pride in being the last outpost of the world; they thought their country fronted right on the great beyond. The royal coat of arms depicted the Pillars of Hercules, the great columns guarding the Strait of Gibraltar, and the royal motto was "Ne Plus Ultra"—meaning roughly, "There is no more beyond here."

But then Columbus discovered a whole new world out there. The ancient motto became meaningless. In this crisis someone at court had a bright idea, which Queen Isabella immediately adopted: It was simply that the first word, *Ne*, be deleted. To this day the motto on the Spanish coat of arms reads just two words: "Plus Ultra"—"There is plenty more beyond."

There really is "plenty more beyond" for you as well, if like Columbus, you are ready to accept the challenge and seek out new horizons.

Self-Knowledge and Self-Esteem: Knowing You Want a Man

The first step in improving your chances of meeting the right man is simply *being clear with yourself that you really want to.* "Oh, I'm fine by myself," and "I don't need all that trouble" are commonly heard sentiments from the very women who most desperately want a relationship.

For many women who can't admit to themselves that they want a relationship, the problem is self-esteem. Self-esteem is a curious mixture of how you feel about yourself and how you think others feel about you.

Women with high self-esteem, such as Bea, believe strongly in their own attractiveness, kindness, intelligence, and so forth, and trust that the rest of the world views them much as they view themselves. It's not that Bea thinks she has no flaws, but she accepts them and tends to think more about her positive qualities. If life is not going quite as planned, Bea may be upset and frustrated, but she also feels hopeful, because she understands that she has the power to alter her situation. Bea also does not confuse self-confidence with conceit. Many women with low self-esteem mistakenly feel it is a virtue, that feeling otherwise would be conceited or stuck-up.

Women with low self-esteem, such as Kate or Dawn (both of whom you met earlier), dwell on their negative qualities and rarely give themselves credit for anything positive. They believe that something negative happens because they are "stupid," or "unlovable," while a fortunate event is a "fluke" that may never happen again. Some women with low self-esteem may put up a good front and appear self-confident. Inside, however, they fear everyone will discover them for the fakes they really are.

The connection between high self-esteem and finding a mate is crucial. Certainly if you're feeling lousy about yourself and Mr. Right appears tomorrow, you could feel like a new person. But if you're unhappy with yourself, (a) Mr. Right will sense it; and (b) you may not even notice that he *is* Mr. Right!

Self-Esteem Quiz

The following quiz is adapted from *Getting Unstuck: Breaking Through Barriers to Change* (Warner Brooks, 1989) by Dr. Sidney B. Simon. Read the following statements carefully. Many will sound familiar to you— perhaps you've had similar thoughts or feelings at different times in your life. Perhaps you have some of these feelings right now. After each statement you will find three comments. Circle the one that is most true for you.

"Look, there is simply nothing I can do to make a relationship happen. It's not in my hands."

I OFTEN FEEL THIS WAY	I SOMETIMES FEEL THIS WAY	I NEVER FEEL THIS WAY

"Any action I could take to meet a man would leave me worse off than when I started. Better to do nothing than to fail."

| I OFTEN | I SOMETIMES | I NEVER |
| FEEL THIS WAY | FEEL THIS WAY | FEEL THIS WAY |

"I ask my friends for suggestions, but their ideas wouldn't work for me. Maybe someone else, but not me."

| I OFTEN | I SOMETIMES | I NEVER |
| FEEL THIS WAY | FEEL THIS WAY | FEEL THIS WAY |

"I have already tried everything possible to meet a man, but nothing ever works. I will be alone forever."

| I OFTEN | I SOMETIMES | I NEVER |
| FEEL THIS WAY | FEEL THIS WAY | FEEL THIS WAY |

"Sure, there are plenty of ways other women meet men, and I could use lots of them. But I can't figure out which ones I *should* do."

| I OFTEN | I SOMETIMES | I NEVER |
| FEEL THIS WAY | FEEL THIS WAY | FEEL THIS WAY |

"I don't want to make the wrong move. What if I make a fool of myself?"

| I OFTEN | I SOMETIMES | I NEVER |
| FEEL THIS WAY | FEEL THIS WAY | FEEL THIS WAY |

"Ask me to make a decision on the job, ask me what to do about *your* life, and I'm terrific. But when it comes to my own life and problems . . . forget it!"

| I OFTEN | I SOMETIMES | I NEVER |
| FEEL THIS WAY | FEEL THIS WAY | FEEL THIS WAY |

If you have circled "I often feel this way" after three of these statements, it's likely that low self-esteem is holding you back. Here's another exercise:

Self-Esteem Bonbons

This exercise is also adapted from *Getting Unstuck*. Take out a large blank sheet of paper and draw four large rectangles on it.

```
┌─────────────────┬─────────────────┐
│                 │                 │
│                 │                 │
│                 │                 │
│                 │                 │
├─────────────────┼─────────────────┤
│                 │                 │
│                 │                 │
│                 │                 │
│                 │                 │
└─────────────────┴─────────────────┘
```

Three of the rectangles represent people you think have a high sense of self-esteem; the fourth represents you. In the three other rectangles put a circle—a piece of candy!—for every quality that person has that gives them high self-esteem. For example:

- Sense of humor.
- Generosity.
- Always completes the job he sets for himself.

Then see how many "candies" you can put in your rectangle, or "box of candy." This may be hard at first, particularly if you're intimidated by how many candies the other three people you've chosen have in their boxes. But think for a while—you may be surprised to see how many goodies fit into *your* box!

It is human nature to be goal-directed. Establishing that you *have* a goal is the first step. Having a high enough sense of self-esteem to say to yourself, "I want a first-class life, and having a relationship with a man is part of it" is the next.

Of course building self-esteem does not happen overnight. You don't wake up one day and say, "Gee, I really *am* a dandy human being, aren't I?" No, it's a long, incremental process. You don't have to wait until you feel terrific about yourself to look for a mate. In fact, *don't wait*, because the time when you feel you're "just right" is unlikely to come. But always keep it in the back of your mind that you are working, bit by bit, every day, to like yourself more.

Finally remember that finding a man shouldn't be an all-consuming goal—after all, it's a man you are looking for, not a cure for cancer.

So, having established this, here are several suggestions that will help you in your search.

Look in the Mirror

"After my divorce from a promiscuous man who rejected both me and the kids, I sought solace in food," said Ruth. "I ate a lot more and laughed a lot less. Some people turn to drink; I turned to Doritos."

Let's face facts: Your chances of starting a relationship are not terrific if you're fifty pounds overweight. People who have known you for years accept you, but a new man doesn't have those images of you as a slip of a thing to kindle his interest.

In this culture you are deluged with information about how to lose weight, and chances are that if you're unhappy with your weight, you already know quite a bit about dieting and exercise. We can only add that before you start that diet, consult your doctor. He or she will be happy to formulate a program that will work for you. Innumerable studies have shown that successful long-term weight loss is almost invariably accompanied by a moderate exercise program, so now's the time to look into the health clubs in your area, start taking those tennis lessons, or even just begin walking often and briskly. If you've always been the kind of girl picked last for the team, chances are you're not going to discover there's been a Florence Griffith Joyner hidden in you all these years; nevertheless the benefits to your health and mental well-being of a moderate exercise program are enormous.

Finding the Right Exercise for You

Women who have never exercised say to themselves, "Well, it sounds great, but it's too late to start now." These are usually the women who have never asked themselves what kind of sport would best suit their personality; their general attitude is, "Oh, well, everybody's running, but I couldn't do it—it's so *boring*."

In his book *Body Moves: The Psychology of Exercise*, James Gavin, Ph.D., a professor of applied social science at Concordia University in Montreal, suggests that people who want to stick to an exercise program evaluate their personalities first and then find the sport that is best suited to them. For example:

- *Sociability:* Do you most enjoy activities on your own or with other people? Do you make friends easily? Do you enjoy parties? (Golf and tennis are among the most sociable of sports; yoga and swimming among the least.)

- *Spontaneity:* Do you make spur-of-the-moment decisions or do you plan in great detail? Can you change directions easily or do you get locked in once you make up your mind? (Tennis and downhill skiing are most suitable for those who don't mind last-minute changes; yoga, running, and golf are better for those who enjoy routine.)

- *Discipline:* Do you have trouble sticking with things you find unpleasant or trying? Or do you persist regardless of the obstacles? Do you need a lot of support or do you just push on alone? (Running and bodybuilding are ideal for disciplinarians; golf, downhill skiing, and tennis are better for those who like a little help from their friends.)

- *Aggressiveness:* Do you try to control situations by being forceful? Do you like pitting yourself against obstacles or do you shy away when you must assert yourself physically or emotionally? (Martial arts, bodybuilding, and tennis are appropriate for the hawks among us; the doves will probably be happier with swimming, walking, or yoga.)

- *Competitiveness:* Are you bothered by situations that produce winners and losers? Does your adrenaline flow when you're challenged or do you back off? (Although running, cycling, and so on can be very competitive, they usually aren't on a day-to-day basis. Those with the killer instinct will get their biggest kicks from tennis, golf, or downhill skiing. Walking and yoga are better for those who don't care for competition.)

- *Mental focus:* Do you find it easy to concentrate or do you have a short attention span? Can you be single-minded? How good are you at clearing your mind of distractions? (Tennis, golf, and dance require a great deal of focus; with running, walking, and swimming the mind can wander a bit more.)

- *Risk taking:* Are you generally adventurous, physically and emotionally? Or do you prefer to stick to what you know? (Downhill skiing and martial arts satisfy the thrill seekers; yoga, running, and walking make better activities for those who like their sports a little more predictable.)

If you're considering what sport to take up, examining yourself with regard to these character traits may help.

Large and Proud of It

We've talked about weight loss as if it's a must. However, if you're large but healthy and you feel content to remain at that weight, there are many organizations for you. You might want to investigate your local chapter of NAAFA—National Association for Appreciation of Fat Americans. This is both a political-activism group (which takes the stance that overweight Americans are discriminated against) *and* a social organization, designed mostly for men who like their women big. And we do mean BIG; if you've got an extra fifteen or twenty pounds of baby fat to lose, you're probably not large enough for NAAFA men.

Fashion versus Style

Looking good also means knowing the difference between fashion and style.

Fashion is: Buying this year's must-have leather miniskirt even though your knees look like the Pillsbury Doughboy's.

Style is: Eschewing the style-of-the-minute mini for a hem length that better suits you. (On the other hand, if that means getting the mini because *you* have great gams—even though everyone else is wearing hems below the knee—go for it!)

Fashion is: Going to the trendiest store in town, even though its clothing selection may have suited you better back in 1955.

Style is: Finding stores that have clothing you like and feel comfortable in and sticking with them.

Fashion is: Being able to tell your friends you had your hair done by Andre, even if Andre shames you into getting a $150 cut and perm that makes you look like the world's first grandma paratrooper.

Style is: Staying with Gus, the stylist who thinks about how your hair can complement you, not how inconvenient it is that his "creation" has to be perched on your particular head and body.

Discovering your style takes time—and money. Invest in new clothing as much as your budget will allow. Let's face it, most of us weren't born with either a silver spoon in our mouths or a Gaultier gown on our backs. There are a lot of us out there who figure out what matches by looking at flags—"Hey, if red, white and blue is good enough for the United States and France, it's good enough for me."

So, take the time to learn something about style:

- If you don't trust your own taste, go shopping with a friend whose clothing you admire.
- Hate going into stores or live in an area where the height of fashion resembles something you'd see on *Hee Haw*? Get yourself on catalog mailing lists. If you haven't shopped by catalog for years, you're in for a pleasant surprise. Dozens of catalogs, such as Brownstone Studios and Spiegel, have gone upscale, offering great items for mature women.
- If money is a concern, learn to buy your summer clothes when they go on sale in the fall and your fall clothes in spring.
- And when you're thinking of a new hairstyle, find women about your age, with your type of hair, who have haircuts that look especially good on them. Ask them where they got the cut, and go there!

Bea was worried when she decided she wanted to do something to change her looks. She is petite, about four foot eleven, and dresses very conservatively. But she always wanted to feel as tall and striking in her clothes as she felt in her head!

First she decided to stop dying and straightening her hair. Her friends were horrified. "I *like* gray," she insisted, "and I'm not fooling anyone with this straight-hair stuff." In fact her short gray afro, although it wouldn't have suited everyone, looked just right on her.

She then examined her wardrobe and figured that she didn't have enough money at the time for a complete overhaul. Her job as a vice president of an upscale clothing manufacturer required subdued dress, but now she always includes some brilliantly colored article of clothing or jewelry—a print scarf, a handkerchief, a Swatch watch. They say, "I'm not just this stodgy little person in a gray flannel suit. I'm fun."

Whether we like it or not, exterior presentation is important when first getting to know another person. How many times have you said to yourself, "Gee, he seems like a nice guy, but what can he be thinking wearing that seventy-five-dollar suit?" Everyone wants to be loved exactly the way they are, but no one controls what they are and are not attracted to. You improve your chances of meeting someone if you look reasonably attractive.

Reasonably attractive doesn't mean looking like Cher; it means looking as good as *you* can look. People respond not to perfection but to what you project about yourself. One woman we know who always turns heads is about sixty, and if you studied her objectively, you'd say she had a big stomach and heavy legs. But she wears vivid colors that beautifully complement her dark complexion, and despite a little bulk she carries herself like a sprite. "When I walk, I always try to remember the way Katharine Hepburn came down the stairs in her first appearance on film, in *A Bill of Divorcement*," she says. "It was as if she was walking on eggshells."

Be Out There!

Remember Kate, the woman we introduced in the second chapter, who had never been on a single date since her husband divorced her seven years ago? She is a prime example of a lovely, vital woman who, when it comes to a choice between going to an intimate little party where she knows there will be men and staying at home and watching reruns of "Miami Vice," will pick Don Johnson over a flesh-and-blood male every time!

Because she loves to sing, she is forcing herself to go out to a piano bar in her neighborhood, which she enjoys. But, she complains, "I'm so out of practice just talking to men. It's *not* like riding a bicycle, which you learn once and then never forget. You *can* forget. At least," she adds softly, "I have."

Fear is the byword of Kate's life. If pressed, she could not tell you precisely what she is afraid of; she just lives day by day with the gnawing feeling that life is passing her by.

In *Getting Unstuck*, Dr. Sidney Simon explains eight ways that fear can create roadblocks in your life:

1. Fear persuades you to set easier goals and do less than you are capable of doing.

Kate considers it a major achievement if she goes out to her piano bar every couple of weeks. There are men there, but as soon as the music stops, she leaves. She also goes to a book club, where there are no men and the women are friends she's had for years—but she thinks this is "enough."

2. Fear triggers internal defense systems and fools you into thinking that you have perfectly good reasons not to change.

"Of course it would be nice, but I don't need a man in my life," Kate reasons. "I can get by on my own. It's only women who are weak and dependent who need somebody. I can take care of myself." Perhaps Kate *can* take care of herself, but because she is afraid, she has convinced herself that it's somehow *desirable* to be entirely on her own.

3. Fear—especially fear of failure or disappointment—reduces the number of available alternatives to keep you from pursuing them.

"The singles scene is just not for me, and, after all, what else is there?" Like the women in our last chapter, Kate's fears have kept her from considering alternatives.

4. Fear warps your perception of your life and what you can do to make it better.

"This is just the way I am," Kate opines. "I was born alone, and I'll die alone. It's just the way my life was meant to be, I guess. Maybe I will meet a person who's right for me, but it's in God's hands." Whether you relinquish all control over your life to God or to your shrink or to Harry next door, you're still denying that you have any control. Remember that saying: "God helps those who help themselves"?

5. Fear keeps you from asking for help when you need it or benefiting from the emotional support offered to you.

"Pride goeth before a fall" could just as easily read "Fear goeth before a fall," because they amount to the same thing. Kate is incapable of asking anybody for help or support because she is desperately afraid of appearing needy.

6. Fear keeps you from asserting yourself and persuades you to settle for what you feel you must settle for instead of going after what you want.

If Kate is waiting on line at a bank machine and someone cuts in front of her, she'll say to herself, "Oh, well, he must be in more of a hurry than I am," or "The story of my life! He wouldn't be able to do that to any of the people on that line over there." It wouldn't occur to her that she actually had the power to make the trespasser move to the back of the line.

7. To calm your fears, you develop (and get stuck with) unhealthy habits and behavior patterns.

Kate has developed a series of comforting routines and rituals to get her through the weekends. For example she calls her sister in California every Saturday night at 11:00 P.M., telling herself, "I must be home at 11 every Saturday. She expects my call." If you pointed out that she was using the call as an excuse not to go out, she'd laugh. It wouldn't occur to her to change the phone date.

8. Fear often makes you give up just one step short of your goal.

Kate's fearfulness is evident not just in the arena of meeting men; it permeates every area of her life. She got her driver's permit and took driving lessons, but never made the appointment for the actual test. She decided to go back to school to finish her college degree, filled out all the applications, and actually took the college entrance exams, but then failed to meet the admissions officer for the final interview. Once, in a moment of wild abandon, Kate even answered a personals ad, but then refused to talk to the man when he called. Ultimately fear keeps you from taking risks, and risk taking is what a new relationship is all about.

Icebreakers

Many women over fifty claim that they just can't start a conversation with a stranger. After all, they reason, we were the generation that was told it was ladylike to wait until men spoke to us first. Notes Alberta, "I always think of that movie *Summertime*, where Katharine Hepburn was a middle-aged woman alone in Venice desperately wanting to talk to someone but much too proud to let on. That's how I see myself sometimes."

Here are a few ways to break the ice:

- If you're at a lecture or meeting where someone has asked an interesting question or made an interesting comment, afterward go up to the person who asked the question and introduce yourself: "Hi, I liked what you said about that piece by Monet." You needn't worry about rejection. Few things are more flattering to a man than that kind of attention.
- At courses, singles functions, church or synagogue events, and so forth: Walk up to that interesting-looking fellow and say, "Hi, this is my first time here. Is this what the place is usually like?" (And don't be afraid of the tried-and-true opening gambit "You look familiar. Where have I seen you before?" It works!)
- If it's not your first time at one of these events, find someone who does look new and ask, "What brings

you here?" A newcomer will probably be feeling a bit uncomfortable and will be particularly glad for the conversation opener.

But be careful where you ask the "What brings you here?" question. Don't, for example, phrase it this way at a widow/widower's support group or an AA meeting, because you're likely to hear more than you want or need to know at this point. Always keep the conversation light, not confessional.

- If you're at an art museum, sit down next to a work you find interesting and wait for someone to sit down next to you. Ask what he thinks. (After all, that's what those benches in the museums are really for, anyway!)

I discovered my all-time favorite icebreaker while on a brief vacation in France. I had just delivered my umpteenth paper on something-or-other, and needed a break. I decided to go to Paris for the weekend, by myself. I didn't know anyone in the city and didn't speak French. So I simply packed my bags, checked into a beautiful hotel, and immediately registered for a bus tour of the city.

As soon as I sat down on the bus, an interesting-looking gentleman sat down next to me. He was an art historian from the Pratt Institute in New York City. We talked for four hours, and after the tour he invited me out for lunch and a special, by-invitation-only tour of an exhibit at the Louvre.

During the course of the conversation he told me that he signed up for the bus tour whenever he came to Paris. "I have to come here a lot on my own, so here's what I do," he explained. "I'll arrive at the meeting place early and I'll scan the crowd for a person who looks interesting.

Then I'll stand in back of her as we're getting on the bus. Most people go to the window seat, leaving the aisle seat empty. I'll sit next to that interesting-looking person I've picked, and usually, if I'm right about the person, we'll have a great day after the tour has ended."

This gentleman wasn't looking for a date—he saw that I was wearing a wedding ring—but simply companionship and a nice time. And that's exactly what we had!

The key point to remember here is this: Let the world know you're a person who loves interesting, stimulating things. As one woman told me, "When people call, my answer is always yes." This woman has had the greatest adventures and experiences, simply because she's become known as the Woman Who'll Try Anything Once!

What you're doing here is not only looking for a relationship, you're practicing having friends. Having friends is not something you're born knowing how to do, like blinking. Many women who have been married for years have so many of their social needs filled by their husbands that they've forgotten how to interact with people on their own. Before you can be part of a couple again, you've got to learn how to be an "uncouple." This means being able to do things on your own, without convincing yourself that your life is somehow "better" that way.

Beware the Too-Much-Too-Soon Syndrome

While you're practicing what you've read in this chapter, there are three things to keep in mind:

1. Don't think about being out there when you're *really* in crisis.

"When I first began going out, every time a man said, 'Tell me something about yourself,' I would burst into tears," says Ruth.

You must be in a reasonably positive frame of mind. This doesn't mean you should wait until you've just won the lottery. It just means you must at least have enough inner peace to be capable of having a good time.

2. Tone down the anger. You are too angry to be out there if:

- Every time a man says hello, you think, "What does he mean by that?"
- You find yourself making mental notes of his every flaw and comparing him to men you could have gone out with, if only . . .
- You find yourself saying things like "God, the way you [chew, talk, breathe] reminds me of my ex-husband."
- You expect him to misunderstand you, and when he does, you're furious.

You may have every reason in the world to be angry at your ex-husband, but direct that anger to appropriate sources. Don't let it infect a new relationship. That sweet fellow sipping a piña colada across the table isn't your ex, and he isn't All Men—he's just a guy with an umbrella in his drink. So realize where your anger is coming from and don't assume you'll be mistreated before you are.

Anger without apparent motivation is not attractive,

and a man could argue just as forcefully as you that historically women have given men a hard time.

3. Don't reveal everything immediately. Intimacy, like the aging of fine wine, cannot be rushed. You may believe that telling a new man about your dead husband's battle with cancer or your ex-husband's battle with you in court will help you both "get to know each other better." Quite the contrary; it creates barriers, because too much knowledge too soon puts most people on their guard. He reasons (and quite rightly), "If she tells me this stuff and I barely know her, imagine what she'll divulge about me to virtual strangers." Small talk is important at this juncture.

Probably the best piece of advice we can give you is to be out there. To someone like Kate, for example, being out there probably came naturally to her when she was eighteen but has evaporated as a social skill now that she's fifty-three.

Being out there means:

- Looking people in the eye—and smiling!—when you walk down the street.
- Chatting with men at the grocery store, on the bank line, on the bus—anywhere that pleasant everyday social interaction is possible.
- Accepting invitations to events or activities you might not have thought to attend on your own. So what if you don't know a titmouse from a bald eagle! Go on that bird-watching expedition—at least once.
- Going to those professional conferences and seminars you've been hemming and hawing about.
- Entertaining. Lise has at least one dinner party at her home every month, usually with couples that

she and her husband knew before he died. This sets up a system of reciprocity, so that those couples have Lise in their minds when the question "Who can we fix Harry up with?" arises.

- Volunteering—for charity committees, political organizations—whatever is your area of interest.
- Traveling (even if it's just a getaway weekend).
- Not giving yourself flimsy excuses to stay out of potentially intimidating social situations. Got a headache? Take aspirin. Tired? Have a coffee and a shower.
- Saying yes when you feel like saying no!

Being out there improves your skills in talking to men you don't know. Just talking to a man, any man, makes you less awkward and apprehensive in male company. Soon after being divorced, when she wasn't dating anyone, Lise liked to go to her local doughnut shop for coffee every morning about 8:00—"when I'd run into the businessman crowd," she explains. "I made it my goal to go every day and talk to at least one person—any person. It helped me get over the horrible shyness I felt with all men after my husband left me." Even now that she's actively dating, Lise still goes many mornings. "I know the crowd there, and besides, I feel it keeps me in good shape. I'm sort of flexing my conversation muscles first thing in the morning."

In the next chapter we're going to examine what you're looking for in your new relationship—and what kind of compromises you should (and should not) make.

6

Good Girls DO:
New Dating Rules for
the Nineties

At sixty-three years of age, less a quarter, one still has plans.

—COLETTE

Even when she was little, Jacqueline was always known as the girl who knew "the right thing" to do. In fifth grade while others were giving Valentines only to the good-looking kids in the class, Jacqueline gave one to everybody, endearing herself to her classmates; in high school she was the only cheerleader who would talk to the pimply, adoring boys on the chess team. An eager student, she sailed through her early academic years; her teachers loved the way she would sit in the front row of class in her argyle sweaters and perfectly creased skirts, pens and pencils lined neatly in a row, with her huge, beautiful doelike eyes focused intently on *them*.

She married Stuart, fifteen years her senior, during

her sophomore year of college at Vassar, dropping out to follow him to Madrid, where he was beginning a promising career in the diplomatic service. It was a whirlwind romance—so whirlwind in fact that years later Jackie couldn't remember when or where Stuart had proposed. Without thinking too deeply about "love," she just knew it was the "right" thing to do.

After marriage Jacqueline worked hard to be the perfect wife and mother; she was the hostess who always made sure everyone at her elegant, intimate parties enjoyed themselves. She also turned her back on her husband's ever-more-frequent philanderings with a veritable conga line of fiery Spanish beauties. After all, she had been taught that men were just "like that."

Years passed. Returning to the United States, Jacqueline's kids were now going on to college. The dashing young man she had married, the rake who couldn't resist a lovely señorita, was now as stuffed and comfortable as an old couch. Jacqueline even felt he was getting underfoot. Despite his protests that he "needed" her at home—years of high living had taken their toll on his health, and now he suffered from gout and a bad liver—she went back to college, eventually earning her MBA and then taking a part-time job selling real estate. Life finally seemed to have settled down just the way she had wanted it. There was plenty of money, her children were away, her husband had lost his desire and ability to pursue other women. Cozy, she thought. Just right.

And then, disaster. Stuart died of pancreatic cancer, and Jacqueline found herself completely, utterly alone. Most of her friends were really business acquaintances of her husband; her children were busy leading their own lives; she had only started working, and even with their savings and her husband's government pension, she wasn't sure if she'd be able to support herself in the style she had become accustomed to. But her lifelong ability to recognize and "do the right thing" didn't fail her now. She increased her time at work, settled her husband's finances, even looked up old friends she hadn't seen in twenty years. For two years she wore the mantle of widowhood beautifully, just as she had worn the roles of pretty coed, mother, and wife.

And then a man, one of her husband's lawyer friends, asked her for a date.

For the first time in her life Jacqueline was stymied. In the past there had always been some model for her behavior. But here was someone she had known for years who had always struck her as gentle, kind, shy, sensitive—and he wanted to take her on a *date*. He was not only younger than her husband, at forty-nine he was actually three years younger than she was.

Jacqueline had always had exquisite timing. She knew when to get married, when to have children, when it was time to work—and she had gone about all these life decisions with perfect equanimity. But what was the right time for dating? Had she been a widow for an "appropriate" period?

And how did people date these days? How was she supposed to act? She couldn't play the demure ingenue anymore, but neither was she anybody's old granny. Yet at her age there was something so . . . undignified about it.

She used to leave all the planning to the man—and now here was Mark asking *her* to pick the restaurant and movie. Wasn't that his job? And, good Lord, he asked her to pick him up at his house—his car was in the shop. There was something almost . . . masculine about it. Still, he had asked her out, so that was the way things were supposed to be. But then, she decided as she wrapped a lemon silk scarf around her thin, delicate neck, just this one night she wouldn't worry about the way it *should* happen. What was that song? Oh, yes. "Let it be," she hummed, as she started her engine.

Even women like Jacqueline who always knew the right thing to do can lose their moorings completely when it comes to dating in the later years. Because, let's face it, when you were a teenager, women your age were *old*. The thought of a forty-nine or fifty-year-old woman going out on a date was laughable, and maybe even a little gross. You'd think, "God, what are those geezers going to do with each other? Are they going to make out in the back of the movie theater? Think of all that old flesh rubbing up against each other—yuk!"

The change came in the 1970s. Not only was there a 35 percent increase in people over seventy-five, but also, for the first time in this nation's history, there were more people over sixty-five than there were teenagers. And, you realized as you looked around you, many of those people were healthy, vigorous, and attractive.

Today there is a new legitimacy to dating over fifty that didn't exist before—and a world of people who are actively dating.

Still, at first, dating at this stage in your life will probably feel all wrong, like wearing size 7 shoes when you're really a size 8. It is, partially, a result of your age and experience—perhaps you're not "carefree" anymore. (But then, you'll soon realize, you don't have to be.) It's also that uncertainty that comes from being out of circulation for a very long time.

There's nothing unusual about wanting a man in your life. You're not sick, dependent, man-crazy. In fact if you've gotten to the point where you're ready to date, congratulate yourself! You are brave, and even if it all feels terribly awkward, it's a sign that you're moving forward.

Think of it this way: Even though it is easier to, say, go to college at eighteen or nineteen, there are a growing number of people who are going back to school in their forties and fifties. Either way you still end up with a college degree.

While human nature hasn't changed much, the rules of dating really *have* changed, although in some ways they are as rigid as when you were a girl. If you have kids who have gone through the usual dating trials and tribulations in recent years, you are already aware of these changes, but you may not know how they apply to you. So, if you have any doubts, here's a little taste of what's been happening during all those years you've been in hibernation.

Step One: The Little Question

If the Big Question is the marriage proposal, the Little Question is the request for a first date! Who pops the Little Question these days? Does it still have to be the man? If it can be you, under what circumstances is it appropriate? And how do you know if "Want to go out to dinner?" is a request for a date or merely for a dinner companion?

At a time when our lives are increasingly dominated by our telephones and answering machines, there are a few rules of etiquette that have evolved around the new technology. Answering machines have become very useful devices for the shy man who wants to ask you out but is too nervous to risk direct rejection. He'll leave a message, and calling back soon (but not too soon—some things never change!) is de rigueur. The machine is also useful for the cowards among us who want to let the other person down easy: "Hi, this is Judith, I can't go out with you tonight or, um, any night, because you ... well ... I never told you this, but you look exactly like my ex-husband. Actually, you could be his twin and it just bothers me and I'm so so so sorry and (*BEEP*) . . ."

You may meet a man, and he may call—but this does not a date make. "I met Peter at a friend's cocktail party. He was tall, good-looking, but obviously troubled—his wife of twenty years had just left him," said Charlotte. "This was one of the first men I had met and actually liked. It was one year after my husband's death." He asked for Charlotte's number, which she reluctantly, and fearfully, gave him. "But then I began to hope for his call. I sat by that phone for one solid week." Finally Peter did call, and he and Charlotte had a wonderful conversation about a mutual interest, movies. "I thought, that's it, this is really the beginning of something," she said. "I was pretty scared, but also excited." Charlotte decided the first movie they would see together would have to be something by Eric Rohmer—French, frivolous, romantic. He called several times, and each time she waited for him to ask her out. He didn't. "I began to think of him as the Voice," Charlotte recalls. In the last year their phone calls have become a regular Saturday afternoon date—but Charlotte realizes that, for now at least, nothing will progress beyond this point, and she is continuing to see another man. "I can talk about a couple of men I've gone out with, but he never discusses other women. I don't think he sees anyone, although I bet he has lots of telephone dates. I think his wife's abandonment just shook him up too much. It may be *years* before he's ready."

Meanwhile, though, Charlotte has made a very good friend. She has an important place in Peter's life, although it's not the place she might have liked. "It's difficult to understand him completely, but it's still lovely to have someone I know I can talk to," she adds softly.

Other women find that the Big Date is really no date at all but simply the man's desire for companionship. "You know, when we were young, men and women didn't just hang around together. If you were going out, everyone knew what the reason was," says Jacqueline. "But now you can never tell."

After several months of dating, Jacqueline met a man she felt immediately attracted to, a recent widower. He happened to mention how much he missed his wife's cooking, so Jacqueline, herself no slouch in the kitchen, invited him over. As usual, she worried she was being too forward, but squelched those worries in a flurry of chopping, boiling, and baking. At the end of all her preparation Jacqueline had to admit she had really outdone herself and was quietly confident she would bowl this fellow over with her culinary talent. She did— so much so that at the end of the evening he hinted around that he'd like to do this again. After talking to him about his tropical-fish collection for three hours, she wasn't quite so sure they had a lot in common. Still, it was kind of fun, and she said, "We should do this regularly."

Jacqueline lived to eat her words—or rather *he* ate her words, every other Sunday for six months. There was no suggestion that he take *her* out, no spark of romance. Their conversations became more varied and more engrossing, although she knew more about carp than she cared to. Jacqueline realized she hadn't done anything "wrong," but she still felt rebuffed—particularly when he began to come over, eat dinner, and then turn on the TV, settling himself in for a few hours.

Finally she gathered all her courage and suggested to Dick that maybe, just this once, they could go out to dinner? He took her out once and almost immediately afterward began to hint that he really could use a home-cooked meal. Jacqueline bought him a wok and sent it, with a kind note, to his house. Dick got the message, and since then, they've alternated—two dinners out for every one dinner Jacqueline cooks. "Of course it's not ideal," she explains. "I'm still looking for other men for a relationship, but in the meantime I have this very sweet, appreciative man who eats everything I put in front of him. And I have to say, I've become a first-rate cook!"

Of Course If He Insists on Paying . . .

The most irksome problem for women who aren't sure if they're actually *on* a date is the money question: Who pays? "Men get away with murder!" is a common lament for women just entering the dating scene. "You want to hear Horror Date—I'll give you Horror Date," says Erica, warming to her subject. "I meet Harold at his loft. He's handsome in a kind of bohemian, long-gray-haired, I-don't-give-a-damn-about-my-appearance kind of way. He picks the restaurant, a kind of Middle Eastern affair with belly dancers who somehow remind me that I could use a tummy tuck. He drinks liters of sangria, all the while explaining to me how he wouldn't be a word processor if the New York art world would simply come to its senses and recognize him for the world-class genius he really is. Then he describes how he's been gluing live fish onto his canvases, how that really makes a statement.

"Then he begins to look a little green, says 'Oops,' and rushes to the bathroom to throw up. The staff come over to ask if they can help, and I'm whispering, 'Check, please.' One waiter puts the check in the middle of the table, and when Harold returns, he murmurs, 'Oh, hey, thanks for getting that.' I do pick up the check, and even though he has a car and it wouldn't be that far out of his way to drive me home to Brooklyn, he asks me what subway stop I'd like to be dropped off at."

Fortunately most women don't have to endure this combination of insult and injury. But women can no longer take for granted that the man will pick up the check. There is, however, an advantage to the new money rules. When you tell a man you'd like to split the check, that should be a clear sign to him that romance is not in the offing. Most men will get the picture immediately, without additional explanation.

If, however, you're with a man you suspect is a bit tight with money but you otherwise like him, you might suggest making him dinner before going out with him. This way the issue of money doesn't come up right away—and you can see if he has other redeeming qualities. (Of course if he turns out to be incredibly stingy and doesn't create an opportunity to reciprocate for your dinner invitation, then you've learned· what you needed to know!)

Date Gradations

Date gradations are a relatively recent phenomenon. In your youth there was nothing unusual about a first date on Friday or Saturday night. Now, more and more frequently, a dating situation might start with meeting for coffee, then lunch, next drinks on a weekday, then weekday dinner, then Friday, and finally Saturday. Somewhere along the line men and women have gotten the message that Saturday night equals commitment.

"With one man I was seeing it took three months before he gave me one of his Saturday nights," complained Erica. "But I've caught on to this little game." (Before you get your dander up about being invited to lunch, be forewarned that this is not a rule that applies everywhere. For some reason date gradations tend to be more common in urban areas. So don't cancel that lunch date so fast!)

Where Has Chivalry Gone?

In addition to not paying for meals, a woman can no longer take for granted the gallant little gestures she grew up to expect were her due: a man helping her on with her coat, opening doors, or pulling out chairs. It's not that men have become more boorish, it's just that during the past two decades many older men who practiced these little niceties have been told, "Please, don't do that" by younger women, who find these gestures patronizing.

"I used to do all those things as a matter of course," said Jay ruefully. "I didn't mind a woman's occasional indifference, because I assumed most women knew I was just trying to please them. But a couple of years ago I was crossing the street, and I made the terrible mistake of helping a young woman who was trying to manage her large dog with one arm and her groceries with the other. I took her groceries and offered to help her carry them home. She said she could manage very well on her own, thank you—and then her dog growled at me. Since then I've learned my lesson."

Of course today many young women have changed their minds about this behavior and are enjoying this kind of special attention once again. But too many men have found themselves snarled at too many times. So, you can no longer judge a man's character by whether he exhibits these so-called old-fashioned manners.

It is also not necessarily significant if a man says he'll meet you at the theater or a restaurant rather than picking you up. He may or may not be regarding the evening as a date. "When we were young, being picked up by your date was a sure sign that the boy was trying to impress you," says Jacqueline. "It was a way of saying, 'I'd go out of my way to be with you.' And if you still lived at home, showing up at the door meant, 'I want your family to see what a fine, upstanding young man I am.' Now picking you up has no special meaning attached to it."

Driver's Ed

Who drives is yet another delicate part of dating etiquette, since it gets back to that fundamental problem many older women have with being (in this case literally) "in the driver's seat." "When Edmund and I were first getting to know each other, I thought he was a bit of a wimp: He always wanted me to drive," says Frances.

Eventually, however, Edmund admitted to Frances that, like many men his age, he had difficulty seeing at night. "He had been ashamed to tell me," she explained. But for this couple the driving difficulties didn't end there. "After I finally became comfortable with the idea of driving everywhere—when I realized it wasn't an affront to my femininity—he became more and more critical of my driving! Can you imagine! Finally I said that I was going to start driving with my feet if he didn't lay off. That quieted him down for a while."

Yes, It Is Okay To . . .

Although it may have created a few misguided notions along the way, happily we do have many things we can thank the women's movement for. For instance there is really no longer any stigma in being a woman who wants to take an active role in the courting process. An informal survey reveals that most men would be delighted to be asked out by the right woman. The operative phrase here, unfortunately, is "right woman," because few things make a man more nervous than refusing a woman he doesn't want to be with. So simply calling up and asking a man you hardly know for a date on Saturday night is out; the following, more subtle approaches, however, are in:

• When you meet someone interesting, you MAY follow up with a phone call to pursue a topic of mutual interest.

   Susan, sixty-one, is an attractive, formerly athletic but now obese widow who has recently joined Weight Watchers, Overeaters Anonymous, and a mall walking club to help her lose weight. She met Matthew on one of her first mall walks, and they discussed recent political developments in the Mideast as they scooted around the mall. He seemed as interested in the discussion as she was, and every other day they would talk about world politics on their jaunts. Finally Susan decided to take the discussion beyond the mall; gathering up all her courage, she called Matthew at home. They talked on the phone for two hours and agreed to meet for a (low-cal!) dinner.

   They are still building a friendship, but Susan suspects that as the pounds slowly come off, Matthew's interest grows!

• You MAY invite a man to dinner, making the invitation as informal as possible—as in, "On Monday nights a few people from my apartment building get together for dinner. Just a casual, everyone-pays-for-himself thing. Want to come?"

• You MAY invite a man to your house for dinner, again, making the invitation very casual: "You know, it's no fun cooking for one person." Or, "I'd love to practice this new dish I've learned, but it isn't the same for one person. Want to come over and try it?" It will feel awkward initially, but at worst the gesture will be appreciated, and at best—who knows?

But DON'T make a huge, elaborate dinner with candlelight and soft music for someone you barely know. This kind of effort can backfire in two ways. "I used to do that sort of thing all the time," says Lorraine. "And generally I would get one of two reactions: either abject fear, as if I'd laid some sort of trap; or wolfishness, as if the candles and the music were the green light to pounce on me. Either way it wasn't such a great idea. I learned to be a little more low-key."

Another don't: DON'T plan that first date-meal for a weekend. Remember the rule about date gradations. A weekday meal says, "I want your companionship." A weekend meal says, "I want your companionship and maybe your body."

• You MAY approach a man seated alone at a restaurant—provided of course you have at least some intuitive sense that he'd like company. The first couple of times Lise did this at a busy time at a gourmet commissary she discovered that the men were just waiting for their dates. "One was upset because she was late, and the other was just furious at womankind because he was being stood up. Either way neither of them was in the mood to talk to *me*."

The third time, however, Lise got lucky. "He looked a bit sad and pensive, and I said, "You look like that fellow in *Moonstruck*, the NYU professor who'd just been ditched by his bimbo date. Can I play Olympia Dukakis?" He laughed, and asked me to pull up a chair. Turns out I was right—he had been ditched. We had a marvelous evening, giggling about it, and we saw each other for several months after that. He vowed he would never play around with younger women again, and I think he actually kept his promise. Unfortunately he left *me* for an older woman!"

- You MAY buy theater or concert tickets and invite the man of your choice to accompany you. When Jacqueline's husband was alive, they would go to the opera with friends of his; when he died, she missed going terribly, but she didn't want to go by herself or with the other couple. So, when she began dating, Jacqueline would take a different escort every month. She was particularly glad to take a man who worked with her—it gave him a chance to see her in an entirely new light.

  Another strategy is an age-old trick that works as well today as it did when you were a kid: If you have your eye on a man who, for example, likes tennis, buy two tickets for the World Cup finals and say, "A friend of mine was going to go but couldn't make it. I wonder if you'd like to join me." (The worst that would happen is that you'd be stuck with two tennis tickets, which you could probably easily sell to someone else; or you could ask your second choice.)

- You MAY show off some of your talents without being a show-off! Sheila, one of Frances's friends who runs a small catering business, discovered that her next-door neighbor was going through his second divorce. Half the time he spent meeting with lawyers, trying to get custody of his two young children; the rest of the time he spent moping around the house, not knowing what to do with himself.

Feeling sorry for him, Sheila baked a loaf of her finest bread, put a ribbon around it, and left it on his doorstep—but she was a little too embarrassed to leave her name. The next day she thought he looked a bit more chipper.

So she left another loaf, and then another. This continued for about two weeks, and whenever she saw him, he looked cheerier—and more curious, as if he was trying to solve a riddle. Finally she decided to leave a silly note with her bread: "I know this is a hard time for you, but I'd loaf to talk when you're feeling better." Her neighbor came over that day—and, as they say, that was the beginning of a beautiful friendship!

- You CAN invite a man to a party. Phyllis was never much of a party animal herself, but when she was invited to what promised to be a particularly exciting New Year's Eve party, she quickly accepted. She had just broken up with a man she had been seeing for several months, though, and she had the no-New-Year's-Eve-date blues.

  Getting to the party meant a drive from her home in outlying Philadelphia to the inner city, and she hated to drive on that night. So she called her hostess and asked if anyone else was driving in from her area—particularly anyone single. As it happened, there was a single man, who was happy to take her. The arrangement worked quite well—he wasn't a date, but (a) she arrived feeling like part of a couple; (b) he asked her to dance and talked to her, easing the initial awkwardness of the party; and (c) he called and asked her out the next day!

• Men have always initiated conversation based on their interest in a woman's looks—*you can do that too*. Many women think there is something shallow or nymphomaniacal about approaching a man because of the way he looks. Some women even think that if a man is particularly good-looking, that's reason enough *not* to talk to him. As Lorraine said, "Hey, if he looks like a man who knows more about hair stylists than I do, I steer clear."

But that's just our conditioning, and after all, what's good for the goose is good for the gander. Just think of his looks as one small piece of information you have about him—and that your mission (should you choose to accept it) is to collect more data!

Margaret, for instance, was in an airline terminal waiting for the fog to lift so that her flight could take off. She spotted an elegantly dressed middle-aged man and walked over to him to tell him she admired what he was wearing. He laughed with embarrassment, but when she started to walk away, he stopped her; they talked for a while and then continued their conversation for four hours on the plane; they even saw each other for drinks the next day. "It turned into a really fun trip," Margaret recalls.

But beware the young flirt. Sometimes younger men will flirt with an older woman just as a way of flexing their "flirting muscles," as it were—the way a young female assistant might flirt with her older boss. This is particularly true when the woman is in a position of power over the younger man. One fiftyish woman, a partner in a major law firm, was flattered and pleased by the advances of a thirty-two-year-old rookie. He even took her out and sent her flowers on her birthday. She soon realized, however, that he was playing the age-old game of getting ahead in the firm—only now that women are in the boardrooms, it is sometimes the men who are blinking their baby blues!

• You MAY buy the man you like little presents—with an emphasis on the word little. The idea of the gift is to show you're interested in him and that you believe that the two of you share mutual interests. For example send a funny, appropriate card that might relate to a conversation or incident the two of you shared, or a book the two of you discussed. (Do *not* send a card that is overly suggestive, even if bed is somewhere you'd eventually like to end up in. Erica still cringes when she thinks about the time she sent a man she had met at a party a card that read, "I think of you often. Sometimes even with your clothes on.") Videos or cassettes you think he might like would also be fine. Loaned books and videos are best, because it's a way of giving him an easy excuse to come back to you. But don't give anything that sends too obvious a message; save movies about lonelyhearts finding each other or *Debbie Does Dallas* for later!

The Third-Date Rule

If you have a pretty open relationship with your kids, you may have heard about the "third-date rule." This is a tacit dating law that's emerged during the last few years that says that if you don't sleep with the person on the third date, it's over. Fortunately AIDS and fear of other sexually transmitted diseases are changing that rule somewhat. (Now many young daters claim that by the third date they have extracted from their partner a chart of his or her sexual history, in an effort to make sure that bisexuals and drug users aren't on the list!)

Of course this rule need not apply to you; for most older women (in fact for most women) the third date is much, much too soon. But the positive side of this rule is that if you want to sleep with a man on the third date, you don't have to make any excuses for yourself. As outlandish as it may seem for women who grew up believing they should wait until their honeymoon, it is far more common for sex to be an appetizer in a blossoming relationship rather than the main course. (A recent survey of over four hundred thirteen- to seventeen-year-olds across the country revealed that the overwhelming majority could not even conceive of marrying someone without first knowing if they were sexually compatible, pointing up how the times have changed.)

As for the specific etiquette rules of sex (how you introduce the subject, can you buy condoms?), we'll explore them in depth in later chapters.

Man As Woman's Best Friend

What if a promising dating situation fizzles out—if you or your gentleman seem more interested in the restaurant or the movie than in each other? When we were younger, most of us would have walked away from the situation, just chalking it up to "no chemistry" and letting it go at that.

But now friendships are more important than ever before. If there's a chance that your common interests will create a new friendship, it's an opportunity that shouldn't be passed up.

Lise is still trying to find the right man, but in the meantime she has found one very special friend. He is married and has children who are grown. "Patrick is in a very bad marriage, but feels he married forever and couldn't abandon his wife at this stage in their lives." There has never been any sexual relationship between Lise and this man, but they meet every Monday morning for breakfast, have lunch together at an elegant restaurant twice a month, and talk on the phone for hours, two to three times a week. As she says, "I adore him and he adores me. He is there for me no matter what I need. My philosophy is: When life gives you lemons, make lemonade."

When you start considering the possibility of platonic friendships with men, many new avenues open up to you. "Sometimes I'll bring the handsomest man I know to an office party!" chortles Erica. "People can *think* what they want—and somehow it gets the attention of both the women and the men in the room!"

Until she met Rob, her current beau, Phyllis had a platonic traveling companion. "I'm kind of a worrier and a crank on trips. I want to do just what I want to do. In my experience my women friends are equally headstrong." So one day, just on a lark, she asked her young, attractive bridge teacher to accompany her. She knew he was pretty broke and offered to pay the $449.00 airfare—in exchange, he would be a companion and make the traveling much easier. He said, "You're on!", and they proceeded to have the greatest two-week trip to London she had ever had. "We turned lots of heads, because he's about twenty years younger than me. But he was easygoing, affable, and put up with all my moods. I also never had to carry a bag during the entire trip. It was the best $449.00 I ever spent!" says Phyllis enthusiastically. In fact they've already agreed on another trip in the fall, to Istanbul.

In chapter 8 we'll talk about one of the most profound changes over the last twenty years in the rules of relationships: living together without marriage.

The Ten Most Important Tips for the Successful First (or Second or Third) Date

1. The greatest obstacle to a successful first date is how it is perceived. Ideally, it's a potentially pleasant social interlude for two people, during which you exchange information and entertain each other. (Usually of course, it's a living hell, but we're talking *ideally*.)

Repeat these words to yourself, like a mantra: IT'S JUST A DATE.

2. At the beginning of dating, people tend to go to extremes of the behavior spectrum: They either put up a

front and reveal nothing or they tell their complete life history in the course of a few drinks and a few hours. (Men tend to do the former; women, the latter.) Neither extreme is useful. Look for a balance so that the other person can get to know something about you without being frightened or intimidated by knowing too much too soon.

3. When you're feeling lonely, your self-image tends to be skewed. You start to believe you are alone for a number of pernicious reasons—you're unattractive, uninteresting, and so on—that may have little to do with reality. The most fabulously beautiful, talented, intelligent people have *all* gone through periods of being alone—sometimes long periods—because finding the right mate is not as easy as finding the right car (and think how hard finding the right car can be!).

Demanding perfection from yourself or comparing yourself with others leads to negative thoughts, which promote bad inner feelings, which invariably influence how others will feel about you. Self-acceptance and happiness with yourself almost always must come before finding the right man.

4. You cannot assume responsibility for anyone but yourself. Your partner's feelings about the date will contribute to its outcome, but you have no control over these feelings.

5. Many people believe that a first date must be followed by other dates in order to be called successful. However, if you and your partner had a good time together, you had a successful first date. There may be many, many reasons why it might not lead to a long relationship, but they do not cancel out a positive learning experience.

6. Leave your mental "dream person" checklist home. You may be pleasantly surprised.

7. Dress to present yourself at your best.

8. Limit your first date to a manageable time span or plan it around an event.

9. Keep the cost of your first date moderate. Less expense can result in less pressure on both parties.

10. If you feel there are barriers to having a successful first date, communicate your concern in a gentle, undemanding way.

First-Date Questionnaire

Maybe the most important lesson to learn about first dates is that they can't be taken too seriously. Here's a little quiz about that first time, concocted by David Galef, an English professor at the University of Mississippi, who's seen more than his fair share of first dates. To bring the point home, as you'll see, it's about as serious as your first date should be.

1. The last time I went out on a first date was
   A. Last week
   B. Last month
   C. Last year
   D. More than five years ago

2. The average time I spend preparing for a first date is
   A. Five minutes
   B. Two hours
   C. All day
   D. What's time, really?

3. Ideally he should
   A. Show up on time
   B. Show up just a bit late with an apology
   C. Show up

4. When he rings the bell, he should be
   A. Carrying flowers
   B. Carrying car keys
   C. Carrying himself well

5. My idea of a romantic evening is
   A. Dinner and dancing
   B. A dark movie
   C. A long car ride to nowhere

6. He should show that he admires
   A. My sexy body
   B. My superior intelligence
   C. My great sense of humor
   D. My bank account

7. The uppermost thought in his mind should be
   A. How to show me a good time
   B. How to show that he cares about me as a woman
   C. How to seduce me

8. The uppermost thought in my mind should be
   A. How to seduce him
   B. How to show him I'm interested in him
   C. How to get him to divorce his wife

9. I can trust a man whom I know pays
   A. For the check
   B. For the evening
   C. Child support

10. A perfect evening should end
    A. With a second date planned
    B. With a smoldering kiss
    C. In bed

11. If we go by car, he should
    A. Drive with a certain flair
    B. Let me do the driving
    C. Be able to fix a roadside flat in an emergency

12. If we go dancing, he should
    A. Hold me close
    B. Be able to foxtrot, tango, and rumba
    C. Avoid stepping on my corns

13. I want him to smell
    A. Not at all
    B. Ever so slightly of sweat
    C. Of bay rum

14. The worst part about first dates is
    A. Asking the same dumb questions
    B. Answering the same dumb questions
    C. The fear of stark silence

15. Acceptable topics for conversation are
    A. Politics
    B. Religion
    C. Sex
    D. None of the above
    E. All of the above

16. Unacceptable topics for conversation are
    A. His ex-wife
    B. My ex-husband
    C. Sex

17. If he has a line, it should
    A. Appeal to my baser passions
    B. Appeal to my maternal instinct
    C. Not be about his ex-wife

18. The usual mistake I make on first dates is
    A. Telling too much too quickly
    B. Letting him control the evening
    C. Forgetting to buy condoms

19. First dates are
    A. An opportunity
    B. A testing ground
    C. Torment from hell

20. My greatest first-date fear is
    A. Being stood up
    B. Not being able to deal with his sexual advances
    C. Fear itself

In the next chapter we'll deal with everything you need to know about dating but were afraid to ask—from who makes the first phone call to the first kiss.

7

Should You Accept the Less-Than-Perfect Man?

The older I grow, the more I distrust the familiar
doctrine that age brings wisdom.
—H. L. MENCKEN

You've been giving a lot of thought to where you can
meet a man and how to improve your chances of spark-
ing his interest. So far, so good; but have you defined
what your goals are in a relationship? As we've said
before, what you need from a mate at sixty is simply
not what you needed at twenty-five or thirty. Some
women have trouble accepting this notion, because they
think that not demanding the same things of a man at
this stage in their lives means they've "settled"—
perhaps because they're not desirable or "good" enough
to demand more.

But before you tell yourself you're "settling," consider these statistics collected in "Love, Sex, and Aging," a Consumers Union report based on a survey of
the life-styles of 1,844 men and 2,402 women over fifty
(the majority of whom were in their fifties and sixties):

- For every unmarried man over fifty in the United States there are 2.7 unmarried women.
- After age sixty-five the ratio is steeper: 3.3 unmarried women for every unmarried man.
- About half of all women are widowed before they turn fifty-six, setting middle age as the time women deal with this loss, and old age as the time they integrate their widowed status into day-to-day life.

Furthermore, as the Consumers Union report points out, "The official figures seriously understate the problem. They take no account of the fact that more unmarried men than women (57 percent versus 33 percent in our sample) are already involved in an ongoing sexual relationship and are therefore unlikely to be available, nor do they take account of the fact that more unmarried men than women (10 percent versus 1 percent in our sample) consider themselves homosexual. If these percentages from our sample are applied to the official date, the ratio that emerges is *more than five unattached heterosexual women for every unattached heterosexual man over fifty.*"

Why this disparity? Because of what we all know but usually don't think about until it affects us personally: Women live longer than men, so they outlive men of the same age. To aggravate the problem, many women marry men a few years older than themselves, thus becoming widows even earlier.

How do we cope with this imbalance? One way is by *not* waiting around for Mr. Perfect. According to Consumers Union, of 160 unmarried older women in ongoing sexual relationships:

- Forty percent had taken married men as lovers

- Twenty-five percent had taken lovers who were five or more years older than themselves
- Twenty-nine percent had lovers five or more years younger
- Fewer than 1 percent had female lovers

At this stage in your life you have a whole new dimension of needs to consider—so relationships other than marriage or total commitment may actually better suit you. At least they can provide you with a transitional relationship that will bridge the gap between being alone and being married.

First let's discuss the various kinds of relationships you can develop with a man. Then we'll home in on several "types" with one or two prominent character flaws, and you can ask yourself, "If I were otherwise enjoying this relationship, would these flaws be acceptable to me? Or would I rather be swimming in a bathtub of piranhas than get involved with a character like this?"

A Man to Get You Out of a Woman's World

Charlotte, as you may recall, had four children with her beloved husband, Edward, before he became ill with a serious organic disorder at sixty-four. After Charlotte spent two years caring for him, he finally had to be hospitalized. During the years of his illness she managed their financial affairs, sold their house, and learned to relate to their couple friends alone.

Two years later Edward died. As a widow, Charlotte

had reluctantly gone out on two dates, and both times, although the men had shown some interest, she had shut them off.

In the meantime, however, Charlotte was not averse to male company—she just felt too fragile to have emotional demands placed on her. Recently she has actively cultivated a friendship with her sister and brother-in-law. Like Charlotte, they like to attend the theater and the symphony. Charlotte is slightly handicapped; chronic arthritis makes it somewhat difficult for her to get around. When she, her sister, and her brother-in-law go out, *he* will buy the tickets, drive her right up to the door of the theater, park the car, and in general act quite gallantly. Charlotte adores all these little gestures and, as she points out, "If you're traveling with another woman, you can't expect her to park the car!"

Sylvia is fifty-nine, with lustrous black hair streaked with gray. She has a slight stoop and hides her strong, handsome face behind Coke-bottle glasses. The model daughter, Sylvia grew up in a household with an acquiescent mother and a formidable father. Her father, in fact, demanded everything of her right up until the day he died in her care. Sylvia lived with her parents until both passed away, and then with her sister until last year, when her sister developed Alzheimer's and had to be institutionalized. It was, Sylvia affirms, the worst year of her life.

Known as the shy, mousy girl with the heart of gold, Sylvia has never married or had a real boyfriend, and worries that it may be too late to start now. Nevertheless she has started a behavior modification program to lose weight and has shed twenty-six pounds, although she hasn't quite gotten the self-confidence to buy clothes to show off her new figure. But she's working on it and after years of therapy, she has decided that while her goal may not be a husband, it definitely *is* establishing some relationships with men.

Sylvia has worked in the same office for thirty-five years, starting as a bookkeeper and working her way up to office manager. Over that time she had become very friendly with her young boss; she looked forward to their regularly bimonthly lunches. They made a point of not discussing work but rather world events and politics, subjects of mutual interest. When her boss finally moved on to another company, Sylvia was more upset than she wanted to admit: "I spent virtually all my time talking to women, and John gave me a man's perspective on things," Sylvia recalls.

It took her a year to buck up her courage, but finally Sylvia called John—and they've resumed their bimonthly lunches, even though he works at another company across town. Recently Sylvia was delighted when John invited her to his wedding: "I was the only person from his old workplace he felt close enough to invite," she says enthusiastically.

Many women who are not involved with a man complain that they are always thrust into a "woman's world." This does not necessarily mean that they yearn to discuss how the Lakers' starting lineup looks this year but that they miss the male perspective on everything from automobiles to Zaire.

Both Charlotte and Sylvia want more from a relationship with a man than they have now. But in the meantime they are forging bonds with men who aren't suitable for romance but who fulfill other needs in their lives.

A Man's Advice

In this age of female empowerment, where women hold positions of power and responsibility in traditionally male fields, it seems outdated, almost quaint, to admit that you value a man's advice just because he's a man. But it is certainly not unusual for a woman to derive a sense of comfort from having a man's opinion on matters that are not in her area of expertise.

When Jacqueline's husband died, she turned to Mark, her husband's second cousin and also her husband's partner in his law firm, to help her clear up many of her financial difficulties. "I had a lawyer and an accountant, but I loved knowing there was a man around who would look after my interests just because he cared. Even though he was a few years younger than I was, it was like having a big brother," she remembers. (Eventually she and "Big Brother" started seeing each other.)

Lise also has a special male friend who is her "protector." Unhappily married with three grown children, Patrick comes from the kind of Catholic background that dictates he will never leave his wife. But he has enmeshed himself in her life. "Patrick is there for me no matter what I need, whether it's buying a car or getting directions to New York City."

You don't have to feel like you're a "helpless female" just because you solicit and appreciate a man's advice. First of all, you can reciprocate with a small gift, a dinner invitation, whatever—just to show your gratitude. And second, as we all know, advice is something most men love to give! (But don't forget that old proverb, "Ask advice but use your own common sense.")

A Man for Companionship

The hit 1989 movie *When Harry Met Sally* explores the question, Can a man and woman ever truly be friends without sex being involved? The movie never answers the question definitively because best friends Harry (Billy Crystal) and Sally (Meg Ryan) eventually *do* end up in bed together. But, as they say, that's entertainment. In the real world I believe that the answer is, most emphatically, yes.

As obvious as it may seem, many women who grew up in the forties and fifties cannot quite accept this concept; there is, they believe, always an underlying sexual tension that prevents true friendship. Or if that tension is *not* there, there's something a little insulting about it. As Alexander Pope once said, "A woman never hated a man for loving her, but there are many she hated for wanting to be her friend."

Moreover, a relationship that *does* end up in bed doesn't have to end when the sexual element does. Some women have a knack for converting that Lothario into the guy next-door, available for weddings, family gatherings, and other occasions that require a suitable escort. As one woman, a lawyer, told us, "Jim fell in love with himself at first sight, and it was a passion to which he had always remained faithful. So there wasn't much room in his life for me. But as a 'walker'—a man who looked good in an expensive suit and would go anywhere—he was perfect."

Gay Men

It almost sounds patronizing (and plays on certain stereotypes) to say that gay men make better friends than straight men, but many women find that some of their most rewarding friendships are with gay men. For some women, particularly those going through a difficult time in their own relationships, a man who provides pure friendship without even the slightest hint of sexual tension may be comforting. And, as one woman with many gay friends reports, "It seems they enjoy and *value* the company of older women more than most straight men." (Why? There may be any number of reasons, but for now we'll take it at face value and not get into the Freudian implications of this observation.)

We know dozens of women who have benefited from their friendships with gay men. When Susan bought a condo, for instance, the first neighbors to welcome her were two men living across the hall; they knocked on her door with an Apple Brown Betty and a smile. She had never known any gay men before, and initially bothered herself with all sorts of questions about the "morality" of their life-style. But she was lonely, and they invited her to dinner. She reciprocated, and within months the three of them were eating dinner together several times a week. "And we would watch reruns of 'Dynasty' together," Susan added.

Paul, Walter, and Susan also go to the theater together every two weeks—something that always makes quite an impression on Susan's friends. "They're a little jealous that I have such attractive male companionship," says Susan with a little smile. "Of course everyone knows they're a couple, but there's something about the three of us going out together that creates a certain visual impact.

"They've become the most supportive friends I have," Susan continues. "When I complained incessantly about trying to lose weight, it was Walter and Paul who convinced me to join the mall walkers' group; if it hadn't been for them, I would never have lost all this weight and met Matthew [Susan's romantic interest for almost a year]."

Before Naomi, the wealthy twice-divorcée, met Bob, her constant companion was Arthur. Arthur, a social worker, doesn't have nearly as much money as Naomi, so she would usually pick up the bill when they went out for the lavish kinds of evenings she enjoyed. "We had similar tastes in theater and opera, but Arthur couldn't afford to indulge too much on a social worker's salary. I was thrilled to have such a handsome and grateful companion."

If Arthur didn't contribute to the relationship financially, he was nevertheless utterly generous with his time and energy. Naomi owns an apartment in Florida; she likes to have all the comforts of home around her, but she hates to drive. Every winter Arthur would drive all her belongings down from New York to Florida. He would stay for a week of sun and come back. In the spring he would drive back to Florida, pick up her stuff, and return everything to New York. He got a couple of weeks of vacation; Naomi got a devoted friend and companion. "The best part of the arrangement was that some people down there thought he was my lover—and I never bothered to correct them!"

A Man for Sex

"Look, I know most women my age don't feel this way, but to me sex is as important as eating or sleeping," says Bea. "At many points within the last few years I've been willing to sacrifice certain things—such as commitment, and yes, sparkling conversation—for a really good sex life."

We'll be talking about your changing sexuality in much greater detail later. Some women feel that menopause diminishes sexual desire; others say that without fear of pregnancy or worry about possible discovery by young children who may open the bedroom door, they feel more sexual than they've ever felt.

Bea becomes involved with much younger men; other women find themselves gravitating toward men who may not make suitable partners when they're vertical but do just fine when they're horizontal. "It's been acceptable for years for a man to have a pretty young thing on his arm—why not for a woman?" Bea asks. "There should be a male equivalent to a bimbo."

Most women probably won't feel quite as comfortable with this idea as Bea, but nonetheless, looking to a relationship primarily for sex is perfectly valid, provided you're not lying to yourself about your motives. If, in other words, you're convinced you can turn Mr. Studcakes into Mr. Rhodes Scholar, or simply into the perfect mate, better steer clear. Only *you* can judge whether a relationship that is primarily sexual will work for you.

Some Sample Male "Types": Who Can You Accept?

Remember Lily, our fifty-five-year-old divorcée who, fourteen years after her marriage ended, had not yet had sex—or even a mildly intimate relationship—with another man? Lily was the kind of woman who always believed what her mother had told her: "Someday your prince will come. Just wait."

And so, thinking the right man would come to her magically, Lily waited. And waited. It took her fourteen years to finally add her own line to her mother's motto: "Now," she says, "I feel that in order to find my prince, I may have to kiss a few frogs."

The types of men discussed here aren't frogs, but they *do* have certain froggy traits that you may or may not be able to live with. Of course we're being simplistic when we refer to "types" of men. There is plenty of overlap, and probably no man fits neatly into any of these categories. We're just giving you some general guidelines to follow.

After the description of each "type," we've included several questions for you to ask yourself that may better clarify your feelings toward this kind of character. Answer them as honestly as you can and see if you can gauge whether any of these types of men exhibit the kind of personality traits you can cope with.

Mr. Tightwad

CRIMINAL: This is a stickup! Your money or your life!
JACK BENNY: [long pause] I'm thinking, I'm thinking.

How many men do *you* know who might hesitate before making this choice? It takes a comedian of Jack Benny's stature to make cheapness endearing; in real life it's anything but.

The Tightwad. We all know him. He may be that blind date who brings out his pocket calculator the moment the dinner check appears. Or your ex-husband, who would walk a mile for a can of tomato sauce that's ten cents less than the sauce on sale down the block. Or an ex-lover, who would borrow little items—your books, your VCR, your credit card—and conveniently forget to return them. (This is such a universally annoying trait that one culture, the people of Easter Island, has a word for it: *hakamaroo*, meaning "the act of keeping borrowed objects until the owner is forced to ask for them back.")

There are of course the cheapskates of legend, men of huge bank accounts and itty-bitty hearts who continue to intrigue us with their colossal, breathtaking *chutzpah*. Multimillionaire John D. Rockefeller, for instance, swore his employees would rather have a smile and a handshake from their boss than money for their Christmas bonus (his wife gave them cash on the sly). Cary Grant reportedly wore his clothes until they were beyond repair, and then, when they were practically rags, clipped off the buttons with a pair of nail scissors and saved them. Andy Warhol's doyenne- and dollar-obsessed diaries read like one long expense account report: "Later that night we cabbed to Studio 54 ($4.00). . . ."

But a man doesn't have to be Mr. Moneybags for his tightfistedness to make us crazy. He can be just your average, comfortably well-off, workaday Scrooge.

Of course one woman's miser is another woman's intelligent saver, and the only way to tell the difference is to gauge *your* feelings toward his spending habits.

Liz keeps a little poem her boyfriend, Al, sent her pinned to her refrigerator. It's by Hilaire Belloc:

> I'm tired of Love: I'm still more tired of Rhyme
> But Money gives me pleasure all the time.

"Al and I agree there's nothing more satisfying than getting a good deal on something," says Liz with a laugh. "It's interesting how friends who accuse us of being a little cheap are the same ones who are always squabbling about money in their own relationships. Money is actually something that brings Al and me *together*." Liz and Al hate it when they spend more than they should on each other. "One of my girlfriends told me I was nuts, but I made Al return an opal pendant he had bought me after I met a gem dealer at a party who told me he could get it several hundred dollars cheaper."

If your thriftiness is in step with your mate's, consider yourself lucky: That's one huge area of disagreement you won't have to deal with!

If, on the other hand, you feel you have a VIP (Very Important Pennypincher) in your life who's driving you to drink (probably Chianti, $1.99 a jug), there are a few things you should know.

The bad news is that you almost certainly won't be able to change him. The good news is that by understanding him—and trying to view his chintziness in a different light—you may learn to live with (and even laugh at!) the Man Who Would Be King Midas.

One part of the psychology of Mr. Tightwad is his overriding fear that he is being victimized—"taken to the cleaners" is the way some put it. "Oh of course I like to pay," protests Peter, one of the local gray-haired eminences at a Virginia university. "But I deeply resent being *expected* to. When I go to dinner with a woman and she doesn't even reach for her wallet, or when we go to a movie and she simply steps away from the cashier when we get to the head of the line, that's when I get angry." Or as Paul, an advertising copywriter, griped, "Sometimes I feel that I head the committee to Feed the Hungry Women of New York."

The other major problem with the stingy man is that his money style reflects his emotional style: Many Mr. Tightwads exhibit an overall lack of *emotional* generosity. To most women the tie between emotional and financial stinginess is glaringly apparent right from the beginning, though it's something many initially overlook or hope to change. "Every time Paul did something that seemed just this side of absurd, he would have such a good explanation for his behavior that he would make me feel *I* was illogical," says Amy, an auburn-haired advertising-account executive who met Paul at a Clio awards dinner. "Why have two video club memberships when I can use yours?" "Why bring flowers to your friend's house? Everyone knows it's such a meaningless, bourgeois gesture." "Teabags are *made* to be used a few times." "Why should I buy that book if you have it? Any marks I put in it I'll make in pencil so that you can erase them later." This kind of withholding behavior extended to the bedroom: If Amy didn't get things started, they wouldn't start. "He wouldn't put himself on the line in *any* way," Amy adds.

Unfortunately arguing with most tightwads about their spending habits is like putting on a pair of Chinese handcuffs: The harder you pull, the tighter they get. The Tightwad, in fact, is comfortable fighting about money; it pits you against him in a *competitive* situation, and "competitive" is his middle name.

Even the smallest financial conflicts become a game, a battle of wits. One of Paul's mottos was "The one who keeps the best records, wins." If Paul and Amy were on a road trip and they were taking turns paying for gasoline, Paul would always insist he was the last one to fill up the tank—or, even if Amy knew she was the last one to put in gas, Paul would note that she hadn't actually filled it, just put in a few dollars' worth. And if, by some chance, the gas station attendant had checked the oil or cleaned the windshield wipers and Paul got some service without having to pay for it, he was delighted.

"Paul's tightness became just another way to control. When we first began seeing each other, Paul knew that arguing about money embarrassed me. He had no qualms about it, but it made me cringe, particularly if he would start the discussion in a public place."

For Amy, Paul's cheapness was about love. In effect he was saying, "I don't care enough about you to take care of you." But for Paul, saving money was about winning: "It's me against the world, and I'm gonna win."

Once money discussions deteriorate into fights, the Tightwad has got you where he wants you. He is in control. He doesn't have to give up anything, including his heart.

Can You Ever Transform the Tightwad?

Control, Competition, Conflict: These are the Three C's of the Tightwad. But what if, like many of the less extreme Tightwads, he's not stingy across the board, just incredibly parsimonious with *certain* items? And what if he's truly the nonmaterialistic type who believes, as Socrates said, "Those who want fewest things are nearest to the gods"? In other words, if he's cheap not just with you, but with himself as well?

You have several options.

Accept the "Mitigating Circumstance"

One thing you can do is see if there are genuinely mitigating circumstances to account for his cheapness—or at least circumstances that seem mitigating to *you*.

Frances, a physician with a thriving practice, complains her second husband, Ed, is an unbearable cheapskate who cuts his own hair, reuses the paper bags he brings his lunch to work in, and yells at her if she buys a dress that costs more than one hundred dollars— "even though it's with *my* money." But whenever they get into a fight about money, Frances forces herself to think about Ed's childhood. "When he was six, during World War II, his father ran a tourist boat on the Charles River in Boston. Every Saturday his mother would give him a nickel for ice cream. Ed would go down to the piers and check to see how many people were riding on his father's boat. If the decks were full, he'd buy his ice cream. If there were only a few tourists on board, he'd return the nickel to his mother."

Ed, like many men who come from difficult financial circumstances, cannot shake the idea that penury is right around the corner—even if the corner where he lives *is* on Park Avenue.

Don't Take His Cheapness as a Personal Affront

If you let yourself get into a never-ending struggle over money with your cheap partner, you are doomed to lose, because money is not just money to him, it's part of his identity. In some cases it even becomes a potency replacement, so that losing money is losing power. The women who do best with cheap men don't take it too seriously. They don't see it as something directed against them.

See if he'll respond to tenderness and affection. Every time he does something that seems unbearably close to the cuff, say something like, "You know, I think there's more to you than that" or "I'm embarrassed when you do something like that; I'm proud of you in so many other ways." Or "I wish you would try _____; let's see if there are any benefits." Being a tightwad is, above all, a *lonely* life. As Nietzsche once said, "He who cannot give anything away cannot feel anything either." There are some men who want to break out of their pattern, if only they can find someone to trust.

One way to have a satisfying relationship with a Tightwad is to decide, as Frances did, "If you can't beat 'em, join 'em."

Frances and Ed used to argue about how they would travel when they went on vacation; she wanted the Ritz, he wanted Motel 6. Now, to preserve the peace,

Frances will occasionally vacation in high style with friends. But on vacations together, Ed is allowed to have the kind of holiday *he* loves. "We do go more often," says Frances with a grin, "and three trips a year is better than one."

Another way is to reason that you can pick up part of the tab (your part); that way you still have companionship and someone to enhance your enjoyment of the trip.

Can YOU Tolerate a Tightwad?

1. I prefer my mate to be dressed in clothing from
   A. Brooks Brothers
   B. K Mart
   C. This century

2. When we go out to dinner, I am most comfortable
   A. If he pays
   B. If I pay
   C. If we split the check
   D. If we trade off—he pays sometimes; I pay sometimes
   E. If we can sneak out without leaving a tip

3. Given a choice between a lavish night on the town and a quiet night at home, I'll almost always choose
   A. The night on the town
   B. The night at home
   C. The night at home, with most of the lights in the house turned off—electricity is *so* expensive these days

4. Which of these situations would bother you, and which could you laugh off? (Write B for Bothered; NB for Not Bothered.)

_____ He borrows things and forgets to return them.

_____ He's always short a dollar or two.

_____ When he pays at a restaurant, he gently hints it would be a good idea for me to pay the tip.

_____ Although he doesn't need Social Security benefits to live, one of his major objections to marriage is the loss of them.

_____ He empties and reuses vacuum cleaner bags.

_____ He carries only large bills—$50, $100—making it, unfortunately, just *impossible* for him to get change and pay for my cup of coffee.

_____ He always finds ways to meet me "inside the movie theater" or "waiting at the bar" so that he doesn't have to buy my ticket or drink.

_____ He scans the scandal sheets, marveling at the number of times Johnny Carson has gotten married "to all those gold diggers."

_____ He complains that I "spoil" my children by helping them out with their college tuition.

_____ He, after years of knowing him, will tell me *nothing* about his finances

If your answers to the first three questions are C, D, or E and you have a majority of "NB" responses to the last, congratulations! You may just find Mr. Tightwad tolerable for you.

The Ladies' Man

He is impulsive, passionate, and tempestuous. Every date is an event. He takes you to the best restaurants; he buys orchestra seats at the hottest play in town; if you travel, you stay only at the finest hotels. Money seems to mean nothing to him (even when that money is *yours*—some really adept Ladies' Men can make you feel so swept away by their largesse that you forget who's paid for what.)

He remembers all the little occasions, as well as the big ones. He probably has a better sense of style (in both men's and women's fashion) than you, but manages to pull off exquisitely tailored clothing without looking like a dandy.

There's just one thing he doesn't have: a lasting desire to be with you.

There are essentially two popular breeds of Ladies' Man:

1. The one who makes you feel as if you're the only woman in the world for him (even though you know, beyond a doubt, that you're one of five or ten of his "only ones"!). This type is embodied in the movie archetypes David Niven, Michael Caine, Marcello Mastroianni.

2. The one who makes no secret of his penchant for other women, but whom you find yourself drawn to anyway. (Movie archetypes: Warren Beatty, Giancarlo Gianninni.)

For some women the thrill of being with a Ladies' Man seems to override that inevitable moment when he says, "I'm sorry, darling. It's been fun, but it's over." As one woman described her special Ladies' Man, "We soared so high together that even when he dropped me, I didn't mind. I felt like the time we spent together had been an incredible adventure."

The secret of the Ladies' Man? (And a true LM would *never* define himself as one.) If we are to assume that there is a male and female component in every individual, the Ladies' Man has a better-than-average dose of "female nature." Not in appearance, but simply in his uncanny ability to tune in to a woman's way of thinking. (This is not a guy who likes to go out bowling with the boys.) Hence the Ladies' Man will convince you he genuinely understands you. And in a certain sense he does.

He needs action, movement, novelty, attention—and drama. He responds well to fights, jealousy, accusations— up to a point. And that point is where he actually believes you're trying to possess him. If he thinks you're simply putting on a show to demonstrate your affection, he'll love it. And with all his attention, he'll give you the illusion of *safety*—a major factor in his success with women. But remember, it is only an illusion.

One of the greatest fears of many Ladies' Men is that women will find out their deepest secret: They're *boring*. Now, he may not actually be boring to you at all, but many Ladies' Men are terrified of the possibility. He doesn't want anyone to know him too well, because he's afraid she won't like what she finds. More than most men, the Ladies' Man is uncomfortable with his inner self. He will disdain introspection, because he fears that if he looks too closely, he'll find . . . nothing.

And guess what? Your chances of changing him are about as likely as finding a Sumo wrestler who's a picky eater.

Can you have a successful (read "entertaining," "enjoyable," "not serious") relationship with a Ladies' Man? Imagine yourself making these statements and ask yourself whether the following behavior is Acceptable, Sometimes Acceptable, or Never Acceptable:

1. "When we're together, it's my every dream come true— champagne, caviar, and making love next to an open fire. Problem is, we see each other maybe once a month—and in between, he never calls."

ACCEPTABLE   SOMETIMES ACCEPTABLE   NOT ACCEPTABLE

2. "He says he's been married and he's been single, and he simply prefers being single."

ACCEPTABLE   SOMETIMES ACCEPTABLE   NOT ACCEPTABLE

3. "Okay, so maybe my legs don't *really* look like Betty Grable's, and maybe my breasts don't *really* remind him of a ruddy country girl of nineteen. He always says the right thing, whether it's true or not."

ACCEPTABLE   SOMETIMES ACCEPTABLE   NOT ACCEPTABLE

4. "He is technically wonderful in bed—and I have a pretty good idea just how many women he's been with to perfect his technique."

ACCEPTABLE   SOMETIMES ACCEPTABLE   NOT ACCEPTABLE

5. "Even though he knows all the right moves, I sometimes feel the sex with him is a bit, well, generic—it could be good for *anybody*."

ACCEPTABLE   SOMETIMES ACCEPTABLE   NOT ACCEPTABLE

6. "He doesn't try to hide from me how much he adores women, and how I am one of the multitude he adores."

ACCEPTABLE   SOMETIMES ACCEPTABLE   NOT ACCEPTABLE

How many "Acceptables" did you circle? If you circled five or six, you stand a reasonably good chance of having a great time with a Ladies' Man—at least for a while. If you circled lots of "Sometimes Acceptables" or "Not Acceptables," you are probably looking for someone more stable, and all the wining and dining in the world won't make this man right for you.

Peter Pan

"I won't grow up," Peter Pan boasted in the classic children's tale, about a little boy who wanted to retain the freedom of youth forever. Who would have thought Peter would speak for millions of American men? These are the boys who are keeping the plastic surgeons in condos, and keeping their wives, ex-wives, and twenty-five-year-old girlfriends at bay.

Twenty years ago a Peter Pan might have been confused with a Ladies' Man, because of their similar inability to make commitments. But since Dan Kiley wrote his book, *The Peter Pan Syndrome*, this man has come to be recognized as a breed unto himself. For example, a Peter Pan may be a monogamous type; he may even be the sort of fellow to work himself into the bosom of your family. And he may stay put, for years and years. But when it comes to uttering the word *responsibility* or making this arrangement official, you'll probably see him take wing. Peter Pan is only comfortable in a room as long as the window's open; he needs an out.

After Paul, Amy met her Peter Pan at her salon where *he* was getting his weekly massage and facial. "I thought there was something sweet about this big, burly guy getting a facial," says Amy ruefully. "While we waited, we talked." Michael was about fifty-five, a high school teacher, never married. He and his friends had a rock band called the Consenting Adults. "He invited me out for coffee."

That cup of coffee progressed to more coffee, then dinner, at Amy's home; soon they were spending weekends together. Michael quickly became ensconced at her house; the perfect "friend of the family," he took her son to baseball practice and her daughter to her riding lessons. Amy, recently divorced, enjoyed that familiar sense of domesticity that having a man around the house gave her. Even if he didn't contribute much to the family coffers, she liked knowing he'd be parked in front of her TV set, watching his football games every Sunday afternoon. Months, then a couple of years, passed in this way, until Amy's children were about to head off to college. Just at the time she desperately needed her ex-husband to continue paying alimony so that she could help the kids out with their tuition, her ex was threatening to take her to court; he had heard about Michael and was claiming that Amy hadn't married Michael in order to force him to continue to pay alimony.

This was the first time the subject of marriage had come up between them. "Suddenly Michael always had something else to do during the weekend, and then on weekdays," Amy said. Eventually he just stopped showing up altogether. "I could never get a full explanation from him, and several months passed before I heard, through a neighbor, that he had "adopted" another woman and her kids. It was at that point I realized that Michael was in love with the concept of a family, but that actually having to take responsibility for it was beyond him," says Amy.

"I wish the new woman and her kids luck," Amy adds. Michael still wanted to be the little boy, with a mommy taking care of him. Even in bed Michael was a snuggler—but he snuggled like a *kid*. He rarely put his arms around Amy; instead he wanted Amy to put her arms around *him*. He would lay his head on her chest, but would feel uncomfortable if she lay on him.

He craved support and nurturing, as long as no demands were made on him.

Can you play Tinkerbell to your Peter Pan? (Can you be the good fairy who grants your boy all his wishes?)

1. I am sexually aroused by:
   A. Smoldering eyes
   B. Finely sculpted hands
   C. Hair weaves

2. The character Dudley Moore played in Blake Edwards's movie *10* was
   A. Charming
   B. Exasperating
   C. My ex-husband

3. When I hear the word *commitment*, I visualize
   A. Wedding bells
   B. Joint tax returns
   C. The rear end of my man, scampering for the open fields like Bambi

4. My man's idea of a perfect dinner is
   A. Angel-hair pasta primavera, arugula and radicchio salad with crumbled goat cheese in a light vinaigrette, crusty Italian bread, a California white zinfandel, and a medley of raspberries and blackberries in crème fraîche for dessert.
   B. Chinese, Mexican, Thai—anything a little spicy and exotic.
   C. Whatever his mother used to serve him when he was eight years old.

5. Complete this sentence: "A man is . . ."
   A. A man
   B. Always having to say you're sorry
   C. Just a little boy inside

The Silent Type

In the movies he is Gary Cooper or Sam Shepard—a tower of strength who seems aloof and invulnerable. If you were a bad guy, he would just as soon shoot you as look at you; but he's putty in the hands of a Good Woman.

Unfortunately most Silent Types neither look nor behave like our movie heroes. To the Silent Type, the best defense is silence; the less information he volunteers, the less likely it is that he'll make a wrong move.

In fact, rather than being the fearless fellows they are in the movies, Silent Types are often the ones who are desperately fearful of any sort of "scene." And they define the word *scene* loosely. Susan and Matthew were seeing each other for a few weeks before Susan recognized how his quietness masked many fears. "All I have to do to horrify Matthew," says Susan, "is make faces at a baby sitting at a table next to ours in a restaurant or call attention to the fact that someone has stepped in front of us in line. Matthew will look like he'll want to sink into the ground."

The Silent Type may be thinking deep thoughts; then again he may be thinking about how he forgot to deduct pencils as a business expense on his income tax. The point is, you are often confused about exactly what *is* on his mind—and if you tend to be insecure, this will quickly become annoying, if not a little scary. "I didn't mind that Matthew wasn't very forthcoming in his praise, because he also wasn't very critical when I did something he didn't like," says Susan. "I'm a talker by nature, and I just wasn't used to long periods of silence.

When we first started seeing each other, I worried he wasn't having a good time. I got so sick of hearing myself say, 'What are you thinking?' " First Susan used to make a joke of it—she'd ask him if his college major was GSL (Grunting as a Second Language). Then, after a few weeks, Susan began to seriously worry that Matthew was hiding things from her. "He wasn't. It was his manner. But it drove me nuts."

He may love you, but you may never hear it. He may hate something about you, but you may never hear that either. The key to his silence is fear—fear of saying the wrong thing, the right thing, *any*thing that makes him more vulnerable.

Fortunately the Silent Type, much more than the Tightwad or the Ladies' Man or Peter Pan, is subject to change, and a man who never speaks his mind for the first few months (or years) of a relationship *could* become Chatty Kevin with time and TLC.

Is silence golden to you? Ask yourself whether you Agree or Disagree with these statements:

1. "I admire someone who doesn't take a lot of words to say something that could be said in a few words."

       AGREE   SOMETIMES AGREE   DISAGREE

2. "I admire someone who takes no words to say something that could be said in *a lot* of words."

       AGREE   SOMETIMES AGREE   DISAGREE

3. "I admire someone who organizes his thoughts before he speaks."

       AGREE   SOMETIMES AGREE   DISAGREE

True or False:

4. "I have taken lessons in body language."

TRUE   FALSE

5. "People tell me I am incredibly intuitive. I can usually tell what a person is thinking before he says anything."

TRUE   FALSE

6. "I can put down a great mystery novel without bothering to read the last page."

TRUE   FALSE

7. "I get embarrassed over anyone making a big fuss about something I've done—baking a cake, getting a big promotion, setting a new world record for the over-fifty high jump, and so on."

TRUE   FALSE

8. "I like a man who speaks softly and carries a big stick."

TRUE   FALSE

The more "Agree" and "True" answers you have, the better off you are with this man!

The Workaholic

Remember that expression "All work and no play makes Jack a dull boy"? Well, you've tacked it up on his mirror, you've given it to him on a T-shirt, you've crocheted it onto a pillow, and you repeat it to him like a mantra—and nothing, but *nothing*, works. When you first started seeing each other, he told you he hadn't had a vacation in ten years but that this was the time in his life when he knew he could finally begin to slow down. He just needed a little help, and you were just the woman to give it to him.

But now when you try to get him to slow down, to take some time off, he becomes furious, accusing you of not caring about his career, distracting him—or trying to ruin him. You're rarely alone together, and when you are, he's discussing his work. He has a fax machine next to the bed.

You used to think that as long as the next man you met didn't have affairs with other women, everything would be okay. How could you have guessed that having an affair with his work could be almost as bad?

There are numerous reasons for workaholism, but psychologists agree that peer pressure is usually not one of them. The true workaholic is not driving himself because someone is telling him to—so, pointing out that those extra hours won't improve his job performance or ingratiate him with the boss will be entirely beside the point. Usually he's trying to make up for perceived failings in other parts of his life and has the mistaken notion that achievement at work is the way to do it. Just *try* to convince the workaholic that obsession with his career is a way of avoiding real-life problems—he thinks he is the kind of guy who confronts life head-on!

Of course the best way to get along with a workaholic is to be one yourself; that way his obsession won't seem odd, and it won't seem to be taking anything away from you. But if this is not your personality, you may have to reconcile yourself to the fact that his seemingly frenetic pace is essential to his happiness. You can't, and shouldn't, *compete* with his work. The best you can hope for is small, incremental spans of time that you can "negotiate"—a weekend away every month, a fifteen-minute daily phone conversation, or one hour out of the day together when you won't be discussing his job.

But change him? Doubtful.

Will the workaholic work for you? Ask yourself if you Agree or Disagree with these statements:

1. "I enjoy company—company picnics, company parties, company field trips."

AGREE   SOMETIMES AGREE   DISAGREE

2. "I am fascinated by endless discussions of the new global economy, the need for higher quality in American manufacturing and strategic alliances with Third World countries. Love and sex? Well, I can take 'em or leave 'em."

AGREE   SOMETIMES AGREE   DISAGREE

3. "I enjoy cooking for one."

AGREE   SOMETIMES AGREE   DISAGREE

4. "I think the *Wall Street Journal* should be made into a movie."

AGREE   SOMETIMES AGREE   DISAGREE

5. "My idea of a great vacation is attending a spouse program at an annual sales convention."

AGREE   SOMETIMES AGREE   DISAGREE

6. "I don't mind if he works nine to five (9:00 A.M. to 5:00 A.M.)."

AGREE   SOMETIMES AGREE   DISAGREE

Hope you're doing a lot of "Agreeing" if you want to stay with a Workaholic!

The Constant Complainer

His children. His ex-wife. His dead wife (may she rest in peace). His heart. His gall bladder. His kidneys. His piles. The bills always come early, and the checks always come late. He's depressed, or if he's not depressed, he *should* be depressed, because you just won't believe what happened to him today. . . .

Kvetch is the Yiddish word for "constant complainer." After a few dates with this fellow you begin to suspect that if there wasn't something wrong, he wouldn't be truly happy. And you would probably be right.

There are so many degrees and variations on your basic, Grade A Complainer that it's impossible to say whether the complaining is something that can be easily sloughed off or whether it's part of a larger, more worrisome problem. What are his complaints about? If they are about health, does this man just like to talk about the little aches and pains of growing older or is he genuinely a hypochondriac who believes he has one foot in the grave? (If it's the latter, he's probably felt this way since he was in his twenties.) If he gripes about other aspects of his life—his family, finances, job—are the problems real or largely of his own making?

The only question you can answer with certainty is how his complaining affects you. Some women find that a man's constant barrage of complaints throws a pall over their own lives. Others, paradoxically, don't mind being around a complainer, especially if his woes are really a bit comical, because there's something cheering in the thought, "Gee, nothing in life is really *that* bad!" Typically, too, the Constant Complainer isn't looking for someone to save him; he really just wants comfort.

Constant Complainers tend to gravitate toward two types of women: other Kvetches (it's more fun to moan together!) and Fixers. Maria is a Fixer. "In my own family my father was always the complainer and my mother was the problem solver," she explains. "When we came to Florida from Cuba, my mother was the first one to learn the language, get a job, set up the house. My father talked about how difficult everything was. I decided I never wanted this situation in my own life."

The quality that attracted her to her ex-husband was his take-charge personality. "Nothing was a problem for him. Even real problems weren't problems for him." After several years and two children, life with Pollyanna was no bowl of cherries. It was in fact a financial roller coaster, because Juan was always taking the family money and investing it in get-rich-quick schemes that failed. "As soon as another project went belly-up, Juan would smile and say, 'Oh, well, next time.'"

After an amicable divorce Maria took her two children and moved from Florida to San Francisco. She started working as a paralegal, and after fifteen years, at the age of fifty, decided to go to law school. When she met Alex at her high school reunion, she thought, "Oh, no, he's just like my father. Everything was a problem. If he sneezed, he was about to get pneumonia. If his shoes hurt, he was coming down with a rare disease that would make his feet swell to the size of footballs. And even though he was one of the best-regarded biologists in his field, if one of his experiments wasn't working out, I would go over to his house to find him sitting on the floor in a darkened room."

But gradually Maria found she actually got a kick out of Alex's gloom-and-doom. "It's kind of funny, really, such a successful person always convinced he's on the brink of some massive failure." Alex's angst gives Maria a feeling of control she didn't have with a man who was unrealistically optimistic. "Given my personality, it's better for *me* to be the jolly one in the relationship, the one who can make Alex feel better, rather than always being the cautious one who has to say, 'Yeah, but what if. . . .' Alex is cautious enough for both of us!"

Are you right for a Constant Complainer?

1. My favorite topics of conversation are
    A. How doctors rip you off
    B. How AARP dues are too high
    C. Nuclear disarmament

2. I don't get embarrassed when
    A. My dinner companion complains loudly about his hemorrhoids
    B. My dinner companion complains loudly about how much better the restaurant was under the old man-

agement, with the new owner standing two feet away
C. My dinner companion commiserates with me loudly
   about *my* hemorrhoids

3. My favorite section of the newspaper is
   A. Page one/current events
   B. Sports
   C. Wedding announcements
   D. Obituaries

Agree or Disagree:

4. "It doesn't matter if the glass is half empty or half full—
I always spill whatever's in it."

          AGREE   SOMETIMES AGREE   DISAGREE

5. "When life gives you lemons, it figures."

          AGREE   SOMETIMES AGREE   DISAGREE

Complete these sentences:

6. It hurts when I . . .
   A. Run
   B. Move
   C. Exist

7. Things were better . . .
   A. Last week
   B. In the good old days
   C. This is a trick question—things were never better

The Smotherer

You can't believe your good luck: After all those fellows who couldn't make up their minds, couldn't com-

mit, just didn't know, here's this man who *adores* you. For a few months you revel in the overwhelming, candy-and-flowers attention. If you bump your elbow, he oohs and ahs. You read a book together, and even if he disagrees with you, well, of course, *you're* the smart one. If you have a fight with your son, he'll tell you what a fantastic mother you've been and how could that dirty, rotten kid say such a thing?! If you need to go shopping and your car's being repaired, he's there, his car motor purring, almost before you can say, "Bloomingdale's."

What could be more delightful? Then a few months pass. You'd like to spend a weekend with your girlfriends—alone. He pipes up, "Oh, I'll keep you company." If you hesitate, he sulks. Or you'd like to spend a weekend by yourself. Why? he wonders. He immediately concludes you're getting tired of him and steps up efforts to be the all-around Good Guy. Whatever he's doing, he'll drop it to be with you. Nothing, nothing in his life could possibly be as important as being with you.

You begin to wonder if this guy has ... well ... a *life*. At first you enjoy all his piques of jealousy. They make you feel so wanted, so *young* again. And sure, it's wonderful to have someone so devoted, but everyone needs some time alone.

Except him. When you begin to demand a little "space," he panics. He wants to know where you are every minute you're not with him. If you're reluctant to tell him, he's furious and accuses you of things you've never even thought of doing. Suddenly there are lots of hang-ups on your answering machine. You hear a car parked outside your house late at night, and when you look out, it disappears.

If you decide that he's really not the right person for you and you'd like to date others, you begin to wonder if you *can*. All that attention isn't all that flattering anymore. It's a little scary. But how will you break away? Or will you?

Smothering is one of the most insidious qualities a man can have because it masquerades as the thing we all want: love. It becomes somewhat less flattering, however, if you discover that his overwhelming attentions are paid to just about everyone he's ever been involved with.

Many women think the Smotherer would be no problem for them—until they actually go out with one. "For a little while I was seeing a man who had gone through a horrible divorce several years ago and told me his wife had been unfaithful to him," says Dawn, our fifty-five-year-old twice-divorcée. "But then I heard through several mutual friends that, even though he believed this, it actually wasn't true. But I just told myself, well, *they* didn't know, or he hadn't admitted it to anyone but me."

Dawn began to suspect her friends' information was true when she realized Charles was checking up on her in little ways, making sure she was always where she said she was. One night Dawn was at home, but she simply wanted a night alone and had turned on her answering machine to take her phone calls. "I heard the machine click and rewind, and I realized someone had gotten my code number and was dialing in to hear my messages." It could only be Charles; but when Dawn confronted him, he acted shocked and amazed that she could think such a thing, and then accused her of going out with some *other* man who was jealous!

There are, however, a few women who thrive on this

kind of attention and without it feel lost. "After meeting Jack, anything less than 100 percent devotion felt like nothing to me," said Lorraine, who claims her beau would rush over to her house any time of day or night if she complained of so much as a foot cramp. "Of course it's kind of silly, but no other kind of love feels real to me," Lorraine admits. "Often it's annoying, but it's far better to have this kind of annoyance than the other kind—when someone doesn't pay *enough* attention to you."

Sometimes there's a thin line between being adored and being smothered. How do you respond to these questions?

1. I don't mind if a man accompanies me to
   A. The supermarket
   B. A mah-jongg game
   C. A public rest room

2. I enjoy receiving presents for
   A. My birthday
   B. Christmas
   C. My birthday, Christmas, Valentine's Day, Lincoln's Birthday, Halloween, Columbus Day, Arbor Day, National Oral Hygiene Day. . . .

3. My favorite pet is
   A. A cat
   B. A dog
   C. A boa constrictor

4. I like a man who depends on me for
   A. Security
   B. Love
   C. Oxygen

The (Much) Younger Man

In 411 B.C. Lysistrata said, "When a man gets back . . . though he be gray, he can wed a young girl in a minute, but the season of a woman is very short."

Hey, Lysistrata, wanna bet?

Jennie Churchill, the mother of Winston, was sixty-four when she married Montagu Porch in 1918; Porch was forty-one, three years younger than her son. Her reply to critics? "He has a future and I have a past, so we should be all right."

Bea likes to tell the story of when she asked one of her beaus, who was thirty, to guess her age. "You must have some idea," she said.

"I have several ideas," said the young man with a smile. "The only trouble is that I hesitate whether to make you ten years younger on account of your looks, or ten years older on account of your intelligence."

"That," Bea concludes triumphantly, "is what you call a *diplomat!*"

Unfortunately most younger men aren't as diplomatic as Bea's lover. One may find it amusing—and even a little boost to his own ego—that people think you're his mother. Another may have no patience with your political or sexual beliefs, chalking them up to the "squareness" of an older generation. Still another might be insensitive to the physical differences between you, wondering why you don't love being out at parties till three in the morning or why you'd rather take the car to the supermarket "when it's such a short walk." Then there are the economic differences, the role reversals that arise because you have more money, and therefore, he may feel, more power in the relationship.

Most older women are so afraid of the pitfalls of a relationship with someone years younger that they don't even fantasize about one. When they describe their ideal lovers, both men and women—but particularly women—usually depict someone within fifteen years of their own age, and sometimes someone five to ten years older. Very few specify a younger age.

Yet there can be something joyous about being with someone years younger than you, if your expectations of him are realistic. Yes, in all likelihood, he'll move on to someone closer to his own age; and yes, after a while the differences between you will become more and more apparent. But if for years men have enjoyed having a sweet young thing on their arm, why shouldn't you? (After all, younger doesn't have to mean brawny and dumb, or insensitive; he could be a perfectly lovely, sensitive man who just happens to enjoy the company of older women.)

To clarify your feelings about being the companion of a younger man, answer the questions below.

1. "When I'm with him, I'm so happy, I just can't help humming a tune—I just wish he recognized it!"

    ACCEPTABLE   SOMETIMES ACCEPTABLE   NOT ACCEPTABLE

2. "My friends don't understand. They keep telling me I'm old enough to be his mother and that while it's okay for a man to do this sort of thing, it's, well, *perverted* for me."

    ACCEPTABLE   SOMETIMES ACCEPTABLE   NOT ACCEPTABLE

3. "His stamina in bed is amazing to me. Sometimes I wonder how long I'll be able to keep up with him."

    ACCEPTABLE   SOMETIMES ACCEPTABLE   NOT ACCEPTABLE

4. "When we lie together, I look at his firm flesh and I look at my own and I think that at any time he's going to be turned off."

ACCEPTABLE   SOMETIMES ACCEPTABLE   NOT ACCEPTABLE

5. "He's a normal young man who's going to want a wife and kids someday. So this situation obviously has its limitations."

ACCEPTABLE   SOMETIMES ACCEPTABLE   NOT ACCEPTABLE

6. "I like Gershwin; he likes the Rolling Stones. He can sit through ten movies about teens at the beach; just sitting through one sets my teeth on edge. We *really* have a great time together in many ways, but I have to admit that we don't have many interests in common."

ACCEPTABLE   SOMETIMES ACCEPTABLE   NOT ACCEPTABLE

7. "Every time I take him to an office function, I have to explain to everyone that he's not my son. It's awkward for both of us."

ACCEPTABLE   SOMETIMES ACCEPTABLE   NOT ACCEPTABLE

Just Say No To . . .

We've been talking in a lighthearted way about the "types" of men that you may or may not be able to cope with. There are certain times, however, when it's advisable that a woman not consider a long-term relationship for *any* reason. Stay with any of these fellows, and you're not merely asking for trouble—you're *begging* for it.

The Married Man

The fact that so many women over fifty actually *do* have ongoing relationships with married men gives us pause. Clearly, with the odds of the fifty-plus woman meeting an available man so stacked against her, shouldn't married men be fair game?

Our answer is unequivocally no. He may be in a loveless and/or sexless marriage; he may not be able to leave because of his children, bank account, dogs, or whatever; he may in fact love you. He is nevertheless married.

First there's the moral issue. Put yourself in the wife's shoes. What if this woman were you (and if you're over fifty and divorced, perhaps she was in the same boat before she married him)? Second there's the self-destructive aspect of this relationship: With precious few exceptions, you will never come first because you will not be essential to this man's life and identity.

Statistics prove that men rarely leave their wives for other women. When they do leave, it's because they are unhappy to begin with, and the other woman is perhaps added incentive. So we're not saying that your involvement with a married man will cause the breakdown of a happy family; we are saying it's highly probable the involvement will end unhappily for you.

There is of course the chance that getting him to leave his wife is not part of your plan and that you have come to terms with the idea that this is a transitional relationship for you. The arrangement may very well meet your short-term needs. But I hear about the dissolution of long-term marriages on a daily basis, and I can't pretend to be impartial on this subject.

Addicts—Gamblers, Alcoholics, Etc.

I'm equally adamant about the prospects of a successful relationship with an addict of any kind. Two years ago Iris, a fifty-one-year-old divorcée, stepped into my office and said she decided to seek therapy because she was worried that she wasn't assertive enough—and particularly not with the new man she was seeing, Ben. She let him have his way with everything—although of course he treated her beautifully. Her ex-husband, a wealthy businessman, had left her with an enormous alimony settlement—about four million dollars. "But one of the things I love about Ben is that he always takes *me* out. He has money of his own and isn't after mine."

As the months passed, Iris noticed that Ben was as attentive as ever but seemed to be saving his money to spend on something other than her—namely, the casinos in Atlantic City. She always knew he enjoyed gambling but thought it was just a harmless little sideline. Meanwhile he always had a business deal brewing, a new get-rich-quick scheme that never quite panned out. And he always managed to get Iris interested in these deals. At first she just invested a little money. Then more and more. Whenever Ben ended up losing her capital in some mysterious dealing, he would say, "Don't you trust me?" and they would have a huge fight where she'd have to promise that yes of course she trusted him.

Now, two years later, Ben has gone through $3.5 million, most of it at the casinos. And Iris, who looks as if she's aged ten years, feels she's invested too much time and money in this relationship to leave. She is still promising that she trusts him.

Then there's Germaine, a fifty-year-old divorcée who was dating a chronic (albeit functioning) alcoholic. "It was like the Amityville relationship; a voice inside my head kept shouting, 'Get out,' but I didn't listen." Keith, a successful chef, had never had any children, but he had gone through three wives and two small fortunes in a haze of alcohol. A dozen times he told Germaine he would quit drinking; a dozen times she found the bottle of Jack Daniel's hidden under the sink or in the bathroom hamper. "Keith was so lovable. He needed me so much. He assured me I was the one who could change him." For the first year Germaine loved being relied upon so entirely. Keith became sweet, loving, and grateful during his binges. But finally after the police dropped Keith off, dead drunk, on Germaine's doorstep, she lost her cool—and Keith threatened to shoot her with his rifle if she ever left him. "At first I was shocked and brushed off this threat as drunken rambling; then I learned a little more about some of the things he'd done in the past than I wanted to know." Sweet-tempered Keith had a long string of arrests, but no convictions, for violent crimes ranging from public disturbance to assault with a deadly weapon.

Still it took Germaine six months and scores of Al-Anon meetings to get out of the relationship. "I loved him and continued to love him after I left," she says tearfully. "But Al-Anon [a self-help group for friends, family, and lovers of alcoholics] helped me to understand my codependent behavior. They showed me I wasn't helping Keith by staying with him. When I finally understood this, I got up the strength to leave."

While he may appear to be utterly devoted to you, the substance abuser has room in his life for only one thing: the drugs or alcohol. As anyone who's been to Alcoholics Anonymous, Narcotics Anonymous, or Al-Anon meetings will tell you, abusers are especially seductive because they appear to *need you so much*.

So many women are drawn to the idea of "saving" a person, but the chances of you weaning your man away from the addiction are minimal—*particularly* if the abuser has made it into his fifties, sixties, and beyond. Old habits die hard; abusers just die, and they'll take you with them.

If, despite these warnings, you find yourself attached to an addict, put down this book and contact your local Al-Anon chapter. Now.

You can't save him, but you can save yourself.

"Marry Me Today!"

Somerset Maugham wrote a gem of a story called "The Round Dozen." It was about a dull, funny-looking little man, down on his luck, who tells anyone who'll listen about his glory days: He had made all the London papers for his career as a bigamist. He married eleven different woman, all spinsters, stripping them of their money and moving on to the next find. When asked why eleven women married him, he simply replied, "Because I asked them." He went on to explain, quite logically, that they had gotten a great deal for their money: "Romance. . . . Change and excitement." His only regret was that he had married eleven—he wanted to make it "a round dozen." (And of course by the end of the story he does.)

Little has changed since Maugham wrote that story more than fifty years ago. For many women there is still something irresistible about a man who acts so swept away by his own passions that he wants to marry—immediately.

DON'T DO IT. No matter how romantic it may seem, wait. Meet friends, meet family. If a man doesn't understand why you want to meet his associates, be very suspicious. One acquaintance of ours was literally walking up the steps of city hall to be married when the future husband, a man she had known for two weeks, confessed that he had told a little lie about his past—a lie that involved two marriages, three kids, and a mother who expected to live with the two of them when they got married.

Our acquaintance was lucky; her man confessed. They are still dating, and she's taking things very, very slowly.

The Bickerer

"You say tomato, and I say tomahto . . . ," begins the George Gershwin classic. The song is lovely, but imagine choosing a life with a man for whom the most insignificant matter in the world is a major argument.

Lots of women do. Erica is often attracted to men with strong opinions, and Raphael, a professor of Renaissance literature, was no exception. When they first started seeing each other, Erica told herself that here was a man with *passion*. He would dissect endlessly every movie they went to see, every concert they heard, offering up his opinion as if it were law. She loved his conviction; she only wished he would listen to her once in a while—because her opinions were equally strong. Sometimes Erica thought that if he suspected that she was going to agree with him about something, he would actually contradict himself in order to play the devil's advocate.

For the first few weeks their arguing was fun. "It really got my blood boiling," Erica remembers. (In fact Erica discovered Raphael actually had low blood pressure, and they used to joke that if he didn't have something to keep his pressure up all the time, he would just keel over and die.) "And our sexual relationship was extraordinary. We would have a fight over some trivial thing, and we would make up in bed." Erica admits that there was a subtle element of violence to him that was irresistible. "We would be having sex, and every time he moved, he would snarl, 'Wasn't I right? Huh? Wasn't I? . . .' "

But soon it wasn't only books and movies Raphael would argue about. It was the proper way to make a cup of coffee, the appropriate way to arrange bills in a wallet (by denomination of course), the correct number of times to wear a sweater before sending it to the dry cleaner—everything. One night, after they had only been seeing each other for a month, he called Erica at midnight while she was watching a television show she had been looking forward to for a week. When she said she would call him back in half an hour, he became furious. He refused to get off the phone until she talked to him. It was nothing important; he just needed further proof that she would do what he wanted. Somehow that was the last straw.

"I saw that he was not this passionate genius but just an irritating dictator," Erica explains. "What was going on was his incredible need to dominate. The more we fought, the more Raphael seemed to enjoy it, in a certain perverse way. I realized that as much as I enjoyed the sexual part of our relationship, I didn't really want to have to *talk* to him."

Beth and David are another endlessly bickering couple. Beth's the ultimate optimist, David the pessimist— "I always see the glass as half full, and David sees it as half empty," Beth says. Like Erica and Raphael (and other couples who start out together loving to fight), Beth and David had a wonderful sexual relationship until they started arguing about so many things that they are constantly angry at each other. Beth doesn't want to leave, but she doesn't want to marry. She says, "There's a lot less 'making up' now."

Hot-headed fights about trivia are not only okay, they're positively healthy for most relationships; it reminds us that we each have our "sensitive spots." It helps us laugh afterward about the silliness of the "blow up." But if the occasional big, dramatic fight at the beginning of the relationship seems to break down into petty squabbling after a brief time, clear out. In other words, if you *always* say "tomato," and he *always* says "tomahto"—just call the whole thing off.

8

When Saying "I Don't" Might Be Better Than "I Do": Marriage May Not Be the Only Answer

> Marriage is a great institution, but I'm not ready for an institution yet.
>
> —MAE WEST

Happily ever after. That's how people lived at the end of fairy tales. And as all good girls know, happily ever after means one thing: marriage. Did Cinderella and her Prince live in separate-but-equally-lovely-homes ever after? Did they live in-mutual-admiration-and-respect-even-though-they-never-got-the-license ever after? No, sirree. And if Cinderella and the Prince didn't do that, then why should you?

Well, you shouldn't—if marriage is truly the only arrangement that will make you feel secure and loved. After all, yours was the generation that grew up on that popular ditty "Love and marriage, love and marriage ... go together like a horse and carriage." (The song never mentions how often the horse gets lame and the wheels fall off the carriage!)

But now might be the right time to ask yourself whether marriage is the only road to happiness for you. What are your reasons for marrying? Financial security? Companionship? Red-hot passion? Because it's expected of you? Because you're afraid to be alone? Because he's got season tickets to the Flyers? None of these are necessarily "bad" reasons to marry; there are only "good" and "bad" reasons *given the personality and needs of the individual*. It's the old situation of "one man's meat is another man's poison": one woman's perfectly good reason for marriage is another woman's disaster.

At this stage many women who have been widowed or divorced find that deep down they really don't want to be married again, even though they want a man in their lives. But they can't quite reconcile themselves to what they perceive as a contradiction in terms. After all, these are the women who may have railed against the evils of "living in sin" to their children, yet they are realizing that, for a variety of financial and emotional reasons, this great "evil" might suit them fine!

Take Marina, for example. Divorced seven years from a man who made Stanley Kowalski seem like Phil Donahue, the still-stunning fifty-year-old has enjoyed a life liberated from housework and child care, which for years she considered her only option. "I speak several languages fluently, and as soon as I got divorced, I moved from a town in New Jersey to New York City and got a job working as a translator at the U.N. Now the only thing I make for dinner is reservations!"

Still, Marina is terribly frightened of growing older alone, and this year she met a man who has assuaged those fears. "Eckart and I met at Bloomingdale's. I was trying to decide which of two dresses looked best on me, and he was just walking by and gave me his opinion. He said both of them suited me so well that I should have both—and he bought me one! That really got my attention."

Eckart, forty-nine, a former model and now a men's clothing-store owner, pursues the good life with relish: He drives a Mercedes SL, lunches at the Four Seasons, has a season subscription to the Metropolitan Opera (even though, Marina complains, he always falls asleep during the first act). His motto is "If you can't do it first-class, don't do it."

Marina and Eckart have one particularly strong bond: devotion to the mirror. "I'm as beautiful as I ever was, even if it takes me a little longer to get that way," laughs Marina. "I've always cared very much about fashion and my appearance, and so does Eckart. Call it whatever you want—I really love the fact that we make a great-looking couple. It's fun to be seen together."

But Marina is the first to admit that she and Eckart get along best in public. In private he's a traditionalist who thrives on routine: dinner at 6:15; bed at 10:30; sex once a week, on Saturday night.

"When we're not out on the town, Eckart's a lump. I'm a doer; he's a watcher. But he'll pout if I go anywhere or do anything without him. Sometimes the relationship is so boring. But it's also very comfortable."

Lately talk of marriage has been in the air. Every week the person who wants to marry changes; sometimes it's Marina and sometimes it's Eckart. "After so many years of a disastrous marriage, I just don't want to get caught in the same routine again. Behind Eckart's flashy clothes and easy-spending ways, there's another guy who wants his dinner cooked and ready for him on time. But he's so *nice* and *handsome.* He buys me anything I want. If I don't settle with him, who will I marry?"

The question Marina should really be asking herself is: Does she have to marry *anybody?* When will the fun of being seen with Eckart wear off? (And who knows, maybe for Marina it won't.)

At this stage of your life you know what marriage is. You have to look at its advantages and disadvantages, not as a twenty- or twenty-five-year-old but as the woman you are *today.* You may be surprised by what you discover about yourself.

If Marriage Is What It Takes to Make You Happy

You may be a woman for whom marriage is genuinely an essential component of a relationship; being intimate with someone without marriage just feels, at bottom, wrong. Yet many women who harbor this feeling choose to ignore it, even when they begin to date someone who makes it amply clear that he's not interested in marriage.

"I was really taken with Mitchell the moment I saw him. There was something about those huge, smoky, dissipated eyes that reminded me of Al Pacino," said Erica, who had met the fiery Serbian on a vacation in Key West. But I told myself he wasn't a ladies' man; after all, he taught theology. He was a good Christian. So what if he had had two unsuccessful marriages?"

On their second date Mitchell told Erica what a great

time he was having with her and how relieved he was to be separated from his last wife. Then he threw in one of his favorite quotes from writer Max Kauffmann: "I never knew what happiness was until I got married. And by then it was too late."

"As we continued seeing each other, I never mentioned how important marriage was to me," said Erica. "I just figured that if he had been married twice, he would certainly do it again. I mean, I had been married before, and I wanted to take the plunge again. Besides, he just had to be good and faithful; goodness was, in a sense, his business."

Good and faithful do not, however, necessarily add up to marriageable. Erica continued to ignore all the signals, and when the subject came up, Mitchell continued to extol the joys of bachelorhood. His first wife had had affairs for twelve of the fourteen years of their marriage, and his second wife had taken their three teenagers and moved to New Mexico. Mitchell wasn't seeing anyone else other than Erica, but for the first time in thirty years he was responsible to no one but himself and his students.

"We always had such a wonderful time together, and I always knew where he was, what he was doing, and when I was going to see him next. Marriage was the next logical step."

After two years Erica planned an elaborate candlelit dinner and confronted Mitchell with the Big Question: Where was this relationship going? Mitchell looked shocked, then puzzled. "Why does it have to be 'going somewhere,' " he asked. "Haven't I said . . . ?"

Erica practically choked on her crème brûlée. "But what's wrong?" she gasped. "We get along so well. Our children have become friends. Even our *cats* like each other! And you *swore* that you loved me."

Mitchell was gentle but firm. "I do, but at this point in time the relationship we have is enough for me."

Erica, who normally never loses her cool, was furious; and after she threw Mitchell out of her house, she cried herself to sleep. But she had to admit that Mitchell had never lied to her—not that it made her pain any less. "I simply couldn't hear what he was saying, because I didn't want to. It was just so much easier to forget about it." Now Erica wonders if she didn't throw away a perfectly lovely relationship. "Mitchell wasn't doing anything wrong; he just wasn't fulfilling the expectation I was brought up with, about how love must end in marriage."

Erica was probably not wrong in ending the relationship; it was just her timing that was wrong. She waited two years to discuss this issue with Mitchell; six or seven months would have been more appropriate.

Unlike Erica, lots of women refuse to throw out the baby with the bathwater. Betty, sixty-three, a retired nurse, is an avid golfer with an eight handicap and a winning smile that makes her the darling of her country club. Her husband, also a golfer, died several years ago of complications due to kidney failure. Betty coped with her sadness by keeping unusually busy. She was out on the course just days after his death. Two years later she met Ted at her club. Ted was a widower in his early seventies who was also a keen golfer, and an enthusiastic yachtsman. They quickly became friends and began playing golf regularly every Saturday. One day Ted happened to mention to Betty how concerned he was about an upcoming operation to replace an arthritic hip. The surgery was generally very successful, he said, but required a rather long convalescence. Ted was worried that he wouldn't be able to fend for himself and might have to hire a private nurse. Ted told Betty about all this on the third hole; by the eighteenth hole they had agreed that he would move in with Betty during his recovery!

Two and a half years later Ted's still there. "What can I say?" says Betty, laughing. "We started out in separate bedrooms of course. We split all expenses, which I appreciated. It was a little awkward at first, but I took care of him . . . maybe a bit too well!"

Betty and Ted still share all expenses, although Ted will pay for their evenings out and their vacations together. Nevertheless they don't always act as a couple. On holidays, for example, they go their separate ways— Betty to her children and Ted to his.

When they moved in together, the neighbors were surprised, but Betty didn't care—she knew that she was simply doing a good turn for a friend. But when that friend moved into her bedroom, Betty began to think her neighbors had a point. "This is just not how I was raised," she says simply. "Living together? Impossible! Next thing I'd be smoking pot and saying things about how marriage was, like, man, just a piece of paper."

Ted, however, really didn't want to get married. When Betty told him she was worried about what the neighbors—and her children—would think, he just shrugged and replied, "They'll have to get used to it."

When a woman hears "I don't want to marry," she's conditioned to react the way she did when she was twenty: "I know what that means—he doesn't love me, he doesn't really need me, he's going to rush off with another woman." In fact sometimes that's not the case at all. "Ted wants to leave his estate to his children, although he's got a life insurance policy that names me as the beneficiary," says Betty. "I would rather get married," she adds brightly. "But listen, it's not a perfect world!"

When Marriage Isn't Right for You

Read most women's magazines, and you'll see endless articles about how men find it increasingly hard to "commit" and how women have to resort to all sorts of wiles just to get the fellow to say those two teeny words, "I do." But it's not always the woman who is yearning for holy matrimony.

If you're reluctant to get married but feel that lots of well-meaning friends and family are pushing you to the altar, try paying attention to your own gut feeling. Even if you're in love, that song in your heart may be "Born Free," not "Goin' to the Chapel"! After all, there's no biological imperative: You will not have any more children. And while you may look at marriage as a way of easing financial burdens, you know that it's not the *only* way. In fact now more than ever before, it's the woman who has the money in the relationship.

Remember Ruth? She's the very well-off divorcée who adores—but has no intention of marrying and supporting—Ben. Ben has entirely different life-style aspirations and doesn't particularly want to live in the style that Ruth has become accustomed to. Together they have found they enjoy sharing their lives more than sharing their wealth.

Ruth also loves having the freedom to say, "Hey, let's not see each other for a couple of weeks"—which she can do with Ben because they know that two weeks is not forever and that eventually they'll be together. This freedom is not about needing to see other men—it's just about having time alone. And both Ruth and Ben have reached a point in their lives where they can accept, and not feel threatened by, each other's need to be alone. They have come to trust not in marriage but in a relationship that is nonetheless *constant, secure, and joyful.*

Then there's Rachel. This cool, attractive redhead spent thirty years as the right arm of her husband, a brilliant, nationally renowned neurologist. When he had to travel, Rachel made all the arrangements; when he had to deliver a lecture, Rachel organized everything, from the typing of his notes to his lecture fee. When Douglas had a massive coronary, he left his widow extremely wealthy—and extremely indifferent to living. "He was my life, it's that simple," she says, her voice cracking even now, seven years after his death.

Three years ago one of Rachel's friends introduced her to a retired insurance executive whose wife had died several years ago. He took one look at Rachel and he was hooked. "Mel proposed on the second date," she says with a laugh. "After years of loneliness it was the biggest ego trip of my life."

Unlike her former husband, who barely remembered major holidays, let alone their anniversary, Mel is a sentimentalist, a gift giver who celebrates everything from the day he and Rachel met to Groundhog Day. He loves to dance, travel well, and eat in the finest restaurants. For Mel, selling insurance was just a living, and he was glad to have the money to retire—life, he believes, is for fun.

Rachel says that Mel is the best thing in her life

right now, but despite the subtle, yet unrelenting, pressure from friends and family, she refuses to marry him. "He's a delightful person to do things with, but his idea of a conversation is, 'Hey, Wayne Newton's playing at the supper club; let's go.' Like Marina's beau, Eckart, Mel is, according to Rachel, "incapable of a conversation about anything important. If I wanted every night to be Saturday night, it would be great. But I need to be able to just sit around and talk to a man. Mel's not in the intellectual league of my late husband, and I can't see the point of joining my life with his."

Even their intellectual differences might not hold Rachel back if it weren't for the problem of their children. Rachel's son is a veterinarian, her daughter an urban planner. His son and daughter have never quite "found themselves," and his son has had trouble with drugs and minor entanglements with the law. Rachel simply doesn't like his children; they take advantage of his good nature, and she fears that a marriage to Mel would mean some of *her* money going toward bailing them out. "My kids are really scornful of his kids, and I can't say I blame them," Rachel admits. "It doesn't make for peaceful holidays together." Now Rachel and Mel spend the holidays with their own children, and Rachel knows that if she and Mel married, they could never be "one big happy family." "The hassles just aren't worth the public approbation that marriage brings," Rachel explains. "I know some people will always think of me as a kind of dirty old lady, spending weekends with a man I'm not married to, but so be it." Rachel has certain expectations from marriage she can't alter; but, she reasons, just because marriage with Mel isn't in the cards, why shouldn't they stay together?

Children also play a big part in Karen's decision not to marry Drew. As aggressive and independent as she is in the boardroom, this vivacious fifty-one-year-old management consultant, who still wears her wheat-blond tresses in a billowy ponytail, sees herself as utterly dependent when it comes to men. When her husband, Matthew, an advertising executive, was stricken with throat cancer, she was almost happy to know that he would finally have to depend on her. But when he recovered, instead of being loving and grateful to her as she expected, Matthew decided to put this painful part of his life behind him and start anew, leaving Karen for a thirty-year-old nurse he had met in the hospital! Matthew died a year later; and Karen, in a sense both divorced *and* widowed, was utterly devastated. She had just managed to work up enough anger over Matthew's betrayal, when he had the temerity to actually die, making her grieve for a man she had wanted to strangle. Amid this onslaught of mixed emotions Karen found herself alone.

One year later, after endless awkward first dates, she finally met a man she could relax with. Unlike her husband, who was even more driven than she was and never had time for their family, this fellow, an optometrist, was a lap dog. Drew was looking for a cozy place to rest, and Karen's lap suited him just fine.

Drew had been in a loveless marriage for many years, which he finally left, but not before he had accumulated a seemingly bottomless well of guilt toward his wife and children. If the marriage must end, he decided that at least he and his kids would maintain a strong bond. So he worked at it. And worked. As if to make up for those years of lost time when he and his wife were trying to ignore each other, Drew now sees his daughter every day and his son at least three times a week.

"She has him wrapped around her little finger," Karen complains. "He would visit her every single day and always bring her a little present. Drew's not good at saving money to begin with, and he had to give a huge settlement to his ex-wife. So it's not as if he has plenty to spare. He also visits his son three times a week, and he's helping pay his way through college—which would be fine, except that the kid has dropped out of school more often than he's dropped in." Drew insists it's a pleasure to give to his children, but Karen sees them as takers. "They never come to visit him, or bring him gifts. They know he felt guilty toward them and they play on this guilt all the time." His attentions are exclusive, too; when he visited his daughter, he would insist upon going himself. "She needs to know she has my full attention," he would tell Karen. "Hmm!" Karen sniffs. "More like he needs *her* full attention."

Karen's three sons think Drew's a sentimental old fool. "They're much too hard on him, I know," Karen admits. "But with all their complaints, they have a point. First of all, when we're all together, Drew ignores everyone but his own two kids. So my sons think that given the choice between me and his kids, he'd pick his kids every time. Now, I know what it's like to have children, and I really believe that in many ways they should come first. But he shouldn't *have* to make a choice. And if he does, well, then we shouldn't be married."

Even Now Parents Can Come Between You and Your Mate

Kay has been going out for a year with the accountant she hired after her divorce. "It was just so natural to go out with him after all that," she remembers. "After all, your accountant knows all your secrets, just like your psychiatrist." At first glance Richard and Kay seemed polar opposites: Though she had the glamour job as a stewardess and he had the staid accountant's position, it was actually Kay who had led a quiet, retired life, either at home or alone in hotel rooms—and it was Richard who had married and divorced early in life and then fathered a child out of wedlock.

Richard was the first man in years to tell Kay she was attractive; her former husband, resenting the kind of attention she got for her charming, homespun looks when she was a stewardess, withheld all praise. In bed Richard was living proof for a bumper sticker Kay saw one day: "Accountants do it with interest."

In Kay and Richard's case opposites do attract: She was looking for a little of his energy and excitement, and he was looking for a little of her domesticity. The problem? Kay's mother. Kay still lived with her mother, who, although mentally sharp, was frail and had recently broken her hip. She could not care for herself. For financial reasons a nursing home was out of the question; the mother could also not live with Kay's brother, who had some severe psychological problems of his own.

Even though Richard wanted to move in with Kay, he didn't want to inherit her mother, who was, admittedly, not the easiest of personalities to deal with. Kay, of course, couldn't think of abandoning her, particularly since her mother had stuck by her and helped support her during the turmoil of her divorce—even though she herself had lost her husband just two years before.

Kay accused Richard of not loving her enough to make the sacrifice. For some reason Richard could not tell Kay that he had lived with his mother-in-law while he was with his first wife, and he firmly believed this crotchety, demanding woman had contributed to the downfall of his first marriage. He refused to get himself enmeshed in what he saw as a similar situation, but he also could not admit his reasons to Kay. When Richard meekly suggested that it wouldn't be so terrible if Kay's mother moved into a nearby senior citizen's home, Kay blew up. She asked him how he would like it if his kids treated him that way someday, and he retorted by saying he hopes when his time comes, he'll know how *not* to be an interfering old man.

"We acted like a couple of lunatics," Kay says, "until he finally told me what his reservations about the whole thing were. Then I finally gathered my wits and said, 'Wait a minute. *He's* the one who wants to get married, not me. I'm happy with the way things are. Why can't we just continue to live in our separate homes? We could even get married and continue to live in separate homes. What would be so terrible?' "

Once Kay realized that she had options other than marriage/living together or no-marriage/splitting up, she relaxed. Then they both relaxed. At the moment Kay still lives with her mother; Richard lives by himself. They see each other almost every day and spend several nights together each week. There are no plans for marriage.

The real question of course is what will happen when Kay's mother passes away. Is she what's really keeping them from getting married, or is she just an excuse? Perhaps Kay finds it hard to admit to herself that marriage with Richard just doesn't suit her. But in any case, taped to her refrigerator Kay keeps a phrase she read in a book by Jean Kerr, entitled *The Snake Has All the Lines*: "Marrying a man is like buying something you've been admiring for a long time in a shop window. You may love it when you get it home, but it doesn't always go with everything else in the house."

Job Woes

Fortunately fewer and fewer women are having to choose between a man and a career because the man wants her to stop working; most men are only too happy to have a mate who wants to work. Yet attachment to a job can still be a legitimate reason not to marry.

Several years ago Phyllis, the fifty-five-year-old lawyer who lives in Philadelphia, met Daniel, a prominent California surgeon, at a seminar on bioethics in Santa Monica. It was a weekend that any mother could love, bringing together doctors and lawyers from around the country to discuss the various legal and medical ramifications of euthanasia. At one lecture Phyllis and Daniel found themselves arguing heatedly over the rights of a blind, paraplegic woman to commit suicide by "pulling the plug" on all the medical apparatus keeping her alive; Phyllis defended the woman's right to die, whereas Daniel defended the Hippocratic oath as he understood it. They took the argument from the classroom to the local coffee shop, from the coffee shop to dinner, from dinner to a bar, and finally, at 2:00 A.M., from the bar to Daniel's hotel room. As they lay side by side in the dark, Daniel confessed that when his wife had been terminally ill and she asked him to discontinue life-support systems, he couldn't do it. Weeks later, after she finally died, he wondered if this had been a selfish decision. Phyllis wondered if she could be in love.

The meeting ended the next day, with Daniel demanding to see Phyllis again—and soon. They arranged to meet again in a month, in a central location. They had a glorious weekend in Chicago; "I became a Cubs fan forever," she says, laughing. Within a few months they were crisscrossing the country for weekends together. Occasionally Phyllis worried where all this would lead. She was having an increasingly difficult time juggling her thriving law practice and her weekend getaways, but she decided, for once, she should just relax and have a good time. After all, Daniel was a fascinating, successful man, and nothing had to be too serious.

But "serious" was just what Daniel had in mind.

They were eating salmon and drinking Dom Perignon in a cozy seaside restaurant on Laguna Beach when Daniel "popped the question." He had had enough of this traveling back and forth; they loved each other; he had all the money either of them would ever need; what was stopping them?

It was, Daniel explained, "out of the question" for him to move to Philadelphia. He was medical director of one of the largest hospitals in Los Angeles. But what was stopping Phyllis from coming there? Phyllis asked herself the same question. She had been practicing law in Philadelphia since she was twenty-five, and she had the respect and envy of the legal establishment there. Moving to California meant studying for and passing the California bar. It meant, at fifty-five, building up a practice all over again. Or it meant—and this is something Phyllis couldn't even imagine—not practicing law anymore.

Phyllis thought about Daniel's proposal for one month. She decided she couldn't uproot. Eleven months later Daniel was married to someone else.

As troubling as Phyllis's situation seems, it was perhaps the only choice she could make. Being a lawyer was a crucial part of her identity. Marriage would in this case mean losing that identity. Several years later she has met another man.

"Why can't I meet someone I love in Philadelphia?" Phyllis asks with a chuckle. "Rob lives in New Jersey, and I still have to worry about time spent with him versus time spent with my practice. But at least I know that a life with Rob won't mean giving up my life entirely, because practicing law *is* my life."

There's a good chance Phyllis won't end up with Rob either. As articulate a woman as she is, she still cannot put these thoughts into words; like most of us Phyllis has been conditioned to believe that marriage is the goal every normal woman strives for. Yet in the final analysis marriage may not be worth the sacrifice.

Concerns Over Health

Liz, as you may recall, has been going out with Jay, the lovely widower she met through a personals ad. While she couldn't be more thrilled with him, she can't seem to overcome her fear about being with a man who is twelve years older (she's sixty, he's seventy-two) and has had three coronary bypasses. "I had to watch my own husband become ill and die, and now I've got to worry about Jay," says Liz, her brow furrowing. "Sometimes I think it's better not to invest too much. I just couldn't take it if anything happened to him."

Lately Jay has been bringing up the subject of marriage. He feels wonderful after his last operation, which was only three months ago; he believes "getting a new lease on life" should be accompanied by having a new wife. This last operation was terrifying for Liz, but bad as it was, she believes that if they'd been married, it would have been far worse.

Now Jay's better, but Liz still can't stop herself from watching over him constantly. "I know I'm a pain in the neck; I'm not letting him forget for one moment that he has an illness—and that's wrong. The doctors say he's amazingly well; he should just be allowed to *live* and enjoy life. But every time he eats the wrong food—he *loves* french fries, and he's always trying to sneak butter into everything—I scream at him like he's just swallowed arsenic. I don't like myself this way, but I can't help it." Jay maintains that they might as well marry, insisting that they already *are* emotionally invested, so what difference would marriage make? "But to me it's another whole level of involvement," says Liz. "Even the word *husband* has great meaning to me. It would be horrible enough if something happened to Jay; but I don't think I can live through the death of another *husband*."

Remember, there is nothing inherently "selfish" about you if you question the idea of marrying someone because of health problems. Many women have a Florence Nightingale complex, imagining how lovely it will be to give themselves entirely to a man who has some debilitating illness, how everyone would admire them, admire their sacrifice.

Nothing could be more disrespectful than marrying someone you feel sorry for. A person with a handicap of any sort doesn't need your pity—he gets that from the rest of the world, from people who don't know him. And in fact usually people with any kind of physical difference are aware of the difference, without having to be reminded of it. They want *normalcy*, someone who'll yell at them when they're being jerks and laugh at them when they're being silly and generally treat them *just like anybody else*. If you love a man who has a disability and you've thought the matter through very carefully, marry him. Otherwise don't. You know what you can cope with—and what is too much!

His Age, Your Age

Generational differences—being with someone considerably older or younger—*do* matter. For Bea the issue that has kept her from marrying is age; she is undeniably attracted to men much younger than herself. "I'm honest with myself about my desires. But on two occasions, when a much younger man was interested in marrying me, I knew in my heart he was more interested in getting a mother than a wife." Bea, however, hopes that she won't always feel this way. "It's conceivable that a relationship with someone from another generation could work out fine. It works out well for many men, after all. But I just haven't found this situation yet."

When Everybody Thinks It's a Great Idea—Everybody But You

"He's a catch!" "Don't pass up this opportunity!" "How many more chances do you think you'll have?"

These are the typical responses of well-meaning friends who think they know what's good for you—better than you know for yourself. It's easy to fall into the trap of listening to them. Easy, and self-destructive. As Rachel said about Mel when she returned his engagement ring, which all her friends urged her to accept, "As soon as I accepted the ring, I began to have bad dreams. I wondered what was wrong with me; after all, I was over fifty-five, I had beaten the odds, I had found a man! Wasn't I lucky? Wasn't that what all my friends told me? But night after night I dreamed about being locked up in a cage. You don't have to be Freud to figure out what that means. I enjoyed spending time with Mel; he was sweet and easygoing, but he was boring. *Bor*-ing. And I knew he deserved to be loved, not just accepted. It took me several months of agonizing to admit that I just didn't care for him that much, and even if it's tough out there for women my age, *it's as immoral to marry a man you don't care for at fifty-two as it is at twenty-five.*"

If You Have Serious Questions About Why He Got Divorced

I have a longtime close friend, a physician, who has been married three times. His first marriage was when he was still in his twenties, to a lovely woman; after one year of marriage she had a nervous breakdown and had to be hospitalized. They got a divorce, and five years later he married another lovely woman, with a master's in music, who taught piano. After three years of marriage she had a psychotic episode and had to be hospitalized. Again divorce.

Fifteen years passed. By this time my friend was understandably wary of marriage. But he finally found the woman who seemed absolutely right for him, and all his friends agreed—a sweet, articulate, eminently sensible journalist.

Two years later she was committed to a private hospital.

Now, the question is, Is this man unwittingly drawn to extremely fragile personalities, or is there something in his personality that drives reasonably strong people over the edge? No one knows for sure; what is quite certain is that he's not a great bet for marriage.

Unfortunately in matters of love people tend to repeat their mistakes, so if there are obvious patterns in a man's previous marriages—or in yours—you should be on the lookout for them. For example, what is his relationship with his former wife, or wives? How about his children? (Like a number of women who marry a man for financial security, one woman who came to me discovered, with a shock, that the Mr. Moneybags she married was really practically broke; he had had to turn over his trucking business to his past two wives, who were milking the company's assets. He was also sending all four of his children to college, something he "forgot" to mention until he was married and needed to borrow money from his new wife to keep up their college expenses!) While past patterns aren't a perfectly reliable indicator for future behavior, for most men they're important information to be carefully digested.

Whatever the reason for not wanting marriage, it's *your* reason, and only you can tell whether it's preventing or promoting your happiness. But ultimately, isn't it better to marry for positive reasons ("Marriage gives me X, Y, and Z ...") than negative reasons ("I'm afraid that *without* marriage, X, Y, and Z will happen ...")? So many women end up marrying out of *fear*—fear of being alone or fear that they will not be able to handle on their own certain demands that life places on them. Yet many of these women underestimate their ability to function independently.

Ruth Thone, a writer, teacher, and certified values clarification trainer in Nebraska, has developed this exercise to assess the areas in which you feel responsible for your life and the areas you feel you need assistance from others. After thinking about each of the following areas of your life, ask yourself:

a. Do I handle this now?
b. Could I handle this alone if I had to?
c. Is this an area I need to work on, to be able to handle it more independently?

Once you've thought about each category, look back over the list and see how many areas you handle independently or feel confident you *could* handle independently. Then see how many areas—and which areas—you don't feel you could handle alone. Think about the areas where you may need to develop more confidence, or work out strategies for increasing independence, and discuss them with people close to you.

	Finances	Leisure Time/ Social Life	Trans- portation Needs	Health Needs	Food	Travel
Do I handle this now?						
Could I handle this alone If I had to?						
Is this an area I need to work on, to be able to handle it more independently?						

We're not suggesting it's somehow preferable to cope with everything in your life by yourself. We just want you to think about what your capabilities are.

You may be much, much stronger and more autonomous than you think.

The Nontraditional Marriage

Probably the most common (but rarely discussed) reason for not wanting to remarry is the fear that this marriage will be like the last one. As one woman put it, "Just when I'm finally free from all those years of housework, I'll have to tie on my maid's apron all over again." If you are divorced—or even if you were happily married and are now widowed—you might feel that the

Living Arrangements	Organization	Legal Matters	Alone Time	Chores	Relationships— Family	Relationships— Friends

role of Wife is just too much of a burden at this stage in your life.

The idea of the Wife, however, is constantly being redefined and reevaluated and certainly doesn't have to be what it was the first time you walked down the aisle. For one thing childrearing responsibilities are over; for another the burden of household tasks is not likely to fall entirely on your shoulders anymore. Many men—even those of your age group—are increasingly receptive to the idea of shared responsibility in the home.

Marina and Eckart finally did decide to marry. First, though, Marina sat down with her fiancé to discuss the fears she had of repeating her last, extremely conventional fifties-style marriage—especially at this stage in her life, when she finally had the freedom to work at a career she loved. To her surprise Eckart was more responsive to her feelings than she thought he would be. "He admitted that he *would* prefer someone who would take care of all the household chores, because it was just so ingrained in him that this was 'correct'—even though he was actually a better cook than I was. So we made up a plan where we divided household chores, and I told him if he followed through with it for six months, we could talk about marriage."

The wedding took place in July 1989. Marina hired the caterer and the musicians; Eckart had grown the flowers in their backyard.

9

Sex, Single, and Over Fifty

In olden days, a glimpse of stocking
was looked on as something shocking;
Now heaven knows;
Anything goes.

—Cole Porter

Admit it: If you're standing in a bookstore, trying to decide whether to buy this book, you probably looked at the table of contents and flipped immediately to this chapter! In this society we are inundated with information about sex and sexuality. You watch TV and one ad tells you, "Buy this supersexoglamoglitz product and you'll have all the men you want." Two commercials later you're being told, "If you've had too much sexual contact with too many different men and now you're in trouble, call this special toll-free hot line."

But for all the information available to us, and for all the different ways advertisers have found to reach us via our libidos, we are still desperately curious about our own sexual natures. This is just as true for women over fifty as it is for girls fifteen or twenty—maybe even more so, because there is still so little information available about sexuality after fifty.

It's only within the last few years, with the popularity of beautiful older women such as Jane Fonda, Linda Evans, and Joan Collins, and with the success of magazines such as *Lear's*, that the sexuality of women over fifty has begun even to *exist* in the popular media.

In the next three chapters we'll be discussing Everything You Always Wanted to Know About Sex as it relates to your body and your life NOW, not as they were thirty years ago. And remember, satisfying sex, particularly as we get older, does not just mean intercourse ending in orgasm. When we talk about "sex," we're not referring simply to the act of intercourse but to the whole spectrum of sexual behavior, which includes touching, hugging and kissing.

Yes, there are differences between Then and Now. But they may not be the differences you think.

How the Body Changes Sexually—At Fifty, Sixty, and Beyond

A recent Consumers Union study—a fifty-question, open-ended questionnaire of eight hundred people, aged sixty to ninety-one years—obtained the following results:

Ninety-five percent said they liked sex

Ninety-nine percent would like to have sex if it were available

Ninety-nine percent of the women said they were orgasmic most of the time or always

Eighty-three percent considered touching and cuddling important

Seventy-five percent were as sexually satisfied now as in younger years

Ninety-one percent approved in principle of older people having sex and living together unmarried

Eighty-two percent accepted masturbation in principle, but only 46 percent said they masturbated

Of course, a survey like this is self-selecting. That is, people who don't have an avid interest in sex are much less likely to take the time to fill it out. Still, the results are intriguing. The results tell us interest in sex among the over-sixty crowd is much, much stronger than sex therapists once thought.

A related Consumers Union study concluded:

- Fifty percent of women are sexually active throughout their sixties.
- Fifty percent of men are sexually active through their seventies. So, sexual responsiveness as well as sexual interest does not necessarily decrease with age.
- In 1966 Masters and Johnson studied the sexual response of thirty-four women aged fifty-one and older and compared it with that of younger women. For both groups sexual response has a keen effect on a number of the body's systems and organs, including the breasts, clitoris, outer labia, inner labia, vagina, and general muscle tension.

- In foreplay and early sexual response nipple erection occurred with the same strength and frequency whether women were twenty years old or seventy.
- In the secondary (plateau) phase engorgement of the areolae, the tissue surrounding the nipples, was not as intense for older women as it was for younger women.
- General muscle tension also decreased with aging.
- Clitoral enlargement and excitation DID NOT change across age groups.
- The major and minor labia do change with age, losing some of their elasticity and fullness.
- The vagina also changes. In younger women Masters and Johnson observed an expansion of the inner two-thirds of the vagina; the expansion also occurred in older women, but at a slower rate.
- Rate and amount of lubrication does diminish with age—although apparently the more active the woman's sex life throughout her life, the less this diminishment occurs.

An earlier Kinsey study, in 1953, also analyzed the effects of age on sexual activities on women up to age sixty. The study showed no decline in frequency of orgasm reached through activities that were not primarily dependent on males, such as masturbation. In fact Kinsey's measures of orgasm and frequency of masturbation declined steadily for men in this age range, but remained constant across age groups for women. Frequency of orgasm through intercourse or other activity that depended on a sexual partner *did* decline steadily.

From this data Kinsey and his researchers concluded that for women in this age group there is no age-related decline in sexual *interest*—and that *decline in activity was more often than not attributable to the male partner.*

What does all this mean? With women the incidence of sexual intercourse does decrease with age—*but not because the woman is no longer interested.*

Which reminds us of an old story: Mary Garden, the astounding Metropolitan Opera soprano of the 1920s, was as lovely to look at as she was to hear. Once, seeing her in a gown with a pronounced décolletage, a distinguished man-about-town asked her what kept her dress up. She replied, "Two things. Your age and my discretion."

Thus the decrease in a woman's sexual activity is usually on account of the absence of a sexual partner or because the *man* in the woman's life is no longer interested. In comparison the amount of sex men have later in life decreases less, because there are more men over fifty living with wives or partners as compared with women over fifty. Men are conditioned to declare that they want and need sex, whether they do or not; and women are conditioned to declare that they *don't* need it, whether they do or not!

Let's examine some of the factors that may affect your current (or potential) sex life.

Health

Reasonably good health—not only yours but your partner's—is important for an active sex life. Energy levels *do* diminish, and if you're in poor shape, it stands to reason that a night parked in front of the television with a bag of Pepperidge Farm cookies is going to have a lot more appeal than sexual acrobatics. Henry VIII notwithstanding, serious obesity can put a real damper on a man's libido. Notes Lorraine, "Until Jack finally lost those extra forty pounds I had been nagging him about . . . well, let's put it this way: If it was late at night and it came down to a choice between me and a Big Mac with fries and a Coke, the Big Mac would win every time."

There are some medical problems that can genuinely prevent sexual functioning. With chronic diabetes, for example, peripheral nerve damage can prevent erection, and while there are medical solutions to this difficulty (the insertion of a prosthetic device into the penis, for example, which will help maintain an erection), the problem itself is a physical reality.

More often, however, a health problem can trigger a sexual problem because of *fear*. Many believe sex is dangerous if you have been sick or had surgery. In fact while pain and bodily malfunction can certainly deter the libido, more often than not sexual activity of one form or another can be resumed.

Recently Jay, Liz's seventy-two-year-old lover, had a coronary bypass after having his second heart attack. He has always been an extremely athletic and sexual man. "Sex," Jay always told Liz, "is as natural and important as breathing." Even though his doctors have told him he can resume all his normal activities, he is frightened of sex—even of touching and kissing. "Jay used to joke that he always wanted to 'die in the saddle,' " says Liz ruefully. "But once, soon after his operation, when we were kissing, he had a little chest pain, and now he's afraid that anything sexual will trigger another heart attack." Jay is extremely depressed about the lack of sex because he equates it with lack of intimacy.

Like Jay, Liz is a worrier, but her bright button eyes shine with optimism when she discusses this current "bump" in their relationship. "We think this is a temporary stage. I think if we just take things slowly, he'll realize that walking fast is actually more stressful on the heart than sex. And in a strange way there's a bright side to all this," says Liz cheerfully. "Jay makes me feel like a real vixen—one touch from me is so exciting that he'll die!"

Liz herself is not free of health problems: Years of uncontrolled high blood pressure have caused some permanent damage to her vision. But Liz likes to think her ailment has actually *helped* her sex life. "I used to have such great vision—I could see everything. Sometimes that made me self-conscious during sex. Now things are . . . well, a little softer around the edges. The less I see, the less self-conscious I am!"

Your Man's Aging Process

Even with the healthiest partner, as a man gets older, it generally takes him longer to achieve an erection, and that erection may not be as firm as it was in his youth. At fifty-four, Lise, once no stranger to the game of musical beds, talks about the Erections of Yesteryear. "It was all so easy when we were young," Lise recalls, smiling to herself as she runs her hands through her thick mane of curly brown hair. "You went to bed with a man and there was one thing you could pretty much rely on. I mean, it might be awkward; you might not know what to say to each other; or he might think "clitoris" was the name of a small Greek island. Whatever. But you could also guarantee he would get an erection. And in your mind that meant he wanted you, and if he didn't get an erection, it meant he didn't want you. It was that simple." Lise remembers a joke she heard at a comedy club recently. The comedienne said, "Wow, there's something about young boys ... they can do it all night. They don't know what they're doing, but they can do it all night!"

How things have changed. "Now if I go to bed with a man, an erection is the one thing you *can't* rely on. Sex is generally so much sweeter, more meaningful now. I would never go to bed with anyone I didn't care for a great deal. And with experience, most men know how to please a woman—or if they're not sure, at least lots of them have the courage and maturity to ask. But an erection is a much more timid creature these days ... and what many women don't understand is that if he *doesn't* have one, it doesn't mean he doesn't want you." As Shakespeare said in *Henry IV*, "Is it not strange that desire should so many years outlive performance?"

"At this stage, there are just a lot more factors that come into play," Lise continues. "Of course that doesn't stop me from worrying and wondering: If I were twenty and cooing over what a big strong man he was, wouldn't he get hard just like *that*?"

There's a saying a lot of men over fifty hear—and believe: "Fear is the first time you realize you can't do it the second time. Panic is the second time you realize you can't do it the first time." In some ways sex is an even scarier prospect for older men than it is for women. Women can fake their excitement (and unfortunately many do!). But if a man isn't aroused, you both know it!

Many, many men have grown up to believe that their erection *is* their manhood; when they can't rely on it, they become frightened and feel they can't truly satisfy a woman. Perhaps some of them would be interested in a survey done several years ago by advice columnist Ann Landers.

A woman wrote to Landers, complaining that there was such a to-do about intercourse but that what was really important to most women was the affection that was part of sex (and that men tend to think of as the appetizer, not the main course!). Ann opened this issue up to her readers, asking them to write in and tell her what aspect of the sex act was most important to them. To her surprise she was swamped with over 100,000 letters! While some women talked about intercourse as absolutely necessary to their happiness, the vast majority agreed that intercourse was not particularly important. Many of the letters began, "If my husband just hugged me and held me, or put his arm around me, or kissed me . . ."

Your Looks

Liz jokes about the loss of her eyesight, and Lise about her effect on a man's erection; but in fact their worries—that the inevitable wrinkles and sags of encroaching age will inevitably repel a man—are among the most common reasons women stop being sexual as they grow older. After all, if everything in society says aging is disgusting—especially in women—and if *you* look in the mirror and are frustrated and unhappy with what you see, what will your man think?

It would be silly to deny that how you look affects your sex life, because your looks affect your feelings about yourself. If you look in the mirror and like what you see, chances are you'll feel more sexy. But what's important is looking *your* best, not trying to measure yourself against the women you see in magazines. Fred, a forty-five-year-old Boston gem dealer, is one of the most eligible men around. He regularly dates women ranging in age from twenty-five to sixty-five. "Sure, I'm sometimes attracted to firm young bodies, but I would much, much rather be with a woman my age or a bit older. Forget about wrinkles. If the woman takes care of herself and has pride in her appearance, she is sexy."

Menopause

Remember the first day you got your period? Most women do, not because it was necessarily a happy occasion (so many girls are frightened, embarrassed, or just plain ignorant) but because you knew it was the *beginning* of something—even if you weren't quite sure what that "something" was! Almost every culture has some ritual to accompany this entry into the club of womanhood. In some primitive societies it was (and still is) enforced isolation for the duration of the period. During the 1940s and 1950s in this country many girls received a slap on the face, along with a little "now you're a woman" speech from mom. Still others receive little keepsakes: Erica's mother, for example, gave her a tiny gold teardrop that she wears to this day.

There is no such ritual for the onset of menopause. (Ever seen a Hallmark card that reads, "Congratulations on those hot flashes!"?) While there are certainly mixed signals given to young girls about their periods (it's a nuisance, it's messy, it's sometimes painful, but it's the beginning of your sexual power as a woman), there is no such mixed message for menopause. Menopause is BAD, BAD, BAD.

Many of you have already gone through menopause. (The average age is between fifty-one and fifty-two.) Some of you were probably not thrilled about it. It seemed like the end of things. Perhaps your children were leaving home. Perhaps your husband was thinking about retirement; perhaps you were. It was the end of fertility, the end of your desirability as a woman. The end, in fact, of life.

As I've discussed before, this was not an unreasonable assumption as recently as 1900, when a woman's life expectancy was forty-eight years and menopause really *did* signal approaching death. But now, with women living an additional thirty or so years after menopause, what does the event mean? And how does it affect your sexuality?

Here are the physical realities of menopause:

- Usually your period does not stop all at once, but rather over time. Sometimes you'll skip a month or two; sometimes your periods get lighter and lighter until they stop.
- There is a marked decrease in estrogen levels in the body. Estrogens are steroid hormones produced in the ovaries. They are responsible for the development of a woman's secondary sex characteristics (breast development, swelling of hips, pubic hair

growth, etc.) in puberty, and they control the phases of the menstrual cycle.

For some women lower estrogen levels result in a slight loss of elasticity in the walls of the vagina, meaning there is a loss of vaginal depth. It also means less lubrication when you become sexually excited. This does *not* diminish your level of sexual excitement, but it can account for the "dry" feeling that bothers some women and makes intercourse painful. As we'll discuss later, this lessening of lubrication can easily be made up for by using a lubricant.

• Androgen levels do not change (androgens are male hormones, which all women produce in small amounts) but they increase relative to the amount of female hormones. A very small minority of women report increased hair growth or some deepening of the voice after menopause. It's not that the woman is becoming "masculine"; it's just that the body may be responding to changes in the male/female hormone ratio.

• Seventy-five percent of all women report hot flashes (a vasomotor phenomenon that is experienced as a sudden onset of warmth in the face and neck, usually progressing to the chest and lasting several minutes), dizziness, weight gain, and mood swings. Just as there's a wide range of discomfort levels during a woman's menstrual flow that ranges from virtually no discomfort to severe cramps, nausea, and diarrhea, these common symptoms of menopause vary greatly in degree and severity.

Menopause does bring about physiological changes. Some of these changes can affect sexual functioning.

But the vast majority of women are capable of enjoying sex, emotionally and physically, as much—or more than—they did when they were younger.

How menopause affects your sex life depends less on physical changes than on your psychological attitude. Is it, for you, an end, or is it a transition?

For Dawn, a stunning brunette, menopause was one of the worst phases of her life. "It's funny. I slept around so much when I was younger, and I wasn't always too careful with birth control," she says grimly. "So getting my period always filled me with such a sense of relief. First, it meant I wasn't pregnant—but it was also a signal to me that I was still, I don't know, just *female*, I suppose."

Dawn's periods had always been very regular, and at fifty-one, when she started missing periods, she panicked. "I knew what it was, and I just couldn't face it. I wasn't . . . a woman anymore. I looked at myself in the mirror, and I swore I could see new wrinkles every day." Dawn always had dressed rather provocatively, but now, to make up for her feelings of unfemininity, she really put on the glitz. "I was wearing so many frills and poufs, I was beginning to look like Dolly Parton—and those were the clothes I wore to *work*." Meanwhile Dawn found herself turned off to the man she was seeing at the time. "Len was about five years younger than me. How could I let him touch this old lady?"

They began to fight and soon broke up. Dawn found herself back where she was when she was twenty—cruising the bars. "I wouldn't let Len touch me, because I felt disgusting, but somehow I felt I belonged in a bar." As attractive as Dawn is, the bar scene was not exactly the ideal place for her to meet men while her self-esteem was particularly shaky. Dawn's eyes still well with tears when she remembers that year. "I would often be the last person to leave, and sometimes I felt like going home with anybody who asked."

Dawn began drinking more heavily, and she felt an overwhelming need to prove herself. On several occasions she did go home with men she didn't know. "I had always heard that menopause means less pleasure in sex, and at the time it seemed to be true. No matter what we did, I never had orgasms anymore; I would leave the situation frustrated and angry with my partner. But I figured this was the way things were supposed to be." Eventually Dawn realized that it was her compulsion to prove her sexuality with everyone, not the onset of menopause, that was harming her natural sexual impulses.

Dawn realized her drinking and her cruising were a vicious cycle; she vowed to stay away from bars and casual contact—and she has. "Maybe it was inevitable that I would go through this stage at some point, but it all happened around the time of menopause. I had always put so much stock in my looks, and I saw it as a signal that my days as a 'real woman' were numbered. But I'm working through these feelings, and these days I feel there's life after menopause."

For many women menopause is not an end (like it seemed for Dawn), but a beginning. With children gone and finances more secure, there's a great freedom to pursue career, education, or other interests; maybe, too, grandchildren are arriving on the scene. Some women also report feeling calmer and freer about sexual activity—no more chance of unwanted pregnancy, no chance of interruption by children.

"For me menopause was a sexual awakening," says

Naomi, who has six children. Today Naomi seems, by anyone's standards, the proverbial tough cookie. She comes by it honestly: She grew up poor and struggling in a religious Jewish home on New York's Lower East Side. But at sixty-five the money from three marriages—and the freedom she has painfully acquired— has now given her the poise and self-assurance she never had.

In her marriages she was, by her own reports, utterly pliable. "Although I'm not religious, my first two husbands were Catholic and didn't believe in birth control. So I wasn't allowed to use it, even though I never really wanted to have more than one or two children. I love them all dearly of course, but I remember a time when I had five kids all under ten and a sixth on the way, and I just wanted to pack up and leave the whole whining, snotty-nosed pack. After the first two every time my period was a day late, my heart sank." Naomi was forty-two and on her second marriage when menopause began. "Friends were commiserating with me about how early my menopause had started, but I was elated. My youngest was ten years old, and my new husband was making noises about how it wasn't too late to start a family with him, and I was having visions of myself as a cover story in the *National Enquirer*—"Oldest New Mom on Long Island Gives Birth to Quadruplets." Fortunately my period stopped; unfortunately my husband decided he wanted his own kids, and if I wasn't going to give them to him, that was that."

Going through menopause and another divorce simultaneously was painful, to say the least, but Naomi was not exactly a shrinking violet. "I waited five years until after my second divorce—I was forty-eight by this time—and then I started dating with a vengeance.

Older men, younger men, anything I could get my hands on. I wasn't exactly picky, and I didn't approach these fellows with thoughts of a relationship in mind. Some of them were so obviously after me because of my money it was pathetic. My children were mortified. They would tattle on me to their fathers. But I didn't care. I felt I had devoted my life to raising them and now I was going to *live*. I'm afraid I wasn't much of a mother at this point."

Still Naomi feels that this time was just about the best time in her life. A life-long swimmer, she was in great shape; her children were away at either boarding school or college; she had plenty of money; and although she wanted adventure, she wasn't interested in falling in love. "For the first time sex was about enjoyment, about having fun; it wasn't, 'Oh, no, maybe we shouldn't do this, I think I'm ovulating now'; or, 'Can you hurry up and finish, dear, I think I hear one of the children knocking on the door.' "

Naomi didn't settle down with another man for years, until, several years ago, she met Bob. "Now I'm sixty-five and I think this one's gonna last. And Henry's seventy-one. As Mrs. Allonby said in Oscar Wilde's *A Woman of No Importance*: 'I delight in men over seventy, they always offer one the devotion of a lifetime.' "

Keeping Informed About Sex and Sexuality

For those of you who want to learn more about sex and sexuality for your age group, there's a newsletter written by a team of sex therapists in North Carolina. Titled, appropriately enough, *Sex Over 40*, the monthly newsletter features articles such as, "Why Morning Sex Can Be More Fun for Couples Over Forty," "How to Help Your Partner Get Firm Erections," "How to Fondle and Caress More of Your Lover," "What They Didn't Teach Us When We Were Growing Up About Oral Sex," "What Effects Does a Hysterectomy Actually Have on Your Sexuality?" and "How to Get Through the Times When You Don't Have a Sexual Partner (Or Your Partner Is Ill or Unavailable) Without Losing Your Sexual Ability."

For more information, write to:

> *Sex Over Forty*
> P.O. Box 1600
> Chapel Hill, North Carolina 27515

(No need to worry about receiving a big envelope that screams *Sex Over Forty*. The publishers have thoughtfully made the symbol for their newsletter a little more cryptic: "S/40"!)

10

Myths and Fears About Sex

Kids think parents old and dull
On matters lewd or sexual
They of course don't know the truth—
Libido is perpetual!
>—GERTRUDE SMALL,
>unpublished poem (1971)

As we've seen, the physical aspects of aging need not have any effect on your ability to maintain and enjoy an active, healthy sex life. Just because your legs aren't as strong as they were when you were twenty or thirty doesn't mean you give up walking or running. You're headed for the same place; it's just that at sixty or sixty-five it may take you a little longer to get there! Psychologically, however, there may be barriers that are holding you back. If the mind truly is the biggest erogenous zone, it can also be the biggest deterrent to sexual pleasure.

This was it. Yvonne was prepared in every way she could think of. She wore a bright yellow dress which complemented her handsome dark features. She had even styled her straight no-nonsense black hair into a soft perm. Now she sat bolt upright on her living room couch waiting for David to materialize. If only she could stop trembling.

Approaching the fourth anniversary of her husband's death, Yvonne, fifty-five, had been convinced by friends and family that an evening out with a new man wouldn't be so bad. So she allowed herself to be talked into a date with David, a well-to-do widower who attended her synagogue and shared her love for opera.

As she waited, the sweat began to break out on her brow. In her head she carried on a conversation with her dead husband: "I'm sorry, darling. I know I look silly sitting here. I hope you can forgive me." How could she do this to him? He was the kindest, sweetest . . . actually she had to admit that their marriage had had its problems for many years, but . . . no, he had been wonderful.

And this fellow David? Her pulse raced with fear. "What will we talk about? What if he thinks I'm a complete bore? What if I think he's boring? What if I spill my wine in my lap at dinner? Will he think I'm an alcoholic if I drink wine? And at the end of the evening . . . ?" Yvonne thought about her marriage at nineteen to the only man she had ever slept with. "What if he tries to . . . ?"

Here Yvonne's imagination failed her. The possibilities were just too mortifying. Despite her friends' urgings, three years after the death of her husband Yvonne was still not ready for a sexual relationship with someone new. For many other women three years would seem like a long time; but for Yvonne and others like her, three years seems like the blink of an eye.

But chances are very good that soon Yvonne *will* be ready—she just isn't now.

For widowed or divorced women who have been without partners for some time, the prospect of a sexual relationship looms like a dark cloud on the horizon. If a man becomes interested in them, the first thoughts are likely to be:

"I haven't made love in years. Can I do it again? Maybe I've forgotten how."

"I've only been with one man my entire life. Can I adjust to a new one? An *old* new one?!"

"God only knows what will be expected of me in bed nowadays!"

"I want to hold hands, hug, maybe kiss—but *sex*? That's for the young."

"Can I? Will he want to?"

The answer? He'll (almost definitely) want to. And yes, you can.

No doubt about it, a physical relationship is scary—it was when you were twenty-five, and it's even more so now. When I'm conducting one of my classes, "On Being a Golden Girl," I must be very careful about the way I discuss sex; to many women a discussion of the subject seems like a personal violation. (After one class that had some somewhat graphic sexual talk, I asked everyone how they felt the discussion had gone. Everyone politely said it was wonderful and informative. Then I asked them to write their responses without signing their names. Cloaked in anonymity, most admitted feeling embarrassed and angry!)

Some people are so frightened of sex they avoid dating altogether because they fear what it will lead to. Perhaps your last sexual experience was a few months ago; more likely it was a year ago, or perhaps even five or ten years ago. Kate still has not gotten over this hurdle.

"When the sexual revolution was here, I was in the kitchen, not the bedroom," she says. "I was raising two small children and caring for my husband. The last time I went on a date, during the fifties, a kiss was a big deal. Now I feel comfortable talking to attractive men in a group situation, but the thought of being one-on-one . . . forget it. I imagine I'll open my mouth to speak, and no words will come out . . . just a sort of raspy croak."

Yet for most people a sexual relationship, if available, plays an important role in psychological well-being and happiness. If you are faced with the possibility of a sexual encounter but are ambivalent about getting things started, how do you cope with your questions and fears? The first step is to examine the beliefs you may be harboring about human sexuality in general, and your own sexual nature in particular. Accept this idea now: Even if you are the most experienced and sophisticated woman in the world, when you've been out of action for a while, sex is not going to be as easy for you as making pancakes.

Myth: "Sexual feelings and fantasies are not normal for older people."

Fact: They are! On her eightieth birthday Nancy Astor said, "I used to dread getting older because I thought I would not be able to do all the things I wanted to do, but now that I am older, I find that I don't want to do them." There are any number of things we think are terribly important to do in our thirties that just don't seem quite as urgent in our sixties. For example, somehow you know your whole world won't collapse if you never, ever, go skydiving, or rafting down the Amazon, or make slow, passionate love to Paul Newman in the backseat of a stretch limo. But for most of us sexual desires and fantasies stay with us—often until the day we die. The *frequency* of these desires may lessen, but they are there, all the same.

"I would be walking down the street, and suddenly see a handsome young man in tight-fitting jeans, and wonder . . . which way is he, you know, *hanging*," says Jacqueline with a nervous little giggle. "I would get so angry with myself. My God, I could be a grandmother, how could I possibly think things like that? But then I think, gosh, I'm entitled to think any way I want. As long as there still are no mind police, like in George Orwell's *1984*, what difference does it make if I have a little fun?"

"Whenever I say something even vaguely sexual to my daughter, Amy, she cringes and yells at me, 'Mom, that's disgusting!' " says Alberta. "I don't blame her really—that's the way I used to react when *my* mother said anything slightly risqué. But on some level I resent the fact that so many thirty-year-old women act as if they invented sex. Even if there are a lot of things I think about but wouldn't necessarily like to try, I'm kind of proud that my imagination about sex is as active as it ever was."

Many older women fear their own needs and desires because they've been told for so many years, by their husbands, friends, and family that those things are "undignified." As Erica reported, "For years there was something I wanted to try with my husband—my *hus-*

band, for goodness sake—that he absolutely refused to do, and I had never done before my marriage. I wanted him to perform oral sex on me—cunnilingus. He said it was dirty—even the *name* was dirty, according to him. And only sick men wanted to do that to their wives. Of course what I didn't know at the time was that he was probably doing it to lots of other women—but not his wife, not the mother of his children, oh, no. I mentioned it several times at the beginning of our marriage, but then I just forgot about it. And later, when I began to see other men, I couldn't believe some of them fantasized about it. By this time I thought it was dirty too. I'll never forget how shocked I was when the second man I went to bed with after my divorce told me that he loved my natural taste and smell. I still don't entirely believe that a man can enjoy a woman in this way."

Myth: "Sex is for the young and pretty."

Fact: The Japanese have a word, *shibui*, which basically means "the beauty of aging"—that is, the beauty only age can reveal, or the feeling one gets at looking at the face of a particularly beloved older person.

The analogy might best be understood by thinking of the face of one of our great actresses, Jessica Tandy. As a girl she was magnificent: soft, dewy, the very embodiment of the stage ingenue. Now, in her seventies, her face has become beautiful in an entirely different way: wise yet electrifying, full of vitality and depth.

It's interesting that we don't have the equivalent expression in English. Attitudes toward aging are not "natural" but learned; they're as much a part of a culture as attitudes toward birth, death, and taxes.

The United States probably has one of the most age-phobic cultures in the world, and nowhere are these fears more prevalent than in the area of human sexuality. From an early age we've imbibed the lesson that people over a certain age are not supposed to be sexual.

"A man couldn't help but be disgusted if he saw me nude," says Alberta, who has taken all the full-length mirrors out of her house. Alberta, fifty-seven, was divorced five years ago and hasn't made love for seven years (although she says she very much she wants to). "I'm not so sure how much I'd like seeing the body of an old man either. I've gone on a few dates, and I find that within a few minutes I'm finding something about the person's body that drives me crazy. Last time it was this fellow's nostrils. I don't know . . . they seemed pale pink, shiny, like a rabbit's. If I could shine a light on them from a certain angle, I'm sure I could see through them. It was *horrible*."

We have all grown up with a lot of ideas about sex being for the young, partly because this is how we see it portrayed in advertisements, movies, and MTV, and partly because we've been trained to think of sex only in terms of procreative sexuality. Some women claim the thought of an old body—particularly *their* old body— "doing it" gives them the willies. As Alberta told us, "Sex looks silly enough even if your body is young and firm. But every time I visualize someone my age having sex, I think of those old *National Geographic* films of two rhinos laboriously going at it in the mud. It's kind of disgusting, and more effort than it's worth."

Most men will readily admit they have the advantage in the aging process. Says one fellow of our acquaintance, "You don't hear anybody referring to a woman's gray hair as 'distinguished.' A man with jowls can be weighty and authoritative; a woman with jowls is an old cow. Let's face it, the physical and personal qualities this society often considers attractive in men— a certain "cragginess," experience, maturity, and so forth—are often accentuated with age. The qualities traditionally considered attractive in women—'dewiness,' innocence/naiveté, helplessness, playfulness—are diminished with age."

We can't deny the biases of our culture. There is even something of a self-fulfilling prophecy in the notion that older women inevitably grow less desirable: If you are thoroughly convinced that the key to being sexy is owning one of those pert young bodies displayed in every advertisement, chances are you won't be sexy. Of course we're not suggesting that you can act like the coquette you were at sixteen; as your appearance changes, the nature of your sexuality changes, and the way you present it must change. It is, after all, the same with men: we all know a sixty-year-old man can be very, very sexy, but not if he's trying to imitate Tom Selleck!

Personal attractiveness at fifty and beyond has less to do with wonderful features and perky breasts than it does with grooming and presence. Who, for example, would have looked twice at Diana Vreeland when she was a young girl? She was positively strange-looking; yet as she got older, the renowned socialite and editor of *Vogue* in its heyday developed a distinctive style and character of her own that made people speak of her as an extremely beautiful woman.

Oddly enough, women who do take pride in their appearance are often given a double message at this stage of their lives. While it was perfectly acceptable to be fussing with hair and makeup at twenty, now, your friends may insinuate, it's a little unseemly. "I'm beyond all that—or should be," some women say. Many feel "damned if they do and damned if they don't"—criticized for not caring at all and also for caring too much. We all know women who look like they're "trying too hard." But that's usually because they're trying too hard to look half their age. What's wrong with looking your absolute, sixty-five-year-old best?! It's true that you'll have more wrinkles. It's not true that you'll feel less sexy or less interested in sex.

Myth: "Good girls are not sexual; or if they are, it is only within the confines of marriage. If you're good, you're sexual with, at most, one person; if you're bad, you're sexual with everybody."

Fact: Good girl/bad girl; you're Sandra Dee, or you're Marilyn Monroe. And remember the male ideal?: "a lady in the kitchen and a whore in bed."

This dichotomy about women's sexual nature is probably the most prevalent myth embraced by women of your generation. (Or indeed of women of most generations throughout history; even with the you've-come-a-long-way-baby feminism of the last twenty years, the good girl/bad girl is still a part of the psyche of today's average twenty-year-old.)

The rules for "good" and "bad" behavior were clearly defined. No kissing on the first date. No touching below the neck—unless you were going steady. No touching below the waist—unless you were engaged. And if you were engaged, and the wedding date was set, then, maybe . . . but really it was much, much better to wait. Good girl or bad girl; there was no in-between.

Even though you might know intellectually that things have changed, that virtually no one will think you're "bad" if you're in a sexual relationship outside marriage, you may still be filled with qualms. This is particularly true if, like many women of your generation, you have known only one sexual partner.

It took Yvonne over a year to justify her feelings for David. "I told myself that after my husband died, I could never want someone in 'that way' again," says Yvonne. "And for three years I didn't. But one day I rented *Annie Hall* and I heard Woody Allen tell Diane Keaton that a relationship was like a shark; it has to keep moving or else it will just die. 'So, I think what we have here,' Woody Allen said, 'is a dead shark.'

"Now, I can't say that movie turned my life around, but it did wake me up," Yvonne explains. "I felt like that dead shark. In my grief I had stopped moving forward. I was raised in a strict Orthodox Jewish family, and everything in my background told me that in order to be a 'good woman,' I was supposed to love one man and only one man till the day I died. Then I thought about my marriage vows—'till death do us part.' Well, it didn't say anything about '*after* death do us part.' I'm making this sound like a sudden revelation, and it wasn't. It took me a long time even after that to even *entertain* the thought of being with another man." Yvonne still can't get herself to say "making love."

Of course it's ideal to be in love with a man before you sleep with him, but as long as there's caring and respect why shouldn't you be able to make love with someone you're not "in love" with (or, for that matter, who isn't in love with you)? True, some friends or family members may object. But this is a new phase of your life, with new rules; you can give yourself permission to do some things you wouldn't have done when you were twenty. And if you explore some new terrain and find that you don't like the feel of the ground under your feet, you can always go back. You will not be a marked woman, a Hester Prynne with a scarlet *A*; you'll simply be a person who explored something new and decided she didn't like it.

Going to bed with someone has nothing to do with being "good" or "bad"—in fact the most common reason a man strays is that his "good girl" isn't interested in dirty things like sex. (Or he doesn't think he should do certain things with his "good wife"—look what happened with Erica!) So whenever you start thinking of yourself as too much of a "good girl" to do this or that, remember humorist Fran Lebowitz's definition of the word *lady*: "most often used to describe someone you wouldn't want to talk to for even five minutes."

Myth: "Nobody my age really likes sex very much anyway."

Fact: If a woman says, "I'm just not interested in sex anymore" and really means it, chances are she never was. These are often the women who tolerated sex because, as Kay told us, "My husband needed it. He was an incredibly sweet, devoted man, and tolerant of my little eccentricities." Kay is a sleek, willowy blonde renowned for her beauty, an Ivana Trump look-alike who always took great pains with her appearance, sometimes at the expense of common sense. "I remember one time when he drove me ninety miles, in a blizzard, just so I could keep an appointment with this very famous hairstylist. Anyway, whenever he did anything like that, I'd make sure we'd have sex that night. It was my way of saying thanks. I never denied it to him, although it meant nothing to me."

You can guess the outcome of Kay's marriage. After twenty-four years of marriage he left (for a woman who was in fact a year older than Kay but much more sexual); Kay was devastated. A lot of marriages where sex is the husband's "reward" for a job well done—and not a mutually pleasurable experience—end in divorce.

Some of Kay's friends would kid her about her lack of libido. But many women who claim to be indifferent to sex are simply frightened, or have had many years with a partner who was less than scintillating. Therefore they really have no idea what all the fuss is about.

Even if you've never cared for sex, are you basically a sensual person? That is, do you enjoy experiences of the senses, such as eating, touching, pleasant smells, the softness of a cashmere sweater, the color and solidity of a piece of rose quartz in your hand? If the answer is yes, you may be more sexual than you think. *Just because you have never been particularly stirred up by sex before doesn't mean you can't learn to enjoy it now.*

Myth: "You can't teach an old dog new tricks."

Fact: Have you ever actually *tried* to teach an old dog new tricks? Fact is, you can—if the dog is smart to begin with! Ask any dog trainer—the learning curve of an older dog doesn't go down. What's harder is not teaching new tricks but breaking old habits!

It's the same with you. Perhaps you feel you only know *this* sexual position or *that* technique. Or you've had a sexual relationship with only one person and it's too late to get used to another. Of course you can adapt. The hard part will be allowing yourself to develop your sexuality—and to see yourself in a new light.

Take Jacqueline. As you may recall she finally began dating Mark, a partner at her late husband's law firm. Mark, who had been divorced ten years ago, had never remarried. Without boasting about it, it was quite obvious that he'd had more than his fair share of experience in the bedroom. "He's had lots and lots of women telling him what to do, what makes them feel good, and I've only had one man telling me what's right—and I have to admit, my sex life with my husband was not the best part of our marriage."

After many months Jacqueline finally decided she cared about Mark enough to sleep with him. Nevertheless she was frightened. She drank several glasses of wine to calm down; she made Mark turn off all the lights; she insisted they keep the music turned up rather loudly, in case someone could hear them. And when it was all over, did Mark turn to her and say, "You're incredible"? Yes—but not quite in the loving, satisfied tone Jacqueline would have liked to have heard.

"He actually turned to me, laughing, and said, 'Wow, you're incredible. Incredibly *naive*,'" remembers Jacqueline with a shudder. "For a moment I was mortified. It was my worst nightmare come true. And this was just one of those matters that, in my previous life, I would have never, ever talked about. But you know what? I *was* bad. I really didn't know what I was doing. With my former husband I had always thought of sex as a 'gift' I gave him—my job was just to sort of lie there and 'accommodate' him. I knew that this time around I would have to loosen up.

"So I told Mark, 'You're right. I am.'" Jacqueline blushes as she says this, noting quietly that in fact there were many things she really *didn't* do then. "'I only know how to do two things—take my clothes off and put them back on. You've been with all these women, and I haven't been with anybody but my husband, and I have no idea how to please you. But I want to learn.' " From that moment Jacqueline and Mark started talking about what they wanted in sex, and within minutes they had collapsed into giggles. "I mean, let's be honest, sex is really silly, it's *absurd*," Jacqueline says. "You can't take it too seriously." Meanwhile Jacqueline has been learning, and Mark has been a very willing teacher. "I can't quite say I'm Jane Fonda yet, but I'm working on it!" And apparently she'll have a chance to work on it for a long time: Three weeks after we spoke to Jacqueline, she and Mark were engaged.

Like Jacqueline, many women who have been out of a relationship for a long time fear being "found out." "It will be obvious I haven't done this in a long time" is the classic response.

"The first time I went to bed with a man after my divorce, I lied about my experience," notes Erica. "I found myself boasting about all my conquests, like a teenager. These conquests were nonexistent, but I wanted to convince this new man what a great catch he had. I didn't fool anybody—certainly not the man, who thought he was getting a kind, smart, discriminating person and found himself going out with a woman who only talked about performance."

If you're worried about inexperience, or the amount of time that has elapsed since your last sexual experience, remember that you don't have to be a Michelle Pfeiffer to be a wonderful sexual partner. You just have to be able to *talk* about your man's needs and desires. Let him feel comfortable telling you what he likes, because that's the only way you'll feel comfortable telling him what *you* want.

Even if you are naive in some respects, you certainly have some idea of what's right and wrong for you. Don't be coerced into anything. If your lover favors some form of sexual activity that doesn't appeal to you, something you think might be painful or harmful, you have the absolute right to refuse.

But what if it's something you've just never tried before? Many women, for example, have been conditioned to believe that oral sex is wrong. Typical responses? "It's unhygienic," "it's degrading," or "I'll choke." In fact fellatio is one of the most attention-getting sexual skills you can develop; many men over fifty claim to prefer oral sex to intercourse because of the extra degree of stimulation it affords. It is also extremely erotic for many women; as one woman told us, "At first I was really a bit put off—how was I going to fit all that into my mouth? But now, going down on him ranks a ten on the one-to-ten intimacy scale. And it gives me an incredible rush of power, a sense of my womanness."

So, if there's something you think you haven't liked in the past but think you *could* enjoy, something that might broaden your horizons, why not give it a whirl? (After all, lots of people think they hate opera, until they hear Pavarotti sing *Pagliacci!*)

Myth: "If I go to bed with someone before we're *really* serious about each other, I'm just going to be used. He'll lose all respect for me and then he'll never be serious about me."

Fact: One of the major changes in social mores since you were growing up is that sex is not such a delicate hothouse flower, to be cosseted and protected until it can thrive safely in the greenhouse of marriage. *Most people don't marry for sex anymore.*

Says Marybeth, a fifty-three-year-old Catholic widow

now going out with (as she describes him) "a nice Jew-ish boy," "When I first got back into dating after my husband died, I was sure everyone wanted to 'take ad-vantage' of me just for sex. In my mind they saw me as the poor, pathetic widow looking for love in any way she could get it. Mostly this image was in *my* mind. But I was so convinced it was in everyone else's, I would lash out angrily at the first hint of a pass—even though I really did want a sexual relationship. It was as if people were inviting me into their homes, I would ring the doorbell, and then I would slam the door in *their* face and stalk away before I even entered the room."

We're not saying you should be indiscriminate about whom you share your bed with. As Dorothy Parker once wrote,

> Oh, gallant was the first love, and glittering and fine;
> The second love was water, in a clear white cup;
> The third love was his, and the fourth was mine
> And after that I always get them all mixed up.

Men are just as put off today by a woman who seems willing to accept anybody as they were forty years ago. (And after all, aren't *you* a bit disturbed if you discover your man has been promiscuous?) We'd even go farther and suggest that you're better off not discussing *any* of your sexual partners until you've known the new man for some time. Even if he presses you for details or seems eager to discuss past affairs with you, don't di-vulge much. As one man who claims to represent the entire male species told us, "Whenever a man tells you how he wants to know everything about you, he doesn't. Really he'd prefer to think you were born about twenty minutes before you met him."

On the other hand, you shouldn't pass up a potentially satisfying, exciting sexual experience just because you know it won't end in wedding bells and handfuls of rice at the church door. "I like sex. I like it even for the moment," Bea says staunchly. "Since I gravitate toward much younger men, I know that what I have with them isn't going to last. But when we make love, it's one more terrific experience for my memory bank. That's good enough for me."

Yes, by having sex with another human being you are making yourself vulnerable. Yes, you could sleep with a man who will never call you again. Yes, in a worst-case scenario he could talk about it with other people. But ultimately so what? This is the gamble you take if you want closeness in your life. Think about the people you know who are happiest in their relationships. In general do they tend to be closed-in and cautious? Or are they people who reach out, who are risk takers?

Myths & Fears

Myth: "I love all the affection, the touching and hugging, but I want to stop there. I don't see any reason for going farther."

Fact: Certainly there are some couples out there who will be mutually satisfied keeping the physical relationship at that level. But for most men this situation will eventually end in frustration and termination of the relationship. It's not the absence of sex per se but what that absence implies: the woman's unwillingness to abandon herself, to lose control with the person she cares about.

Myth: "Well, if I'm going to be modern about all this, I've got to be *really* modern—and that means I shouldn't mind if he's sleeping with other people."

Fact: This is not modern; this is dumb. While many social mores have changed, the desire for intimacy with *one* person is as prevalent—and legitimate—as it was when you were younger. You have as much right to want and expect monogamy now as you ever had. If the man you're with wants to sleep with more than one woman and you don't want him to, don't even *try* to accept it. You'll just torture yourself.

And there's more good news here: The sexual revolution is not as revolutionary as you may think. Men as well as women are being much more cautious about whom they share their beds with, and for good reason. *You will not be rejected by any reasonable man if you refuse to sleep with him immediately.*

Myth: "It's a dangerous world out there—AIDS, herpes, all those diseases I can't even pronounce."

Fact: Sexually transmitted diseases are a fact. AIDS is a particularly terrifying fact. But look at the real statistics: According to a report in the March 1990 issue of *Sex Over 40*, 97,000 cases of AIDS have been reported in the United States. Ninety-one percent of reported cases are men, while nine percent are women. Eighty-eight percent of AIDS patients are between the ages of twenty and forty-nine. The vast majority of AIDS cases are still within the homosexual and intravenous-drug-using population, although incidence of HIV infection is growing at an alarming rate among teenagers. But unless you're engaged in unsafe sexual practices with a member of one of these populations, your chances of contracting the HIV virus are extremely low.

Interestingly, most women report that they fear contracting herpes not so much because of the unpleasant nature of the (*not life threatening*, but still incurable) disease, but rather because of the embarrassment of telling others that they have it.

The point is that the fear of "catching something" is, 90 percent of the time, a convenient excuse for avoiding intimacy. Insist that your partner use a condom, or you provide one.

Myth: "Masturbation is harmful and 'bad' for older people."

Fact: People masturbate. They just do. Most start when they're babies—before sex is anything more than just 'feeling good down there'—and keep doing it throughout their lives.

In the Consumers Union study we've mentioned, even though 82 percent of the people surveyed accepted masturbation in principle, only 46 percent said they masturbated. There's still a tremendous taboo around this subject.

Masturbation is safe and natural. It's the way humans release sexual tension and learn about their own bodies—what gives them pleasure and what does not. In the (temporary or permanent) absence of a sexual partner, masturbation also keeps the individual in tune with his or her sexual nature. People masturbate for the same reason that if you're not using your car for any length of time, you still occasionally put the key in the ignition and run it for a while—it's good for the battery!

11

Psyching Yourself Up
for Sex

ह्ब

We talked about growing old gracefully
And Elsie who's seventy-four
Said, 'A, it's a question of being sincere,
And B, if you're supple you've nothing to fear.'
Then she swung upside down from a glass chandelier,
I couldn't have liked it more.
                    —NOEL COWARD
                    "I've Been to a Marvelous Party"

Have you ever read the *Kama Sutra*? It's the "lovers'
Bible," the famous ancient Indian text that sets down
the rules and regulations for the art of lovemaking. In
order to be the ideal lover, the *Kama Sutra* says, here
are just a few things a woman should be able to do:

- Tattoo (herself and her man)
- Perform magic
- Balance for long periods of time on her head
- Play musical glasses filled with water
- Know about cockfighting, quail fighting, and ram
  fighting

- Gamble
- Make artificial flowers
- Perform gymnastics
- Practice quickness of hand and manual skill
- Teach parrots and starlings to speak

So you think *you* have it rough! Imagine the kind of expectations the ancient Indian man had for *his* lady!

Our point is simply this: Don't believe everything you read about what you need to be a great lover. If you do, you'll probably end up feeling scared, not sexy.

Sex is not about doing it in 120 positions. It's not about having a body Jane Fonda would envy. It's about communicating with your partner, learning what gives him pleasure and what gives you pleasure. And, as I've discussed, it's also about learning to adjust to the new sexual relationship. There comes a time in the dating process when you must realize that even if you didn't have much of a sexual relationship with your husband, sex will probably be an important factor in your new relationship.

There are many tricks to put you (and your partner) at ease those first few times. The following is a list of little situations that might crop up, and practical ways to handle them.

(Here we're dealing with the basics of overcoming the psychological hurdles of a new sexual relationship. It's not a *physical* primer. To learn about various sexual positions and alternative activities in detail, get your hands on a copy of *The Joy of Sex*, which is still an excellent how-to source of sexual technique, sort of a *Popular Mechanics* for the human body.)

If: *You're worried about "what the neighbors will think" if they see a strange car parked in your driveway* *overnight—or a strange man emerging from your apartment the next morning. . . .*

We all have a couple of phrases for this phenomenon—"making a mountain out of a molehill," "creating a tempest in a teapot"—but psychologists call it a cognitive distortion. This is an irrational fear that, if thought about long enough and with enough intensity, becomes real and takes on a life of its own. For example when a teenager has a pimple, she will look in the mirror, see it, and think, "Oh, gross. I'm disfigured." She won't be able to see anything else but that pimple—it might seem to be a hideous disfigurement rather than the small, temporary blemish it is.

Similarly women who worry, "What will the neighbors think?" imagine they have neighbors like Mrs. Kravitz on the old television sitcom "Bewitched"—folks who are sneaking around the home, peeking in the window, eager to spread delicious gossip. The fact is *your neighbors aren't glued to their windows and probably couldn't care less.* It's a fantasy fear.

On the off chance there *is* someone who's paying attention, you can have the man who's staying with you park his car in your garage, or simply leave at two or three in the morning. He may grumble, but you can explain that it's only temporary: Having a relationship like this is new to you, and you need a little time to adjust to the situation. Some men will even find it romantic to slip off into the night—as long as you make it clear you're not ashamed of him and that eventually you'd *like* to wake up with him.

Perhaps, too, you're living with someone—a housemate, an adult child—and you're not quite ready for him or her to know about your romance. Although most women prefer starting a new sexual relationship in fa-

miliar surroundings, there's always the option of going
to his place. One woman who admits she's not exactly
the most enthusiastic housekeeper told us she always
initially preferred staying overnight at the man's
house. "If his place isn't in great shape, I couldn't care
less. But if mine isn't, I feel guilty. So if I go to his
house, I can concentrate entirely on the experience and
stop worrying about things like, 'Did I clean the bathtub?' "

If: *You have this image of him taking one look at your
naked body and running shrieking from the bed. . . .*

You're not Gypsy Rose Lee, and you don't have to
pretend you are. If it makes you more comfortable, get
undressed in the bathroom—or have him get undressed
in the bathroom and be waiting for him under the covers. You also don't have to make love naked: You can
wear a fetching new nightgown and your most sensuous perfume.

Seeing yourself as a participant in sex, not an
observer, will go a long way toward easing your self-
consciousness. So if it makes you more comfortable,
why not have sex in the dark? As humorist and poet
Bert Leston Taylor ("B.L.T.") said in his poem "The
Passionate Professor,"

> Love, it is night. The orb of day
> Has gone to hit the cosmic hay.
>   Nocturnal voices now we hear.
>   Come, earth's delight, the hour is near
> When Passion's mandate we obey.
>   * * *
> Candor compels me, pet, to say
> That years my fading charms betray.
>   Tho' Love be blind, I grant it's clear
>   I'm no Apollo Belvedere.

But after dark, all cats are gray.
Love, it is night!

In the dark both of you can concentrate on the tactile
sensations; looking becomes secondary. Ruth, for instance, had enormous, pendulous breasts and simply
couldn't stand the thought of anyone seeing them. So
when she and Ben first started sleeping together, she
would always wear a beautiful lacy bra; the act of re-
moving the bra—in the dark—turned Ben on.

For women who are seriously bothered by sagging
tummies and breasts, saddlebags, and the like, there
are alternatives. These include exercise and weight reduction—and I do not want to exclude the possibility of
cosmetic surgery. It can't work miracles, but it can
make you feel better about your body and yourself. And
isn't this, after all, the point? But surgery is no pana-
cea. If correcting one or two obvious flaws will satisfy
you, fine; but if you're unhappy with yourself and your
sexuality in general, no amount of nipping and tucking
will make you feel confident. That confidence has to
come *first*. It really is more than skin deep.

If: *You can't be sexual in a place that has past associations with your dead or divorced husband. . . .*

For some women, becoming comfortable with sexuality has less to do with physical confidence than with
changing patterns in day-to-day living. We all know
how we attach importance to certain objects. So, for
example, many women cannot contemplate making
love with a man other than their husband in the bed
they once shared with someone else. A possible solution is to buy another bed or to solve the problem the
way Marybeth did. She simply switched the side of the
bed she slept on, so when Irving was in the bed with

her, she didn't look over at him and immediately think of her last husband, George.

Lorraine, a divorcée, began sleeping with her new love, Jack, in neutral territory: a hotel room. "Because I was so angry at my former husband, a part of me just wanted to drag a man home, any man, and do it right in the bed I had shared with him. I was bitterly unhappy, but in some way I felt I was getting revenge. But when I met Jack, I knew I wanted to put all that anger and bitterness behind me. So we went to a hotel. It was romantic, fun, and had no associations for either of us," she said, adding, "It really got things off to a good start." If you don't want the people at the hotel to know you're not married, register under the same name; no one checks. Or if it makes you more comfortable, take adjoining rooms. The king and queen of England always have separate rooms—if it's good enough for them, it's good enough for you!

If: *You're worried you've never done anything but "the basics"—straight, missionary-style sex—and he's going to expect something more "advanced". . . .*

Ever the good student, Jacqueline was not going to go into her new sexual liaison unprepared. She read the letters column in *Penthouse* magazine. She rented a few porn movies, ignoring the quizzical looks she got at her local video store. She poured over *The Joy of Sex*.

"It's amazing how ignorant you can be about sex, even after years of marriage," Jacqueline explains. "I didn't think I was going to actually *do* most of the things I saw in the porn movies, but I didn't want to be uninformed. As they say, information is power, and I needed all the power I could get."

We're not saying you have to know how to do all the things depicted in sexually explicit material—you probably wouldn't want to—but at least *know* what the possibilities are. Know what anal sex is like, what bondage is, how to give and receive oral sex. It's also important to know all the colloquial terms for sexual acts. Extending your sexual vocabulary is as useful as extending any other part of your vocabulary—it enables you to know more precisely what your man wants, and what you want.

"I know this sounds incredibly naive," one woman told us hesitatingly, "but when he asked me to 'blow' him, I thought he actually wanted me to blow *on* him— his neck, chest, and so on. I didn't understand what was so great about that, but I thought, 'what the heck.' So there I was, huffing and puffing away, and he looked at me like I just beamed down from the planet Zornac. Then he burst into laughter. He explained that 'blowing' was just another term for oral sex, and I was so embarrassed I hoped that a big hole would just appear in the middle of the bed and engulf me."

Being sexually literate does not make you sluttish, it makes you *knowledgeable*.

If: *You're really turned on by him but you're not lubricating enough and you worry that he'll think he doesn't really excite you. . . .*

As we've discussed, the reason for less lubrication is a reduction in the body's estrogen levels. Estrogen therapy for menopausal and postmenopausal women has become an increasingly popular treatment for women who are experiencing unpleasant and menopausal symptoms such as depression, recurrent hot flashes, and painful intercourse. It is also thought to hinder the beginning symptoms of osteoporosis, the medical term for calcium loss in the bones.

But doctors may be administering estrogen therapy too hastily; its long-term effects are still not known, and there are some unpleasant side effects. (Many women report getting their period back again, even if they haven't had it for years. Who wants PMS when she's sixty-five?)

Better than estrogen therapy is simply using a water-soluble lubricant such as K-Y jelly. Before intercourse you insert it into the vagina with a small plunger shaped like a tampon (you can buy the plungers from the pharmacist, or they are usually enclosed in packages of contraceptive jelly). If the lubricant seems a bit messy, try using less of it! In most cases a lubricant will be all you need for easy, pain-free sex.

However, if what you're experiencing is not lack of lubrication but a general tightening of the vaginal muscles ("vaginismus") that prevents a man from entering you, the problem may be more mental than physical. Your body may be trying to tell you that psychologically you're not ready for sex, or at least not ready with this particular man. If the situation continues past the first few attempts at intercourse, you may want to consult your gynecologist, who may refer you to a therapist.

If: *He can't get an erection.* . . .

Twenty-five percent of men over forty have occasional bouts of impotence. So if you're having sex with a man over fifty, there's a good chance that his erection isn't going to appear magically. Or, if it does appear, it may need a bit of added inspiration to stick around. At this age some men need manual stimulation no matter how excited they are to be in bed with you; it's just a physiological fact.

At the moment neither of you know each other well. So if he can't get an erection, don't feel obligated to *do* anything—unless he tells you exactly what he wants you to do.

There are a few things *not* to do. Don't, for example, burst into tears. Not having an erection doesn't mean he doesn't find you attractive; in fact it might mean he finds you very attractive and is just very nervous about pleasing you. And now is not the time to start making comparisons with men in your past. One woman told us she tried to console a new lover with tales about how " 'this always used to happen to my husband before he died, so don't worry about it.' I was just babbling. I can't explain why I thought that bit of information would be comforting to him."

Your best bet? Just don't make a big deal about the whole thing, because he probably feels worse about it than you ever could. Laugh it off and show him that all you're interested in is being with him and learning how to please him—everything will happen at its proper time. Hug him, kiss him, snuggle with him—and tell him, either with words or with your hands, that you'd like to learn just what will give him the most pleasure.

Above all, don't expect grand passion at first. Typically the first few times you go to bed with a new man aren't so wonderful. It's *normal* for sex to be awkward at the beginning. The playfulness and pleasure that make sex terrific do not come on command—they come with experience, with getting to know your partner.

If: *You're worried that he'll be turned off by your inexperience. . . .*

Your most valuable tool in dealing with sex is humor, because no matter how frightened you are, he is probably just as frightened. After all, even though you may be worried that he won't like your body, *he's* the one who actually has to make his work.

If he's revved up and ready to go and you're not, discuss your inexperience or ambivalence. Have a little speech prepared beforehand that doesn't seem to be attacking your man for what, after all, are his natural and desirable feelings. Here are a few possibilities:

The Straightforward Approach: "I'm really excited about this, but I haven't made love to anyone in _____ years/months. So this might take some time. But with you I'm willing to try. I want to."

The Handyman's Analogy: "Look, this is kind of like trying to start a car that's been sitting in the garage for a long, long winter. You've got to let the motor run for a while before you can go anywhere."

Almost a Virgin: "I've had experience with only one man. You've probably had much more experience. I'll be depending on you."

If he wants to try something you've never done before in bed: "Um, you know how Baskin and Robbins has thirty-one flavors? Well, let's put it this way: I've only tried vanilla. I'm not sure if I'm going to like all the other flavors, but I'll try a few—in small bits, please."

The Bait-and-Switch Ploy (drawing attention to your best features): "I've always been told I have the most sensuous elbows. What do you think?"

If all else fails and you're still feeling self-conscious, you can do as one of our friends suggested: Step on his glasses!

Remember, too, that *you* may not be the only one who wants to take your time. "Jack was full of bravado about his prowess—until we actually got to the point where I could consider making love with him," said Lorraine. "Then, all of a sudden, the tiger became a pussycat. He decided we had to get to know each other

better, which was fine with me—except that eventually
it was *me* who had to assure *him* I would respect him
in the morning!"

If: *You've never really enjoyed sex, and you're sure
it's too late to learn to like it now. . . .*

Remember Kay, the woman who always thought of
sex as a distasteful but necessary "reward" she gave
to her husband? After the not-too-frequently rewarded
husband left her, Kay was of course devastated. But
after several years she has found a sexual partner who,
for the first time, has shown her what sex is supposed
to be. She recently told me, "You wouldn't recognize
me. I don't even recognize myself. I can't believe I like
it so much. In the past I was just passive; I lay there
like a log, being manipulated by my husband. My husband was the only man I'd ever slept with—how could
I know there was so much more to sex? Now, in bed,
I'm doing; I'm not being done *to*!" Kay believes she is
a perfect example that just because you never liked sex
in the past, it doesn't mean you can't love it now.

If: *You're worried about AIDS, herpes, or other sexually transmitted diseases. . . .*

As we said in chapter 10, if you are with a heterosexual man who is fifty years old or more, you're not
swimming in very dangerous waters. However, taking
precautions these days is always a good idea. Ask him
to wear a condom. These days 60 percent of all condoms
are sold to women, who are insisting their men wear
them. (Some even come in pink, flowery packaging!)

If he does not like to wear condoms, ask why. It's true
that in some cases wearing a condom means less sensi-
tivity and makes it slightly more difficult to maintain an
erection; for men who worry about performance this can
be an additional, unnecessary hindrance. So do not hesi-

tate to ask him about his past sexual history. Has he ever used drugs intravenously? Has he ever been involved with a man? (Just because he looks and acts like a macho dreamboat, don't take it for granted that he has never "experimented.") The AIDS test is not conclusive, but it might put your mind at ease if he took one.

Regarding herpes, you shouldn't be shy about asking him, point-blank. If your man does have herpes, he has probably lived with this condition for a long time and can tell you about it. Then you can decide if you want to get involved. You may already know—particularly if you have herpes yourself or been with someone who has—that herpes sufferers are only contagious when there are active lesions on the skin (usually around the mouth or genitals). There are many couples where one partner has herpes and the other never contracts it because they don't engage in sexual activity during outbreaks of the virus. You and your partner should discuss the situation *before* you land in the bedroom.

If: *You're convinced the first time you see him in bed will be the last. . . .*

As we discussed in chapter 10, the possibility of rejection and pain always exists; you're taking a risk. Or it's possible that for some reason you may be fine partners out of bed, but you really don't get along sexually.

If you think he'll abandon you because you're "bad" for wanting sex, think again. Women are entitled to their sexual needs as well as men, and the vast majority of men are delighted to find themselves with a woman who's as enthusiastic about sex as they are. It shows you want a mature relationship.

If, on the other hand, you have good reason to believe he just wants another conquest—you've seen him act

this way with other women in the past, for example—
you have to stop and ask yourself why you're sleeping
with him in the first place. Perhaps you just want the
sexual experience, which is fine. But beware if you're
expecting more.

And if, in the worst-case scenario, he does just want
to sleep with you and never calls again, it's probably a
fight-or-flee behavior pattern he's repeated for years.
Nine times out of ten it has nothing to do with you.
Past behavior is a pretty good indicator of present and
future behavior; finding out if he has a history of being
a ladies' man will go a long way toward predicting his
actions with you.

If You Really, Truly Don't Want a Sexual Relationship Now: One Alternative

We strongly believe that a sexual relationship, when
available, is healthy, normal, and adds to a full and
vital life. Most relationships where a woman says she
doesn't want sex will end, because having a physical
relationship is crucial to creating a bond of intimacy
between two people.

However, you may genuinely feel that sex outside
the confines of marriage is inappropriate. This feeling
may or may not have to do with your religious beliefs,
but whatever the reason, a new organization has just
formed that allows you to meet like-minded partners.
Founded by Mary Meyer, the Chicago-based National
Chastity Association believes that any sexual contact—
including kissing, hand holding, and touching—should
be reserved for marriage. The NCA has a list of "nineteen desires" that its members share, among them:

- The desire to be married eventually
- The desire to marry someone who will be "in love" with him or her throughout life
- The desire to marry someone to whom hand holding, kissing, caressing, and sexual intercourse mean special experiences of mutual, exclusive, faithful, romantic love
- The desire to save hand holding, kissing, caressing, and sexual intercourse until he or she is actually married
- The desire to save the feelings of being "in love" until he or she is actually married
- The desire to be very close friends with someone for at least two years before even wanting to marry him or her

If you share these beliefs, you can obtain more information by sending a stamped, self-addressed envelope to:

> The National Chastity Association
> P.O. Box 402
> Oak Forest, Illinois 60452
> (Telephone: 312/687-1767)

Again, we don't share the views of the NCA, but we believe it may be a beneficial singles meeting place for the men and women who do.

Talk, Talk, Talk

Do you like your feet massaged? Do you love having your nipples caressed? Does he like his ears nibbled? Unless you're going out with the Amazing Carnak, your man is probably not a mind reader, and neither are you. If you want him to understand you sexually, you're going to have to tell him. Otherwise you stand a better-than-even chance of being misunderstood.

Kay talked about one of her first postdivorce sexual experiences with Richard, the man she's seeing now. "I was really attracted to him, and I was sure he was crazy about me too. But after we slept together, he dropped me with no warning. I thought, 'Oh, no, this is my marriage all over again.' I panicked and was depressed for weeks. A month later I ran into him again, and I got up the courage to ask what happened. He told me that because I didn't move the first and only time we made love, he was sure I was repulsed by him. So he figured he might as well make it easy on both of us and just get out. I didn't move because, first of all, I wasn't really ready to have sex, and second, I didn't know what else I was supposed to do—that's what sex had always been like for me, and I was afraid of making a fool of myself. But boy," says Kay, heaving a sigh of relief, "we went out for dinner and laughed about the whole thing. How things have changed now!"

You may think, "I'm scared. Am I actually going to have to talk graphically about sex?" Well, there are many kinds of talk, and speech is just one of them. Communication can be tactile, nonverbal. You can show each other what you like by touch, by placing his hands there and saying, "Oh, I like this" or asking, "Do you like that?"

But intercourse does mean *communication*. Don't worry if you have to do plenty of the vertical version before you do any of the horizontal!

12

"I Want You All to Meet Harry. . . . Hey, Where Did Everyone Go?": Introducing Your New Man to Friends and Family

> Govern a family as you would cook a small fish—
> very gently.
>
> —CHINESE PROVERB

Liz, as you may remember, met Jay by placing a personals ad in the newspaper with a bunch of her friends. They received scads of responses and divvied them up according to various tastes and interests. When more than one woman wanted to respond to the letter of a particular man, the group would draw straws to determine the "winner." Jay was a hotly contested respondent, and Liz "won" him.

So when the two met and things began to go so well, the first reaction of Liz's friends was, "You see! It was fate!" As the relationship progressed, Liz's friends began seeing less and less of her, as Jay took up more and more of her time. And soon their happiness for her took another turn: "Darling, don't you think he's a little too old for you?" one purred. "He's a good dancer, or he would be, if he lost thirty pounds," said another. "Oh, this one's sweet, but how can he compare with your husband, God rest his soul . . ."

Meanwhile Liz's son, Eric, much to her consternation, pretty much went off the deep end. "I admit I could have have picked a better day to introduce Jay and Eric. I brought Jay to my grandson's fourth birthday party. Now, Jay loves little kids, but there's only so long a seventy-two-year-old man can play with a bunch of four-year-olds before he gets tuckered out. And Eric and his wife, Lynn, had their hands full, and it was hard for all of us to sit down and get to know each other."

Still, Liz thought the day was going pretty well, all things considered, until her son called her up the next day—and blasted her. "Mother, don't you see what this man is doing? He wants a nurse, not a wife! You're going to end up spending what should be the most peaceful years of your life taking care of *him*. And then when he goes, who's going to take care of you?"

"I hadn't seen Eric so angry since he was a teenager," Liz recalls. "And the funny thing is, because Jay did have a heart condition, Eric managed to home in on precisely that part of the relationship that scared me the most. Still, Eric was acting like an angry child about the whole thing—and he's a psychologist!

"I just don't know what went wrong," Liz adds. "They should have been thrilled for me." Well, they should have been, but they weren't.

He looks like Sean Connery (okay, maybe the economy-sized version). He is kind, sweet, suave, gregarious, smart, loyal, sensitive—and *yours*. So why the doubts? Why the hesitations? "Well, he *seems* nice enough, but . . ." "Mom, he's okay, but what does he *really* want from you?"

Many women expect that when a new man comes into their lives, their friends and family will be as happy as they are. As they often learn from painful experience, this is not always the case, particularly at the beginning, when they are in their period of greatest elation.

Why is it sometimes so difficult for the people closest to you to share your joy? There are many different reasons, and of course they vary depending on whether the person in question is friend or family. Let's look at some of the reasons for both groups.

Your Friends

It's easy to chalk up any negative reactions from your friends to jealousy. If they are married, they wish their lives were as exciting as yours; if they are single, they simply wish they had a man in their lives too.

This is only part of the story. Certainly envy can enter into the picture, and the more attractive the man seems, the more envious friends tend to be.

Jacqueline's closest friends knew much of Jacqueline's married life had been unhappy; affluent and respected though he was, her husband was a philanderer and, at times, a heavy drinker. When he died, they all took great joy in providing support to Jacqueline, dropping by her house with freshly baked cookies, making sure she was included in all their activities, and basically letting her know she always had someone to talk to.

"But there was something else going on," Jacqueline explains softly. "The Germans call it *Schaddenfreude*— the joy that one feels as a result of someone else's misfortune." Jacqueline had always hidden her marital unhappiness even from those closest to her, and now in her grief some of the truth was pouring out. So some of her friends, who had always suspected the truth and resented the fact Jacqueline had never confided in them, were filled with a strange sense of triumph that they never would have admitted to anybody, particularly themselves.

Then about a year passed, and Jacqueline was seeing Mark. She was happy for the first time in years. She wanted to share her happiness with friends, and all of a sudden most of them were gone. Others played that popular psychological game, "Blemish":

"Jacqueline, doesn't it worry you that he's younger than you?"

"He worked for your husband. He has a pretty good idea how much money you were left."

"Well, I heard that he's been out on the town with several older women lately."

With one of Jacqueline's friends envy spilled over into full-blown jealousy. Apparently Mark had gone out on several dates with Suzanne before meeting Jacqueline and had decided, for one reason or another, that they weren't really suited for each other. Suzanne had to assure herself that there must be some ulterior motive for Mark's preference for Jacqueline. So, those reasons quickly became: (a) "Oh, he prefers brunettes, and I'm blonde"; (b) "Well, everybody knows Jacqueline has much more money than I do"; (c) "They live closer to each other; he'd have to go out of his way to get to my house"; and so forth.

Some of Jacqueline's friends *were* envious and jealous. But looking back on the situation, Jacqueline also had to admit that her own behavior played a part in their reactions. "A friend might call me on a Monday to ask me for dinner on Friday night. Before Mark came into my life, I'd simply say yes. After meeting Mark, I'd say, 'Well, can I let you know a little later in the week?' Then I'd wait to see if Mark wanted to do anything that night. If he didn't, *then* I'd call my friend back and say yes. Or if I went out to dinner with friends, I couldn't stop myself from talking about Mark. I mean, he was on my mind all the time. I'm a little ashamed of this behavior now, but at the time I thought everybody would understand."

Your friends *do* understand—on an intellectual level. But this doesn't mean that emotionally they're not wounded by this kind of treatment. Like Jacqueline, many women, when they find themselves wrapped up in a wonderful new relationship, make a terrible mistake: *They treat their women friends as if they were expendable.* Suddenly ten or twenty or thirty years of friendship is put on the back burner for the *possibility* of that one phone call.

This kind of behavior fits into an implicit hierarchy in our culture that says, *In a woman's life, men are more valued than women—because men are scarce, and women are abundant.*

If you find yourself acting in a way that subtly confirms this assumption, we can almost guarantee you will upset and alienate your friends. Even the most empathetic, genuinely happy-for-you chum will quickly tire of always being shunted aside for someone entirely new—for someone who *wasn't* there to go to the police station with you when your ten-year-old ran away from home; someone who wasn't there to hold your hand when your father died, when your brother joined the Moonies, or when your husband was hospitalized. In short your friend's feeling is: "*I* was there. *He* wasn't." And incessant talking about the new man in your life? As one woman put it, "It's like getting together with your old college friends and discovering you're the only one who chose a career over having children. They sit around and discuss their babies, and you just feel shut out."

Additionally women in the first throes of a new romance are likely to attribute others' doubts about their beau to jealousy and not consider that their friends may genuinely be concerned for their well-being.

Irving, Marybeth's new man, was indeed a little different from anything Marybeth's friends anticipated. Here she was, their sweet, placid, home-loving, nice Catholic girl, going out with a Jewish man who made Woody Allen look like the Rock of Gibraltar. Opinionated, stubborn, and brilliant—and somewhat of a hypochondriac, who loved discussing his medical history with anyone who'd listen. He had an opinion about everything, from how Marybeth should wear her hair to what she should read. At first he struck Marybeth's friends as a bully and a whiner. And really, they weren't entirely off the mark. What they didn't see was his sincere fascination with everything about her. After a lifetime of benign neglect from her former husband, Irving's constant scrutiny was extremely welcome! But just *try* to say anything about this man in front of Marybeth!

She was so busy being defensive about Irving, she just couldn't see that her friends had a point. Rather than tell them, "I understand what you're saying," and proceed to explain why Irving was the right man for her, she would simply cry, "You want to spoil my happiness!" and the tears would well in her eyes.

Marybeth also antagonized her friends with her public billing and cooing. She had always been known as a quiet, slightly formal woman, the kind who would think twice before hugging in public. She had always been the first to complain that men she dated wanted to take advantage of her. All of a sudden Marybeth was not merely holding hands with Irving—at social occasions she would practically sit in his lap, kissing and hugging him, barely able to keep her hands off him. At first her friends were amused, then, after several weeks when her behavior didn't change, a little embarrassed. One friend finally decided to put her foot down when she invited Marybeth and Irving to her daughter's wedding and Marybeth had Irving licking the icing from the wedding cake off her fingers. "For one thing it was a little disgusting," the friend said. "And for another it upstaged my daughter; even as a new bride, she wouldn't do that!"

Beyond the occasional touch, pat, and peck on the cheek, overt public displays of affection tend to embarrass people—and, if they don't have a sexual partner in their lives, make them feel the lack even more keenly. So, although most women don't give it a thought in the first blush of love, around your friends these displays can be rather ostentatious, not to mention cruel.

No matter how in love you are with a new man, you

need to maintain your friends. We can't say this enough: *You need your friends.* They're probably more important to you now than any other time in your life. No matter how perfect you and your man are for each other, your life can quickly become tedious without outside connection to friends and family. And the fact is, women *do* tend to become involved with and marry men older than themselves—so, even if the relationship is serious and ends in marriage, your friends are likely to outlive your husband.

Many women mistakenly believe it's desirable, when becoming a twosome, to act like a "onesome"—a single unit that does everything together. Rachel (the woman who called off her engagement at the last minute, to her friends' dismay) found this out when her fiancé Mel, showed her—all too forcefully—the meaning of "togetherness." A recently retired widower, he claimed the main reason for remarriage was to have a companion. So far, so good; but Mel insisted he and Rachel should be able to share *everything.*

Rachel was used to a twice-weekly game of tennis with a woman friend; Mel insisted that Rachel didn't need to play anymore now that he was around. At one point Rachel and Mel planned a trip to Italy together; Rachel, who was extremely interested in art history, suggested to Mel that she leave a week early so that she could take a special tour of Florence Mel wasn't interested in, and then they could meet up in Rome. What was the point of *that*? Mel spluttered. If he wanted to spend time alone, he wouldn't have bothered to get engaged.

"Things went on like that for a while," Rachel says. "I began feeling more and more trapped. I looked at that engagement ring on my finger as if it were a two-

ton anchor. And one day I realized I hadn't seen any of
my woman friends for five months."

That was the end of the engagement. But Rachel had
further troubles ahead. She was still seeing Mel, but
now she wanted her friends back in her life. "They were
hurt. It was very difficult convincing them of their importance to me and that they wouldn't be dropped from
my life again."

Other women find the men in their lives have interests they want to pursue alone or with *their* friends—a
weekly poker game, or just a night out with the boys.
"Jack and his cronies had been going fishing together,
during fishing season, once every two weeks for
years," says Lorraine. "He made it clear, as nicely as
he could, that I wasn't welcome—there was some sort
of superstition among them that a woman's presence
would keep the fish from biting. He needs time with
his friends—that does not include me."

So if you have a new man in your life and you're
angry that your friends don't seem happy enough for
you, think about how *you* may have unintentionally
contributed to the ill feeling. They may feel they're losing you. They may feel betrayed. And if the close friend
happens to be male, there may certainly be an element
of sexual possessiveness, *even if it's always been clear
he wanted you only as a friend.* As one of Liz's best
friends, a happily married man, finally confided to her,
"I know how selfish this is, but I was really hurt when
you started to see Jay. I felt like you belonged to me."

So instead of burning bridges, think of ways to build
them. This might mean arranging one or two nights of
the week that you spend *just* with your woman
friend(s), where the main topic of conversation does not
center around you and all the exciting things you do

with Mr. Perfect. Or it may mean including the friend in activities with you and your mate. (Tread carefully here; you must make sure she doesn't feel like a "third wheel." When possible, it's best to arrange activities in groups of four or more.)

Your Children

If it's difficult for your friends to accept and feel comfortable with the new man in your life, imagine what it's like for your children.

Yes, the vast majority of kids are delighted for their mother, because it relieves some of their worries about you growing older alone. They want you to have companionship, and if you're with someone, it makes it easier for them to go out with you in couples. They may feel that your new partner will reduce your financial worries and will make you less reliant on them for your social life. Most of all, the kids will be happy if you're happy.

BUT—whatever your child's relationship with his or her father, the new person in your life may present new worries: How is this person going to change their relationship to you? We're not talking about five- or ten-year-old children here; even if you have adult children, your new relationship is a major adjustment for them.

It's natural for a child to feel protective of Mom when she's been widowed or divorced; he or she simply doesn't want to see her hurt again. And if in the child's eyes she's a bit overweight, not ravishingly beautiful, or somewhat tiresome, he or she reasons, how could any man really be attracted to Mom? Moreover, even if your children seem as altruistic as Mother Teresa, they may have certain areas of self-interest where you are concerned that color their feelings about the new man in your life.

When your children say: *"How can you settle for this guy? He's not good enough for you."*

They may mean: *"How dare you try to replace my father?"*

Some children whose fathers have died would like you to become Queen Victoria. After her husband, Prince Albert, died when she was thirty-seven, the queen vowed always to wear black and never to smile or dance again. And by golly, she stuck to her word!

Your children think of their father as irreplaceable, and they expect you will too. Even if they know it's not rational, even if they know you're a vital, active woman who wants and needs companionship, they sometimes prefer to believe that you won't need another man in your life. If you have another man, it means seeing you in a way they may never have seen you before: as a sexual person. You are, after all, Mom; how dare you become a bombshell?! No one can be more moralistic than a child to its mother—particularly if that child sees the mother doing things *she* told him or her not to do!

Marybeth explains the problems she faced when introducing her children to Irving. "I admit I was very strict with my four girls. Their father died when they were very young, and when I remarried, I chose a man I thought would be a good, steady, disciplined authority figure for them. I taught them the importance of being virgins before they were married and how wrong it is to get divorced. Of course they didn't listen to me, and when they began doing things like living with their boyfriends, there were huge family arguments.

"Then my second husband asked me for a divorce, and they couldn't believe it. Even though I had always told them divorce was wrong, I guess they felt it wasn't my fault. I was still the mom they knew.

"But when I started seeing Irving, I was so happy, and I guess we were overly affectionate, and we stayed together on weekends. My kids got upset. 'What happened to everything you taught us?' they said to me. It's so tough for me to explain to them that times are changing now for me, just as times changed for them."

If the man you're with also has kids, your children might be concerned about how the two of you plan to integrate. Are you all going to get together on holidays and pretend to be one big, happy family?

This was a particular concern for Rachel and her children. Rachel's son, Adam, is a successful veterinarian; her daughter, Julie, is an urban planner with a plum job in Philadelphia's city government. Sadly, Mel's kids were troubled: His son, Todd, had a history of drug problems and minor run-ins with the law, and his daughter, Tammy, abandoned by her husband and, now pregnant by another man, relied on her father for financial help.

Adam and Julie simply could not understand: After a lifetime with their father—a brilliant, charismatic, take-charge man, one of the leading neurosurgeons in the country—what could their mother possibly see in Mel, a dependent, bald, fat, yet sweet retired insurance salesman? They were not insensitive to the problems of Mel's son and daughter, but neither did they feel any sense of camaraderie with them or with Mel. On the one occasion when Rachel tried to get both families together for a July Fourth picnic, the results were disasterous. Julie and Adam tried to be courteous and engage Tammy and Todd in conversation; Tammy was intimidated by them, and Todd interpreted their politeness as patronage. The picnic ended when Todd, overturning the picnic table, ran off, screaming to his helpless, embarrassed father, "I don't know what you see in that bitch and her stupid yuppie kids."

When they say: *"He doesn't love you for yourself; he only wants you for your money."*

They may mean: *"Will there be enough for me and my children, or will it all go to a stranger?"*

Maybe you've been helping your kids meet the bills. Maybe you've promised to pay their way through college. Up to now it was *your* money to spend as you please; will the new man talk you into doing something else with your money (buying a new house, traveling more, getting a new wardrobe)—something that excludes your children? This is a particularly worrisome prospect when your man has fewer assets than you; the fear of "the gigolo" looms large.

This is how Naomi's children felt about Bob, the new man in their mother's life: Even though he lived comfortably, his income was nowhere near what Naomi's was from her two previous marriages. Her son, Raymond, was particularly disturbed. Of all her children, Raymond was the only one to scoff at material things, saying he would rather spend his life living honestly in a hovel than lead a life of unhappiness and corruption in opulence. Yet suddenly Naomi's son the hippy was more money-conscious than she was.

"Bob is so generous, but my son, Raymond, was always looking for signs of his cheapness," Naomi says with a sigh. "It was embarrassing. Bob and I used to alternate taking each other and our children out to dinner. When it was my turn to pay, Raymond would monitor what Bob was ordering, and report back to me if he thought Bob ordered more expensive dishes when I was paying than when he was paying."

Over time it came out what *really* worried Raymond: He had just returned to graduate school, and his mother was helping him pay the bills. Bob was the type of hale-and-hearty fellow, Raymond believed, who would convince Naomi that it would be "good for the boy's character" to work his way through graduate school. Raymond was not averse to work, but he knew he simply couldn't get the grades he needed *and* hold down a full-time job. "When I put money in a trust for his education and assured him his school bills would be paid no matter what happened between me and Bob, he calmed down. And he finally began to warm up to Bob."

When they say: *"He just wants a nurse and housekeeper."*

They may mean: *"Will you still have time for me and my family?"*

Naturally your children don't want to see you burdened with someone else's health problems as you get older, particularly if they've seen you go through this situation with a husband who died. But they may also be looking for the reassurance that you'll be around for them. Will you still take your granddaughter on that trip with you to Europe? Will you still be coming to your son's house on the holidays? "My daughter, Amy, wouldn't come right out and say, 'Ma, will you still be able to baby-sit for the twins on Sunday afternoons?'

but that's what she meant," says Alberta with a
chuckle.

Working Your New Man Into the Family Structure

Being aware that your children might have problems
with the new man in your life is the first step. The next
is figuring out how best to ease this man into their
lives comfortably and amicably. Here are some steps
you can take:

1. You don't have to tell your kids, or your friends
for that matter, about everyone you date; gushing endlessly about every man you go out with is just crying
wolf. Wait until you feel that a man is going to be a
fixture in your life before you make the introductions.

2. The key is to *do everything gradually.*

Mel Brooks used to tell an awful, and awfully funny,
story about how he introduced Anne Bancroft, a nice
Catholic girl, to his strictly observant Jewish folks. He
was terrified of their reaction; then he had a bright
idea. "First I told them she was black. After I pried my
mother's head out of the oven, I said I was only kid-
ding, she was just Catholic."

Nasty though it may be, Brooks's point is well taken:
Just as it was always better to break news to your parents gradually, so it is with your children and other
family members.

3. If your children's first response is negative, don't
react immediately. *Listen to what they say.* They could
be right! Or they could be right in one sense but still
not quite understand that even if what they say is true,

this man is still good for you. *Amplify* and *clarify* your feelings for him.

Rachel's children asked her, "How could you settle for someone who's not as smart as you? You'll be bored so quickly." Immediately she wanted to jump down their throats, denying what they were saying. Instead she listened, thought carefully for several days, and answered, "Mel is not like your father, that's true. He's not as exciting, and he's not as quick. But at this point in my life I want something different. Your father was a leader; now *I* get to lead. I want a man who'll do what I want, someone who's good to me and values my companionship. Is there anything wrong with that?"

4. Make this point very clear to your children: *This new man is not Daddy. He is Mom's husband (or boyfriend).* No matter how well your man gets along with your children, he is not coming along at an early stage in their lives where he could expect to develop a father-child relationship with them. They should treat him with respect, yes, and ideally with affection, but they are absolutely not obliged to treat him as a father. One woman we know realized she made a grave mistake when she introduced her husband-to-be to her children, in their twenties, as "your new dad." "Somehow the phrase sounded so right, so happy, like something on a fifties sitcom. My kids were disgusted, and now I understand why. Not only was it disrespectful to their dead father, it also showed that I still thought of them as little kids who would be eager to have someone to play the authority/daddy role."

5. At a first meeting between your children and the man, *do something comfortable together.*

- Don't bring him in for public inspection, meeting your kids (and maybe all your other relatives) at one time. It's bound to be a nightmare for both of you. If you're thinking it would be easier to get the introductions over with in one fell swoop, just think of that classic dinner scene in *Annie Hall* where the character played by Woody Allen was on show to all of Annie's relatives. Remember how he felt? Instead plan smaller gatherings. Have him meet each child individually, or each child with the child's own family—wife/husband, and kids. (In fact the presence of your daughter-in-law or son-in-law generally helps to create a balance in these situations.)

- You may not want to set up the meeting in your home, particularly if it's the home where you and your former husband raised the children. Pick a neutral place, such as a restaurant—and *not* a restaurant they used to visit with their father, or a place that stirs up any other kind of memories.

- If your child and your new man have a common interest, you might want to build the meeting around that. One of Naomi's other sons, Daniel, was a competitive swimmer; Bob had won many national swimming championships in his age division. The first place the two met was the local indoor pool. "They talked breaststrokes for about an hour, and then they swam together," Naomi recalls. "Of all of Bob's first meetings with my kids, I think that one worked out the best. Bob still gets along better with Daniel than with any of the others."

- Avoid a first meeting on a family holiday or special occasion that used to be celebrated as a family unit.

One of Naomi's daughters first met Bob at her twenty-first birthday party, an occasion, she later confided to her mother, she would have preferred to celebrate with "just family."

Another woman we know made an even greater faux pas: She introduced her fiancé (he had proposed, she accepted, and they had set a date for the wedding) to her children *on the two-year anniversary of her husband's death!* Her kids hadn't even been warned beforehand that she was dating anyone seriously. "I don't know what was going through my mind," she says ruefully. Three years later this woman is still kicking herself: Her kids *still* hate her husband. They haven't overcome that initial shock.

6. Once he's established himself with your children, remember he still doesn't have to be included in everything, and neither do you in his family's activities. Chances are you simply will not have the same feeling for each other's families as you do for your own. *You are probably not going to be a merged family, nor should you have to be.* Thus you can plan certain holidays separately, and some together. For example, after they married, Irving and Marybeth had it easy: Jewish holidays were celebrated with his family, Christian holidays with hers—and they held the neutral ones, Thanksgiving, July Fourth, New Year's—in their own home. But remember that when the gathering is in your house, the two of you are entitled to entertain whomever you want: his family, your family, his crazy Aunt Edna—*anybody*. You decide whom you want to invite.

7. It's not only your children you have to worry about. Chances are, if you're divorced, your contact

with your ex-husband's family may be strained or absent altogether, in which case the reaction of his family to your new man is the least of your worries. (You must simply act with the same courtesy and restraint you would give to anyone who shows an interest in your life.) But if your husband has died, you probably still have brothers-in-law, sisters-in-law, and maybe an aged mother-in-law to contend with.

Acknowledge their concerns. Like your children, they may feel their brother/son is being supplanted, forgotten. They may resent that the money he's left to you is going toward forming a household with another man. Reassure them. Comfort them. If you have pictures and mementos of him in your living room, don't immediately dump them in the back of your closet. Tell his family, "I had a wonderful life with _____, but I have to get on with my own life now. He'll never, ever be replaced in my heart." Let them know that your late husband is as important to you as he ever was—and so are they.

8. Above all, if the kids say they won't let you see the grandchildren, or you can't visit their home with "that man," *ignore them. Do not listen to threats from anyone.* This is your life now; they must adapt. And even if they make a lot of noise, they *will* adapt. After all, when they did something you disapproved of, didn't you?

13

Twenty-one Questions to Ask (and Answer!) Before You Marry

> DAUGHTER: Do you know, Mom, that in some parts of Africa a woman doesn't know her husband until she marries him?
>
> MOM: Why single out Africa?

Comedian Richard Lewis, whose stage persona is a chronically depressed hypochondriac with girl problems, has a great routine about a woman in the seemingly endless stream that reject him: "I dunno. Maybe I should've known better. The first time we made love, I was kinda looking around her bedroom. . . . I asked her, 'Honey, what's that writing on the wall over there?' "

In fact whether you're on a first date or walking up the aisle, there is always *some* "writing on the wall"— that is, preliminary signs that some area of the relationship will cause friction. Most people ignore the writing (or wait until it's flashing in hot-pink neon

277

every few seconds in front of their eyes) before they do something about it.

This chapter is about seeing the writing on the wall and doing something about it. It's about not letting your relationship with a new mate be tossed by the winds of chance. It's about getting your questions answered before you take the plunge.

The greatest difficulties in marriage are caused not by resolving your doubts beforehand. We're not suggesting you should jump right in there and say, "If you don't answer me the way I want, the marriage is off." You need to take a positive approach: "Honey, I love you and I want to spend my life with you, but I just need to know how certain things will be with us once we're married."

And remember, the idea here is not to reform your mate—because that's not going to happen. *The courting, premarital stage of the relationship is as good as it's going to get!* So if there's anything that drives you absolutely bonkers right now, which you think will change when you're married . . . well, you know that Rogers and Hammerstein tune from *South Pacific*, "I'm Gonna Wash That Man Right Outta My Hair"? Well, time to reach for the shampoo.

Careers

1. *What will happen with your careers?*

2. *Will both partners continue to work?*

3. *If he is retiring, will you continue to work, or will you retire too?*

One of the main reasons Rachel decided not to marry Mel but to continue seeing him was that Mel was retiring and he wanted Rachel to quit her work too. What was the point of marriage, he argued, if they couldn't do everything together? Rachel had spent her life working as her husband's assistant in his medical practice, and for the past few years she had held a responsible administrative position at the local hospital. She was only fifty-two; she wasn't ready to give up work she enjoyed just so that she could be available as a fourth at bridge.

Finances

There's an old joke about the key to a successful marriage being the couple's reliance on two Good Books: the cookbook and the checkbook. The implication here of course is that the checkbook is the man's territory— an outdated notion, to say the least.

The 1989 movie *The War of the Roses* can be seen as a morality tale about the plight of a couple who lets the love of their *things*—their exquisite mansion, his antique car, her one thousand pairs of shoes— supercede their love of each other. We're not implying that you, like the Roses, could eventually become so aggravated with each other that you'll be dividing up your entire house into "his" and "her" territory, or vengefully trying to destroy each other; but we are saying that the economics of the marriage should be worked out before you buy the license.

4. *Will you have joint banking accounts?*
Some couples believe that everything, down to the last penny, is to be shared. Others feel they should pool living expenses but still keep separate accounts for in-

dividual expenses: her tennis lessons, his club membership, presents for her grandchildren, presents for his grandchildren, and so forth. Maybe he has children in college, in which case you can expect a substantial sum of money to be tied up for the next few years. Maybe you're taking care of an infirm parent, so you have little discretionary income. If there is a large inequity in the number of financial responsibilities, do you still feel comfortable pooling resources?

Frances learned the importance of keeping separate accounts the hard way, not because her new husband, Edmund, wasted money, but because he wouldn't let her spend her own! "At first I thought, well, marriage is marriage, share and share alike. So I put his name on all my accounts, and he put mine on his. As a physician I had much more money than Edmund. I never needed money from him, and because he was so frugal, he never needed it from me. I never thought for a minute that sharing expenses would be a problem.

"What I didn't anticipate was that once he began to regard my money as his own, he wouldn't let me spend it. Suddenly we were arguing over every present I wanted to buy for my daughter and every new dress I wanted to buy myself."

Arguing over money became the biggest source of friction during the first six months of their marriage. One day Frances woke up and said to herself, "Wait a minute, *I'm* working for every penny of this, and I'm not going out and spending it wildly. Let him be cheap with his own money." From that day on, Frances established one account to which they both contributed equally for living expenses; the rest of their finances were kept separately. "Other women have the opposite problem, which is worse, I suppose—a man who wants to spend all their money. But it's no picnic living with a man who wants to *save* all your money either!"

5. *Will there be a prenuptial agreement?*

Prenuptial agreements are a dirty word to some ("Such a sign of the times!" "People don't trust each other anymore"), an absolute necessity to others. But at this time of your life they can be a peace-keeping force in families.

For example a woman may want to be sure her estate reverts back to her children and grandchildren, and not to her husband's children, upon her death; the man might wish the same, but, particularly if he is the more affluent of the two, he may want to make sure his wife receives income from his estate, if not the estate itself. Not surprisingly, the woman may prefer that his money go to her, to dispose of in any way she sees fit.

It is reasonable that people have prenuptial agreements in a second marriage that occurs in their middle years, especially when there is a sizable amount of money involved. It is completely understandable for someone to want children and grandchildren to inherit the money. In the case where a man has much more, he can provide insurance on his death and/or the interest on his estate plus a lump sum to take care of his new wife.

6. *How much do we save?*

Have you ever seen one of those bumper stickers on the back of an RV that reads, 'I'm Spending My Kids' Inheritance'? Clearly "to save or not save" can become a very big issue. Now that you've found a partner to share more of life's treats, do you squirrel money away or do you splurge?

This was part of Frances's dilemma with Ed: As they both had such different spending habits to begin with, they had to work out a way of being with each other without infringing on one's right to spend and the other's right to save. "Even though I always paint Ed as the Scrooge in this scenario, he could just as easily paint me as a wastrel. I'm the ultimate impulse buyer, and a sucker for advertising. If an ad tells me that there's a new Q-Tip holder that holds Q-Tips better than any other holder in the history of mankind, I'll have to have it *that day.* So you can imagine how frustrated I got with a man who insisted on cutting his own hair."

Like other couples who agree to disagree on politics or religion, Frances and Ed have agreed not to discuss money—or at least, not to discuss it more than once every two weeks. "We have regularly scheduled meetings where we sit down and air our gripes on the subject. I make a list. Ed doesn't need to, since he's been brooding about my flaws for the last two weeks. Then we sit down, argue, throw out the *really* stupid complaints, and if we're left with anything else, we do our best to talk about it. Usually we don't really solve anything—we *still* hate each other's spending habits—but at least we get things out in the open.

"We have learned, however, that I can spend my income (not including what I contribute to my household) as I please. It may annoy him, but he respects my right to 'my pleasures.' "

7. *Should you buy life insurance plans?*

You may already have a life insurance policy naming your children as beneficiaries. Do you change those plans, or buy new ones naming each other as the beneficiary?

"When Jack and I were discussing marriage, one of the most ludicrous fights we ever had was over life in-

surance plans," explains Lorraine. "We had just
watched, for the dozenth time, one of my favorite movies, *Double Indemnity*, where Fred MacMurray and
Barbara Stanwyck play lovers who plot to murder
Stanwyck's husband and make the death look like a
suicide so that she can claim his life insurance plan.
After Stanwyck gets MacMurray to do the dirty deed,
she double-crosses him at the end. Great stuff, but I
guess it was a rather inopportune time to discuss our
life insurance policies. I wanted Jack to buy a new one
that would benefit me at the time of his death. He acted
as if I was just biding my time until I enlisted some
lover to throw him off the back of a train. It started as
a joke, and somehow it turned into a fight." Lorraine
wisely let the issue cool for several weeks; now they
each have policies naming the other as beneficiary.

8. *Do you make changes in your wills?*
Naomi and Bob rarely have an ill word between
them, but one time they did fight over the engagement
ring he had given her. It was a flawless two-carat diamond, which had been in Bob's family for generations
and had belonged to Bob's late wife. It wasn't the fact
that this ring had once been perched on Bob's deceased
wife's finger that irked Naomi; it was that Bob wanted
to leave the ring to his daughter in his will. With her
wealth Naomi could have bought ten diamond rings
like this one; to her it was the principle of the thing.
"I mean, this ring was a symbol of our union, and I felt
it was a permanent gift to me. What if he died before
I did? Did that mean I had to give up my ring? I really
cared about Bob's daughter, but I felt this ring was
mine to keep, whatever happened."
Finally Naomi relented. She understood there was

family significance in the ring, and she agreed that upon *her* death, but not before, the ring would revert to Bob's daughter.

Who gets the house? Who gets the jewelry? Who gets the stuff the two of you collected before your marriage, and the stuff after marriage? By the time two people get into their fifties and sixties, they've worked very hard for their money and possessions, and they generally have very definite ideas on how they should be distributed. There are endless disputes that can arise over wills, and they should be discussed NOW.

9. *How are the bills of daily living worked out? Rent? Recreation? Vacation? Gifts? Petty cash? When you go out to dinner together, should that be considered a "date" he pays for or part of a joint daily-expense account? If he has no grandchildren and you have six, where does the money from the gifts come from—a joint account or your private one? In short, who pays for what, and when?*

And what if you both like to spend money—on very different things? Jack, as we mentioned several chapters ago, has poured lots of money into the restoration of a Sherman tank; Lorraine would like to see that tank blown up. She had no objection to spending money, as long as it was on the things that really mattered: her books, her records, her children and grandchildren. Oh, yes, and her favorite charity, Greenpeace. The fact that she was a staunch antinuclear activist while her husband, a military-history buff, reconstructed a tank in their backyard struck Lorraine as funny; it struck Jack as a damn shame. Jack made it clear he didn't want one penny of his money to go toward those pantywaist liberal troublemakers, and Lorraine was equally adamant about her contribution toward anything that glorified war. Approaching their first anniversary, the couple have combined most of their finances, but they still keep separate accounts for the expenses that they both call recreation.

Housing

10. *Where will you live?*

His place? Your place? If you move to his place and sell yours (or vice versa), who gets the money from the sale? Obviously most couples choose the home that's largest and/or most convenient. But often there's disagreement about what constitutes convenience.

When Karen and Drew decided to move in together (they had not yet decided to marry), it was clear that Karen had the larger, more upscale home, and she didn't see why she would have to reduce her standard of living if she wanted to be with Drew. Drew, on the other hand, had a home very near his children, whom he visited every day, and *he* didn't see why he should have to tag an extra hour's commuting time onto his daily trip to see his kids. Karen started to nag Drew about why he had to see his children every day in the first place; and the two of them have still not quite resolved the problem. (Friends of Drew and Karen, however, have pointed to the example of Woody Allen and Mia Farrow, who have been together for almost a decade and still keep separate residences!)

11. *Whose furnishings are you going to use?*

Chances are, you and your mate have both accumulated objects that are dear to you. Of course you could combine the furnishings from both households; but what if your taste runs to Art Deco and his to Southwestern? Unless you think you'll be making a new, interesting fashion statement with Tiffany lamps and buffalo skulls, you might want to give some thought to how you're going to make two homes one.

Not only did Lorraine and Jack argue about how to spend their recreation money, they also had decidedly different taste when it came to home furnishings. Specifically, Jack was a hunter and a fisherman, and he had a number of prized trophies he wanted to hang in their new den. Lorraine, on the other hand, felt a dead moose means always having to say you're sorry; she was repelled by the idea of these stuffed creatures in her home. She wanted Jack to throw them away; he wanted them to occupy a proud place in his home. So far the dead animals remain in limbo, banished to the basement but not yet entirely gone. Says Lorraine, "I tell you, some days I want to scream at Jack, 'It's the largemouth bass or me.' "

12. *How will you divide the household tasks?*

He takes out the garbage. You cook. He mows the lawn. You do the dishes. Or maybe *you're* the one who's handy with a lawnmower and he's the one who makes a great pesto sauce—but find out who does what better. You may not even be aware of the kind of expectations you have, and there's an even better chance you have no idea of the kind of expectations *he* has.

The first wife of one man we know had the traditional ideas about the division of chores, and of course cooking was her domain. She was a ghastly cook. He, on the other hand, really loved to cook, but had grown up with the idea that unless you were a chef, this was woman's work. Finally, when his wife died and he remarried seven years later, he was delighted to discover that his new wife was also a terrible cook and she knew it. Cooking had always been the bane of her existence, because she knew she was terrible and had no enthusiasm for it, yet for twenty years in her last marriage she had been expected to cook. The couple agreed; it was such a *relief* to throw away the conditioning of a lifetime and follow your natural inclinations. (Of course if *both* of you hate to cook and both adore, say, vacuuming, well, there's a little bargaining in store for you!)

13. *What are your attitudes about pets?*

Cecilia didn't like company all that much. She was perfectly happy roaming her apartment all day staring out the window dreamily or watching TV. And she really *liked* drinking alone: milk, straight up, hold the Purina.

Occasionally Cecilia would put up with the ministrations of her human, Suzy, who worried that Cecilia spent too much time alone. Fifty-five and twice-divorced, Suzy also worried that *she* spent too much time alone. So when she met Yuri, a bearded, chain-smoking Russian emigré with a booming voice and a generous heart, she decided after three weeks they should move in together and even marry. After all, Yuri needed a green card, and, Suzy thought, she needed Yuri.

Unfortunately Cecilia didn't like this arrangement one bit, particularly since Yuri moved into Suzy and Cecilia's apartment with *his* best friend, Vlad. While Vlad tried to make friends, Cecilia quickly surmised that Vlad was 120 pounds of boisterous, drooling stupidity.

Suzy loved Yuri; Cecilia, Suzy's cat, hated Vlad, Yuri's dog. So the fur began to fly.

If Vlad, feeling friendly, decided to use Cecilia as a furry, animated throw cushion, Cecilia would enact her revenge by peeing in Yuri and Suzy's bed. Suzy interpreted this action as a none-too-subtle complaint, which read, "You got me into this mess. Now you've got to pay." Yuri would scream at the cat, and then at Suzy. Suzy would retaliate by letting Yuri know in no uncertain terms that his dog was not only vicious but ugly and retarded.

Afterward Vlad didn't want Suzy and Yuri to leave him alone in the apartment, and playfully gave them this message by biting Suzy's ankle, breaking the skin. Suzy called the ASPCA to put the dog to sleep. Yuri said that Suzy, who obviously didn't know high spirits when she saw them, might as well put *him* to sleep. That's what she did most of the time anyway, he murmured under his breath.

Things escalated from there. After a few of these disagreements, Yuri actually moved into the living room and began sleeping on the couch—with his dog.

This scenario sounds a bit silly and childish; it is also absolutely true. Many people, particularly those without children or whose children have moved out of the house, deeply identify with their pets. When two people with treasured animals come together and try to build a household, the tensions of the relationship are often worked out in the pet arena, because people tend to project their own feelings onto their animals.

Suzy felt that her cat's rights, and by implication, her own rights, were being infringed upon in her own home. Yuri felt that his dog, and he himself, were being misunderstood. And you can pretty much take things from there.

Yuri did not get a wife or his green card. Suzy did not get Yuri (although recently she met another man who, she is happy to say, is allergic to dogs). This was an extreme case; but still, if one or both of you have pets, you should know where you both stand with your animals.

Family

14. *How do you divide your time with your kids and/or elderly parents?*

Do you expect your spouse to accompany you to all your family occasions? Does he expect this of you? What if it's clear to both of you that your families don't mix well? Do you still gather everyone together and hope for the best, or do you avoid these situations altogether? As the story of Rachel and Mel's children proves, few things are more frustrating than trying to mix oil and water; forced gaiety is no gaiety at all.

As for elderly parents, Richard and Kay are still at a standstill in their wedding plans because Richard cannot reconcile himself to moving in with Kay and her mother, while Kay could not imagine having her mother live anywhere else but with her. Kay is saddened by this situation, but believes their love for each other will win out and that eventually Richard will relent. Meanwhile Richard finds he gets along better with Kay's mother the more time he spends with her. "I begin to find her crankiness kind of funny, and she's slowly learning to accept me," he says. "At least she's stopped referring to me as 'that excuse for a man' every time she thinks I'm out of earshot." Richard and Kay are actively discussing their problem rather than just trying to hide their feelings about Kay's mother from each other.

15. *What's the role of religion?*

As we discussed in previous chapters, religion often does not play as critical a role in a marriage when children are no longer an issue. But if one or both of you have strong religious feelings that do not match, it's best to discuss them now. If, for example, you're Jewish and your spouse is not, would you still like him to accompany you to synagogue now and then? Will you want to keep a kosher home? Or if you're a fundamentalist Christian and your husband is part of another branch of the Christian church, will you feel comfortable going to each other's place of worship, or are you better off going your separate ways? When it comes to religion, it's one thing to say, "Live and let live." It's another thing to actually *do* it.

16. *If you're getting married, what will the ceremony be like?*

Well, at least this time around you probably don't have to have those hideous peach tablecloths your mother was so crazy about. (Now it's probably your *children* who'll be bullying you!)

Will it be a huge blowout or a quiet family occasion? Religious or nonreligious ceremony? Irving and Marybeth found a reform rabbi and a rather special priest to officiate. Because most of Irving's family is kosher, they were going to make the food kosher—but a halfway-decent kosher caterer was so expensive, they finally settled on providing lots of choice vegetarian dishes for his family. ("Besides," sighs Marybeth, "the *really* Orthodox members of his family were boycotting his wedding to a *shiksa*.")

Time Together, Time Apart: How Intimate Is Intimate?

17. *How are you together?*

Tolerance for time spent alone and time spent apart

varies widely from individual to individual. Think of Rachel and Mel: She needed at least one day a week entirely to herself, while Mel thought everything should be shared. "Until I talked to him about this, Mel simply had no respect for my privacy or my need to be alone. It was ridiculous; if I didn't lock the door, he wouldn't think twice about walking in on me when I was going to the bathroom! He came from a family of nine children, and I'm an only child. He didn't grow up with the amount of privacy, or the *need* for privacy, that I have. And whenever I said I needed some time alone, he would take this as a personal rejection."

So that one or both of you doesn't end up feeling like a gerbil in a crowded cage, it's very important to explain your needs in this area to each other. Leave it to chance and you may find one of you turning to the other and shouting, "If you wanted to be alone, you didn't need to get married."

18. *How do you like to spend your leisure time?*

If, like many couples, you met each other playing golf, visiting a Star Trek convention, or what-have-you, you may not run into this problem; with luck you both share an avid interest in *something*. But if your interests don't overlap entirely, it's useful to give each other some idea of how much time you will each spend in individual pursuits. One night a week? Two nights? More? The best thing to do is make your arrangements so that he goes out for bowling night with the men while you go to your book club. The worst thing to do is make each other feel guilty about pursuing hobbies alone. In fact time spent apart is often as important to your relationship as time spent together. Adding to the interest and quality of your life means adding to the quality of his life too.

19. *What kind of boundaries do you have?*

If you're at a friend's party with someone you barely know and he tells an off-color joke, you can kind of roll your eyes and shrug helplessly, as if to say, "So sue me, I'm on a date with a moron." No loss of face there. But what if that date is your *husband?* His embarrassment becomes your embarrassment. Suddenly you're cringing, kicking him under the table, and hissing under your breath that you'd like to see him in the other room, *right now.* Or what if *you've* just told your husband's boss what a cute little daughter he has, and she's his third wife? Does your husband have a right to kick *you* under the table?

You might want to establish ground rules for the way the two of you behave toward each other in company. For example if he's particularly sensitive to public criticism, he may want you to save your lecture about his having one glass of champagne too many until you're home. Or you may want to stress to him, very strongly, that he should not belittle your opinions when other people are around and must, instead, save those differences for private discussion. (On the other hand, perhaps, after some discussion you'll discover the two of you enjoy a little public disagreement, à la George and Martha in *Who's Afraid of Virginia Woolf?*—in which case let 'er rip!)

20. *Under what circumstances can you flirt with other people?*

Setting up rules about flirting sounds a trifle silly; after all, isn't part of the fun of flirting doing something you know is forbidden? Yet vast amounts of time, energy, and ill will can be saved if you discuss this issue before you marry. Because at some time or another he *will* flirt—and you might too. And telling him not to . . . well, you might as well tell a lion to become macrobiotic.

You can't ask him not to flirt, but you can certainly tell him not to do it in front of you—and not in front of your friends. It's usually a bit humiliating, even if it's harmless. You might add that it's okay to notice another woman when you're around, but he can save the "Wow, look at that gorgeous body!" cracks for his friends (if he must say that at all). What are the acceptable rules of flirting in your relationship?

As far as the question of the two of you maintaining friendships with past flames is concerned, this is a tough call. It depends on so many variables: the length of the relationship, the marital status of the former companion, the level of trust between you and your spouse. You are, after all, a unit now, and you should always be acknowledged as such. This does not mean, however, that he's not entitled to have female friends anymore. But talk about these friendships now, not when you've been seething with anger over that lunch date between him and *her* that you weren't invited to.

21. *How do your definitions of intimacy differ?*

It's an old stereotype that for the most part holds true: Men and women have different definitions of intimacy. Women consider intimacy the ability to talk over problems and issues. Men consider intimacy the *doing* of things together. Think about this the next time he offers to take you to the movies. He may want to go, but don't expect a two-hour dialogue. He feels close to you just by the simple act of being together.

Men and women also experience conflict differently.

For most women discussion of a conflict leads to feeling close in the give-and-take involved as well as in the ultimate resolution. For most men conflict is a source of tension and thus something to be avoided. "My nickname for Jack used to be Ray; that's short for 'Moray,'" says Lorraine with a laugh. "Because just like a moray eel he would look threatening when he knew he wasn't facing any opposition—but the moment he realized I might challenge him, he'd slink back into his lair and wait for the trouble to pass."

So it may not be easy to get your man to sit down with you and think about all the questions we've posed here! But try it; it's worth the effort.

A Final, Three-Part Test of Compatibility

1. Go on a vacation together, just the two of you, for two weeks.
2. Spend time shopping for a hypothetical house (or furniture) together.
3. Make a list of each other's five most attractive and unattractive qualities—and discuss them.

Why are we saying you should answer these questions satisfactorily before marriage? It's not because we think you have to be ultracautious or ultracritical. It's just that you're no longer twenty years old. You have a lifetime of likes, dislikes, and habits behind you, and as we'll discuss briefly in chapter 14, they're unlikely to change radically. So know what you're getting into, and then, by all means, get into it!

14

Happily Ever After? Ha!
A Problem-Solving Handbook
for Older Newlyweds

> Marriage is a mutual admiration society. One is
> always right, and the other is always the hus-
> band.
>
> —MARY MARTIN

*This is the shortest chapter in our book, but the one
you should read again and again.*

In a wonderful 1940s movie Rosalind Russell was a
high-powered career woman who met cab driver George
Raft. First she spurns him; yet there's something about
this simple but canny man . . . by the end of the movie,
even though they come from entirely different back-
grounds and have entirely different interests, they get
together and manage to work everything out.

I remember watching this movie when I was a teenager. I remember leaving the movie theater wondering,
"How could they possibly work everything out? They're
so different. I don't get it."

Overcoming enormous social and financial barriers in the name of true love is one of our most pervasive and beloved American myths. (The latest example of this myth in action?: 1990's *Pretty Woman*, where beautiful hooker Julia Roberts is transformed from vulgar street waif into elegant princess by the power and prestige, not to mention the credit cards, of financier Richard Gere. This story speaks to this country's sense of democracy: In the eyes of the one who loves you, you can attain equality, no matter what the circumstances. The idea here is that once you get to the altar, everything will be okay.)

You already know what our response to this is: disbelief! We said it in chapter 13: As people get older, they become more differentiated, because they have tried a lot of alternatives and figured out what they like best. You know you like Total for breakfast, not Special K. You know that the toilet paper roll should be placed in its holder with the free end coming over the top of the roll, not from the bottom. You know precisely the right way your sweaters should be folded in the drawer. And so on.

When I was growing up, one of the axioms in my house was that my father was the sweetest, most flexible, most easygoing man in the world. Some years ago my mother died, leaving my father to fend for himself. He was utterly bereft without her and quickly lost twenty-eight pounds. Alarmed, I decided I would make sure he came to my house regularly for dinner so that at least he would be well fed.

On the first night he came, I served fruit cup for an appetizer, then lamb chops, baked potatoes, and asparagus, and finally cherry pie for dessert. And I made an interesting discovery. My easygoing father didn't eat fruit cup; he would only have cantaloupe or tomato juice for an appetizer. He didn't eat lamb chops, only steak. His potatoes had to be fried, not baked. And asparagus? No way; the only vegetables he ate were peas and string beans. Finally, when I brought the cherry pie to the table and he informed me he only ate apple pie, I was ready to cry. Then I recognized the truth: He only ate about fifteen different things. For all the years of their marriage, no matter what my sister and I had for dinner, our mother would prepare the foods my father would eat specially for him—every night.

So much for easygoing Dad.

The point is most people don't think of themselves as "picky," but they don't realize how people may have catered to them or accommodated their peculiarities. So now as you embark on a new life with someone, the chances are slim that the two of you will do most things the same way.

You have lived separate lives for a long time. If you had been together since you were young, you might have grown to have similar habits, even if your habits were quite different to begin with. For example a couple with a new baby might fret about how disciplined or lenient to be with that child, but they have a whole lifetime to work out their differences.

You and your new mate, on the other hand, have entirely different life histories, different patterns; you probably approach problems in different ways. To compound the problem, you probably went through a period of time before meeting each other when you were newly single and had a chance to do everything exactly the way you wanted!

So if it seems there are a number of insurmountable problems at this point in your relationship, there may not be. You're just discovering that, at this particular stage of your life, love is not enough, and good sex is not enough: there will always be areas of disagreement. The secret is knowing how to work them out, without hostility or animosity, but with patience and understanding, recognizing that each of you is *unique*.

Here are some strategies that work:

1. *Put aside time to talk and air differences.*

Now, there's talking and there's talking; we call the two different messages you convey to your mate "you" messages and "I" messages.

"You always. . . ." "You never. . . ." "You don't come home on time for dinner." "You care about your exwife more than me." "You are lazy." All of these are "you" messages. They threaten. They tell a person what he or she does. They tell a person what he or she is. They are destructive labels.

"You" messages are harmful to a relationship because they become self-fulfilling prophecies, which, as defined by psychiatrist R. D. Laing, occur when a person creates an image of himself or herself that eventually becomes true. Tell a man he's a good-for-nothing slob enough times, and you know what? He becomes a good-for-nothing slob! Most men's reaction to repeated criticism is not to say, "Hey, I'll prove her wrong," but rather, "Well, if she thinks that's true of me already, what can I do?"

Then there are "I" messages. Instead of "You are a pig for leaving your dirty socks on the kitchen table," try, "I am not comfortable with your socks on the table." Instead of, "You never take me out anymore," try, "I was so happy when you used to take me out every Friday night. It really added something to our life together. Why don't we do that again?" An "I" message conveys your feelings about a particular issue and does not shunt all the blame onto the other person (even if he is to blame!).

Remember Betty, the woman who became involved with Ted when he needed a hip replacement and she took care of him in her own home? After Ted fully recovered, he not only could walk around but was actually beginning to play tennis again. But during the many months of his convalescence, Betty and Ted had set up a pattern in which she waited on him because he wasn't able to do much for himself. Unfortunately this state of affairs appealed to Ted, and as he got better, his demands on Betty didn't let up. "He was as gentle and loving as could be, but he still liked it when I fetched him a nice cold beer from the refrigerator so that he didn't have to interrupt his football game," Betty remembers. "Gradually I became annoyed and began dropping hints like, 'You really enjoy being pampered, don't you?' The hints soon became stronger, and even while Betty was continuing to do Ted's bidding, she would call him "lazy" and "spoiled." "And you know what? The more I said it, the worse he became!"

Eventually I told Betty about "you" messages and "I" messages. "Instead of saying 'You are lazy,' I'd say something like, 'Sometimes I feel you don't really care about me when you ask me to do little things you could just as easily do yourself.' Well, the notion that I thought he didn't care about me finally got through to him. He saw the situation in a different light and he started getting his own beers!"

2. *Learn how to "fight fair."*

In his book *Fair Fighting*, psychologist George Bach tells

couples how to fight in ways that resolve conflict, not increase it. Here are four rules of fair fighting to remember:

- Don't judge a man's whole character; just state the specific problem at hand. Jack and Lorraine agreed that every week, on Monday, he would give her $150.00 for household expenses. Jack had a habit of missing payments, so Lorraine would have to remind him. Soon this infuriated Lorraine, who started referring to him as "Mr. Cheapskate." And the more she did it, the later his payments became. "It wasn't that he was actually cheap," Lorraine admits. "In fact he was very generous. It was just that, for some reason, he liked me to ask for the money. It gave him a feeling of control." When she finally realized this, instead of telling Jack, "You're just trying to control me," Lorraine sat Jack down and said, "Look, it makes me uncomfortable and unhappy to ask you for the money when we agreed you would give it to me. Why should I have to ask?" After this the $150.00 showed up on the kitchen table every Monday like clockwork.

- Do not complain incessantly; ask for a change that will relieve the problem. After Betty let Ted know how she felt about waiting on him at home, he did fend for himself; but he grumbled a little, admitting he really felt "special" when she did little things for him that she used to do when he was sick; and he showed signs of slipping back into his old ways. So they struck a deal: Since he loved being pampered when they were at home together, she would continue to play this role if he in turn would play the role she wanted from him in front of her friends. "It's kind of shallow, but I love it when Ted acts the gallant swain in front of my girlfriends—opening doors, helping me on with my coat, paying for dinner, even if we're really splitting the expenses," Betty admits. "They think, 'Boy, does he take care of her.' They should see me some mornings, bringing him his breakfast in bed."

- When fighting, never betray a confidence by bringing up private information that was shared. For instance if he confesses to you that he used to have a drinking problem that caused memory lapses, the next time he forgets your anniversary, don't snarl, "What's the matter? Been hitting the sauce again?" Deal with the specific problem at hand; don't throw the past in his face.

- Finally do not go to bed angry. One day's worth of snapping at each other isn't so awful; but if the problem isn't dealt with, anger mounts up. And one of the first areas of the marriage to suffer will be the bedroom. People tend to punish their partners by withholding sex or affection. Then the partner who is being punished becomes, in turn, rejected and resentful. Once this cycle starts, it's very hard to break. So don't start it!

3. *Learn to be an active listener.*

Have you ever known a person who's always ready with a solution to your problem, even if she barely knows about (or understands) the problem? Many women are afflicted with adviceitis, the uncontrollable desire to give advice when it's not asked for!

When your man comes to you with a problem, 95 percent of the time he is not looking for you to solve his difficulty; he simply wants you to listen. It is, after all, *his* problem.

Instead become an active listener. Feed back to him what you're hearing. After a short time being together, Maria realized Alex, a biologist, was a chronic worrier, yet she could do nothing to help him with his professional difficulties. "He would come home ready to practically slam his head against the wall because some strain of drosophilla fly he had been working on in the lab didn't mutate the way he had hoped. What kind of practical solutions could I offer him?" Sometimes Maria just wanted to shake him and shout, "For God's sake, cheer up!" Instead she became an active listener. While he moaned, Maria would say things like, "You're worried because things haven't worked out the way you expected" or "You think the other guys in the lab won't feel you're pulling your weight."

"Alex didn't want help, and he didn't want to be jollied out of his mood," Maria explains. "He simply wanted a sensitive, sympathetic ear, and that's what I gave him."

4. *Do not try to be a mind reader.*

He comes home, flops into his armchair, and turns on the TV. "Oh dear, what did I do wrong?" you wonder. He starts handing you a slightly smaller percentage of his weekly paycheck. "Who's the rest of that money going to?" you meow.

In case 1, he may not be angry at all, but tired, or angry at himself. In case 2, who knows? Maybe he's putting a little money away in a Christmas-club account. The point is, you are not a psychic. Making assumptions about another person's thoughts or feelings is bound to get you in trouble. "I can read Harry like a book" is a common (mis)statement among mind readers.

If you don't understand what's happening, don't threaten or accuse; ASK. More often than not, your assumption will be wrong, or at least only part of the story.

5. *Do not correct your partner's feelings.*

He should be happy when you make a fuss over his birthday; why is he angry? He shouldn't be upset because his brother lives in a larger, more expensive house; what difference does it make?

Well, when it comes to feelings, erase the words *should* or *shouldn't* from your vocabulary. His feelings are his reality, and there's absolutely nothing you can do to change them.

Irving hated accompanying Marybeth to her huge yearly family reunions. "They hate me," he complained. "They see me coming, and they smile, but they're thinking, Oh, great, here comes that loudmouth." "Ridiculous!" Marybeth would cry. "They love you! They know how happy you make me."

Marybeth's family's actual feelings toward Irving were immaterial; what mattered was that Irving believed they hated him, and nothing could dissuade him. When Marybeth contradicted his feelings, she was, in effect, saying, "That's a dumb way to feel." Instead she could try saying to him, "How did you get the idea that they don't like you?" Or "What would make you feel more comfortable?" Or she could simply not insist that he accompany her to this reunion; if he comes to some but not all of her family occasions, that's hardly the end of the world.

6. *Experiment with your relationship.*

No, we're not talking love fests. We mean, when you want to change one behavior pattern in your relationship, make it clear that it's an experiment, and give it a month or two. (After all, if experimenting works for rocket scientists, why can't it work for you?!)

So if you desperately want a pet cat and he thinks cats are (as comedienne Rita Rudner once called them) a waste of fur, why not take care of a vacationing friend's cat for a month and see how the three of you get along? If he wants to open a joint account for all your household expenses, but you still have memories of your ex-husband taking your share of the money to pay off his gambling debts, then give the joint account a trial period anyway. This is a new man, a new life. And it's true what they say that, if you're thrown off a horse, the only way to get rid of your fear of riding is to get back on.

7. *Try being nice—even if you're faking it!*

She says: "I think we should go out together every Sunday." He says: "I think we should stay home together and watch TV." So what if you and Mr. Excitement don't have the same idea of how to spend your Sunday?

Compromise: Tell him you'll do whatever he wants for two Sundays a month if he'll come with you on the other two Sundays. And even if his perfect Sunday means staying home and watching football games, do it with him—and do it with grace and good spirits. It just stands to reason that when people get what they want, they're kinder to each other and more willing to go out of their way to please.

You've met many different kinds of women in the pages of this book; we hope you recognize some like yourself. Here's where some of them are in their lives as this book went to press:

- After spending months worrying about Jay's health and her own, Liz finally decided to put aside her fears and take the plunge. "Everybody says that because he's twelve years older than I am, I'll end up being his nurse in a few years. Well, I'd rather be his nurse, if it comes to that, than spend a day without him."

- Kate, the Irish beauty who was so frightened of a relationship, makes progress, but it is slow. Memories of her philandering first husband still run deep. "Sometimes I feel like I'm fourteen. I don't trust myself in the company of men. I'm always afraid I'll say or do something that will reveal . . . I don't know . . . everything that's wrong with me. My first husband saw it, and other men will too."

- Ruth and Ben continue to spend most of their time together, as do Rachel and Mel, but will not marry. Ben is content in his relationship with Ruth, but Mel is not as fortunate: Rachel believes he is looking around for a wife, one who is willing to spend virtually all of her time with him. "Ultimately, it seems, there are too many differences between us: our children, our life-styles. I love Mel in my way, and he takes such good care of me, but I can't say I blame him for looking for someone else," Rachel says, her eyes momentarily brimming with tears. "I'm a little afraid to be alone, but I'm less afraid of being alone than spending the rest of my life feeling hemmed in."

- Now seven years after her husband's death, Yvonne keeps company with David; they've traveled around the world together. She has not, however, overcome the physical barrier between them; after one year they have not yet made love. "Still," Yvonne says with some satisfaction, "David will wait until I'm ready—and until he's ready." They may be waiting a long time, but they are best friends and constant companions.

- Recently married, Lorraine and Jack are one of those couples who seem so different from each other on the outside that people look at them and say, "Huh? How do they stay together?" Somehow they do. The first six months were hard, though. "But then, every time we had a fight, I thought of my German grandmother's advice: It's a German proverb that means, "What doesn't kill you makes you tougher."

  Lorraine, incidentally, finally took the plunge and had her face lifted, as she had wanted to for quite some time. She didn't stop there. She was so pleased with the results that she had just about everything else lifted too. "For a while there every night Jack would cower under the covers and yell, 'Help, there's a strange woman in my bed!' He couldn't fool me, though. He liked the results. Boy, did he like the results!"

- When they're not arguing about money, Frances and Edmund enjoy each other immensely. Every now and then Frances exacts tiny revenges on Edmund's cheapness by going on shopping sprees and leaving any bill for more than twenty-five dollars in conspicuous places around the house. Edmund counters by occasionally emptying vacuum cleaner bags and reusing them.

- Bea is seeing a thirty-nine-year-old construction worker and having the time of her life.

- Claiming she was ready to give up on men forever, Lise met Kurt, a sixty-two-year-old Richard Chamberlain look-alike just getting divorced from his second, twenty-six-year-old wife. (His first wife died in a car accident.) "He says he doesn't think he could look at another much-younger woman again," notes Lise, barely hiding the glee in her voice.

- With a combination of Weight Watchers, Overeaters Anonymous, and a mall-walking regimen (and with Matthew as motivation), Susan lost twenty pounds, gained fifteen back, and has now finally taken off seventy pounds. Matthew was not quite as successful and ended up putting on an additional ten pounds. Susan said she didn't care. But instead of feeling happy for Susan's success, Matthew retreated into his shell; they soon split up. "I only found out later that Matthew actually preferred fat women. He admitted to me later that he was going to the mall-walkers' group to meet upbeat women with weight problems!" Susan is now seeing a sixty-year-old widower who runs two miles a day.

- Sylvia has a boyfriend! "Well, not exactly a boyfriend, but we'll see," the fifty-nine-year-old woman says demurely. Sylvia, who claimed she had never had a real relationship in her life, has gone into psychotherapy, lost fifty pounds, bought contact lenses, and splurged on a whole new wardrobe. She met John, fifty-five, at a church singles group; he is a physicist and a lifelong bachelor who, he says, "finally decided to get out of the lab."

- Dawn is also in psychotherapy, exploring the abuse in her past, her history of drinking, and the destructive relationships she had previously sought out. For the first time in years she is not desperately seeking a man. "I want to get off the merry-go-round for a while and see what else life has to offer."

- Last we spoke to Naomi and Bob, they were off on a trip to Papua New Guinea (sans Naomi's children).
- Jacqueline and Mark just married, and, Jacqueline reports, she is enjoying sex for the first time in her life. "I used to worry I was frigid. Now I worry I'm a nymphomaniac." No need to worry, Jacqueline.
- Irving is even more persuasive than Marybeth could have predicted: After they married, Marybeth decided she'd like to convert to Judaism. "What can I say?" she shrugged. "Irving doesn't care, but I'm making his mother very happy."
- Karen and Drew have married, and still live in separate homes!

We hope these women's stories convey to you the many, many options you have at this stage of your life.

What you are looking for is desirable and attainable—if you are not waiting for perfection. As Henry Ward Beecher once said, "When a man says that he is perfect already, there is only one of two places for him, and that is heaven or the lunatic asylum."

The best possible life between two people is one with commitment and a mutual understanding of what that relationship will be. Or, as M. Scott Peck wrote in his *The Road Less Traveled*,

> We're going to love each other
> We're going to work out differences and problems.
> I'll be there to love you—I'll stay
> Hope you'll do the same for me.

About the Authors

MATTI GERSHENFELD is a psychologist and the co-founder and president of the Couples Learning Center in Philadelphia which conducts innovative programs for couples, individuals, and families. She has served as director of several funded projects including The Impact of the Changing Roles of Women on Women, Being Single, Divorced, and the Prime Custodial Parent, and, most recently, Golden Girls, a focus on the adult development of women ages fifty to sixty-five. Gershenfeld is the author of several books including *Making Groups Work* and *Groups: Theory and Experience*, the leading college text on groups.

Dr. Gershenfeld lectures frequently at national and international conferences, and she has appeared on national television programs including "Phil Donahue" and "Good Morning, America." She lives in Elkins Park, PA.

JUDITH NEWMAN is a New York–based free-lance writer whose work has appeared in *Mirabella, Spy, Cosmopolitan, Seventeen, Self, The New York Times, Manhattan, Inc., The Washington Monthly, Newsday,* and many other publications. She is a graduate of Wesleyan University, holds an M.A. in English literature from Columbia University, and she lives in New York City.